SAVORY STEWS

Savory Stews

Jacques Burdick

FAWCETT COLUMBINE

NEW YORK

A Fawcett Columbine Book
Published by Ballantine Books

Library of Congress Cataloging-in-Publication Data
Burdick, Jacques.
Savory stews / Jacques Burdick.
p.   cm.
Includes index.
ISBN: 0-449-90545-4
1. Stews.   2. Cookery, International.   I. Title.
TX693.B85   1995
641.8'23—dc20   94-27242
CIP

Manufactured in the United States of America
First Edition: January 1995
10   9   8   7   6   5   4   3   2   1

This book is for
Billou and Gaga,
the best brother and sister
in the world,
and for Mariluz,
the dearest friend.

CONTENTS

ACKNOWLEDGMENTS

So many friends helped me at various steps in the preparation of this collection that the list of their names alone would be too long to include here. I hope each of them already knows how grateful I am. However, very special thanks are due to a few: to my editor, Joëlle Delbourgo, for the idea of a book on stews and many invaluable suggestions about how to write it; to Amy Berkower, my literary agent, for her unflagging support and enthusiasm; to Jane Mollman for her clarity and gentle persistence in teaching me to tame my impetuous, often intractable prose; to my fellow members at the New York Association of Cooking Teachers for their camaraderie and advice; to Joan-Antoni Draper i Miralles, my Catalan cousin, for sharing his deep knowledge of the Mediterranean kitchen, his vast culinary library, and his indomitable joie de vivre with me; and finally to M. F. K. Fisher, a great stew-lover, for spurring me on with letters and notes. She hoped to read the manuscript before it went to press, but alas, I couldn't hurry enough. Unfortunately she couldn't wait, but I must acknowledge my debt to her as a constant source of humor, encouragement, and delight during the writing of these recipes.

SAVORY STEWS

INTRODUCTION

Stews are a fine invention . . .
Any household that does not know how to
construct a good old ragoût is to be pitied.
—M. F. K. FISHER

This is a book about stews, the best-loved dishes in the entire repertoire of world cooking. For most of us the word *stew* conjures up the image of a great steaming kettle filling the house with delicious odors. We associate stews with comfort, satisfaction, and the warmth and security of home, family, and loving friends. No wonder! Stews are our oldest culinary accomplishment; they are an invention so inevitable, so right, that every culture has developed its own stews, and every cook in each culture seems to have developed his or her own ideas about what a stew should be. There are more recipes for stews than for any other dish in the world. The varieties are almost infinite, encompassing everything from the most elegant ragouts, in which every morsel is done to perfection and holds its own in the ensemble, to the lowliest slumgullions, in which all the ingredients are seethed to a savory sameness.

Our word *stew* is so wide and comprehensive that I have found no exact translation for it in other languages. All the generic words for a stew in other languages are pejorative. You will look in vain for *stew* in that classic standby, the *Larousse Gastronmique*. You will find all the specific *kinds* of stews defined there, just as you will find at least three words for *stew* in most foreign dictionaries. But each word will be more exclusive, more specific, and emotionally poorer than our English word. Accordingly, I have used the most generic English definition in preparing this book. It has given me plenty of room for exploration.

A stew is any dish in which solids are slowly simmered in liquid until they are tender. The solids may be meat, fowl, fish, crustaceans, vegetables, whole or ground cereals, peas, beans, fruit, or a combination thereof. The liquids in which they may be simmered are water, stock, broth, beer, wine, unfermented grape juice and other fruit juices, vegetable juice, or combinations thereof. The solids may be simmered straight away or marinated for as long as several days or as little as a few minutes. There are many stews, such as beef *gulyàs* and Silesian-style short ribs, in which the solids are browned, then braised with a mixture of sautéed vegetables, herbs, and aromatics. The mixture can be simple or elaborate, and at times it may contain chopped ham or bacon, like Roman-style beef with fennel and artichoke hearts. Blanquette and Argentinian *gaucho puchero* are prepared from beginning to end on top of the stove, while old-fashioned Burgundian beef gratinée, Lancashire hot pot, and others are finished by slow braising or quick browning in the oven. Some stews are brothy enough to be called soups. Some are very thick, or, as in the case of the Hispanic paellas, Latino "dry soups" such as Brazilian-style dill-flavored hot pot, and Cantonese short ribs, start brothy and end delicious but almost sauceless.

•   •   •

I have chosen the stews for this book from many places and cultures. Some of them are no doubt already familiar to you, while others will surprise you, and, I hope, become good friends. My main objective was to find recipes that would delight both the cook and the diner. I have remained as steadfast to the original versions as possible, while accommodating them to our ingredients, times, and circumstances. Many of the original recipes came from friends and relatives far and near. The prospect of passing along my versions of their recipes to you delights me.

The late Laurie Colwin, a wonderful, high-spirited cook and a lover of stews, believed that people either came to cooking with an inborn talent, became expert through practice, or learned from a book. I kept

Laurie's words in mind as I prepared this book, striving to address all three types of cooks while keeping the recipes fairly simple. Having been a teacher for almost half a century, I have an affectionate concern for beginners. I want them to use these recipes, too.

Most of the original versions of these stews came from the past, when diners consumed far more fat and salt then we do today, and cooks spent far more time preparing meals than most of us can now afford. However, a quick, lean stew is still an oxymoron. Most stews require at least some simmering, and all meat and fowl must be cooked with a certain amount of fat or they become dry, tough, and tasteless. Consequently, I have suggested many ways to reduce substantially the fat in question at various stages in the stewing, and, for those who must monitor their fat intake very closely, how to reduce the fat even more once the dish is finished. I have compensated for the reduction in simmering time by enhancing some of these stews with stock or concentrates, a standard professional solution. If you simply cannot find the time to make your own stock, many excellent canned stocks and dried concentrates are available today. Most of the manufacturers have reduced the usually high sodium content in their concentrates, and more will doubtless be doing so shortly.

Some of you may live where certain ingredients called for in these stews are not readily available. I have suggested some substitutes right in the recipes, though I encourage you to search for the real article. I have also included a short list of mail-order sources for the rarer ingredients at the end of the book.

It is important to remember that stews are great favorites for very good reasons. They are not only tasty but also provide excellent nutrition, and, for the shrewd shopper, attractive savings. Once you have decided to invest in a stew, it is often wise to opt for a big one. Leftover stew, refrigerated overnight, is even more nuanced and full-bodied in taste than it was on the day it was made, and, if there is still some stew left over the third day, the addition of a few well-chosen fresh vegetables will revive the stew surprisingly.

The choice of stews in these pages is so wide that you can find an appropriate one for almost any occasion. Stews are wonderful for special lunches and informal dinners. These one-dish meals are also perfect prepare-ahead fare for the spring and summer months; they shouldn't be reserved for cold or blustery weather. In Provence one of the all-time summer favorites is the *soupe au pistou*, a scalding-hot stew of fresh summer vegetables laced with a spicy blend of pounded fresh basil, cheese, and olive oil. Here in Manhattan, where the summers sizzle, chilled apricot chicken is a favorite lunch at my house. I have noted other recipes, as well, that can be sampled chilled or cold.

In the headnotes and the notes that follow each recipe, I often suggest appropriate accompaniments for the stews that make it easy for you to use them as the basis for complete, well-orchestrated meals. Many of these stews lend themselves to variations that transform them completely. When I thought it useful, I suggested such variations. In several places I have tossed in, as a lagniappe, a special sauce or unusual bread recipe when I felt it was so closely associated with a particular stew that it would have been a pity to leave it out. Now, have fun with these stews!

I wish you joy in your stew making. I leave you with all these great recipes and this old Dublin grace:

"Bless all that's on your table,
 And what's still in the pot,
 Keep it hot!"

A WORD ABOUT STOCKS AND BROTHS

What has happened to the time we used to spend doing the kind of cooking most of us learned to do and liked to do at home? We might as well ask with Villon, "Where are the snows of yesterday?" We all like old-fashioned stews and braises, yet, crockpot cookery aside, we don't have the time to prepare them nor to make the stocks and broths that were the mainstays of that savory cooking.

Aware of the irony of writing a book on stews for urban cooks, I have managed to shorten the simmering time for many of the stews in this book by as much as an hour. As a compensation, however, I have been obliged to enhance the flavor of the stews with stocks and broths. That can be done with rapid-method homemade stock (I have an excellent generic recipe to propose below) or its many commercial equivalents, the canned stocks and broths or the concentrates, whether liquids, granules, or cubes. I prefer using my rapid-method homemade stock, but I recommend some of the canned stocks and broths, such as Campbell's Healthy Request Ready-to-Serve Chicken Broth, and Swanson's Natural Goodness Clear Chicken Broth or Clear Vegetable Broth, and I often make use of the concentrates produced by Knorr, Goya, and Summit. They are wonderful time-savers. It is good news to those on low-sodium diets that many of these products are now being produced with less salt.

Rapid-Method Stock

MAKES 4 CUPS

*H*ere is my recipe for rapid-method stock. It can be made in 1¼ hours. Chicken is its principal source of protein, but it makes a generic stock that works equally well with almost everything except fish and vegetarian dishes. For those who insist on beef or veal stock, an equal amount of coarsely chopped lean beef or veal may be substituted for the chicken. For vegetarian dishes, substitute ½ pound coarsely chopped mild-flavored root and leaf vegetables, the one exception being potatoes. For fish stocks, see pages 217 and 218.

1 pound chicken parts, such as backs, wing tips, and giblets, skin and excess fat discarded

2 medium-size carrots, coarsely chopped

1 medium-size white turnip, peeled and coarsely chopped

1 small leek, white part only, split, well washed, and coarsely chopped

1 medium-size onion, halved, peel left on, each half spiked with 1 clove

1 coarsely chopped celery rib

1 sprig flat-leaf parsley

1 bay leaf

½ cup dry white wine

Salt

1. Put all of the ingredients except the salt in a medium-size heavy-bottomed kettle with 4½ cups of cold water.
2. Bring to a rolling boil, then reduce the heat to the lowest level. Allow the broth to simmer for 1¼ hours, skimming off the froth that rises during the first 15 minutes.
3. Allow the stock to cool. Salt to taste. Place three thicknesses of dampened cheesecloth in a strainer and filter the stock through it, discarding the solids.

NOTE: Covered and refrigerated, this stock will keep well for a week, provided it is brought to a boil every other day. Frozen, it will keep for 6 months.

A WORD ABOUT FAT

M ost of us are now very conscious of the dramatic role fat plays in our diet and of how necessary it is to our health to keep the intake of animal fat low and the overall percentage of fat (those on low-fat medical diets apart), to less than 30 percent. In keeping with that caveat, I have reduced the fat content considerably in my versions of these stews and braises from what they were in their original forms. Bear in mind, however, that the texture and juiciness of cooked meat depends on maintaining a ratio of 20 to 30 percent fat during its preparation. Never fear: There are many ways of defatting and degreasing stews and braises before they are served, thus ensuring the tenderness and juiciness of the meat while reducing the fat content of the finished dish.

REDUCING THE FAT IN STEWS AND BRAISES

1. Before washing the flesh, cut away and discard the excess fat. Excess means more than 20 percent; any less fat will jeopardize the meat's texture and juiciness. After defatting the flesh, wash it under warm running water, then blot it dry with paper towels. The best implements for this operation are a very sharp boning knife and a pair of sturdy kitchen shears.

2. If the flesh is to be browned before stewing, drain the browned flesh and blot it well with paper towels.

3. Unless otherwise indicated in the recipe, discard all but 2 tablespoons of the browning fat before sautéing the vegetables for the *soffritto*, if a *soffritto* is called for.

4. Skim off and discard the fat, froth, and coagulated albumen that rise to the surface of the stewing liquid during the first 15 minutes of simmering. The best implement for this is a fine-meshed stainless steel skimmer.

5. Spoon off and discard the liquid fat that has accumulated on the surface of the stew around the edges of the kettle before finishing and serving the stew. The best utensil for this chore is a soup spoon. At best, this is a work of patience and persistence. Pass an ice cube over the pesky areas to coagulate them, and use an absorbent paper towel to finish the job and to wipe down the edges of the kettle.

6. If you are not pressed for time and can refrigerate the stew overnight, place the stew in a vessel deep enough to allow its liquid to cover the solids well. The fat will solidify and form a cap, which you can lift off neatly, whole or in several pieces.

CHAPTER ONE

Chicken and Turkey Stews

Introduction to Chicken and Turkey Stews

Because of our long-standing predilection for beef in the United States, we usually think of stew as beef stew. Yet, of all the meats in our supermarkets, chicken and turkey lend themselves best to stewing. They are generally the least expensive of stew meats, and they are certainly plentiful. Both make tasty soups and stews that are most attractive in these fat- and cholesterol-sensitive days, with one proviso: Commercial chicken is often excessively fatty. Consequently, most chicken must be defatted and, in many cases, skinned, before stewing.

Turkey, of course, is by nature leaner than chicken. However, this also has its drawbacks: Turkey quickly becomes dry, so a certain amount of fat—never more than 10 percent of the stew's volume, and usually added in the form of bacon or oil—is needed to ensure that the meat will remain juicy. Most excess fat can be skimmed from the stew during the first 15 minutes of cooking or at the end. If you have the luxury of letting the finished stew sit in the refrigerator for a few hours or overnight, the cold fat can be easily removed.

Our grandmothers seem to have had a proclivity for overcooking chicken. Unless you are stewing an old, tough hen, 1¼ hours should be sufficient time. I encourage you to produce stews in which the various ingredients are not only recognizable but properly done, not overcooked. That means putting them in the pot according to their hardness. Most vegetables require less than half an hour to cook through. Harder vegetables, such as carrots, take longer, and thawed frozen ones require considerably less time. An excellent stew, then, isn't simply a planned medley of tastes, it is also a calculated interplay of textures and colors.

Preparing the Fowl for Stewing

H ere are some basic procedures I strongly suggest you observe in preparing poultry for stewing. Although our main consideration here is chicken, these suggestions are generally applicable to turkey and other fowl:

1. Purchase the leanest, freshest chicken available. (Check the date on the package.) If possible, chicken should be cooked the day it is purchased, or repackaged and frozen at once. White-skinned, white-fatted chickens are considered superior to yellow-skinned, yellow-fatted ones. They are usually a little more expensive because they have been fed a varied diet.

2. The chicken should have no odor—check the cavity as well as the outside. Its skin should be free of bruises, abrasions, and discoloration. Remove any pinfeathers with tweezers, and singe off any hairlike fuzz by holding the chicken briefly over an open flame.

3. If the fowl was frozen, make sure that it is entirely thawed before you cook it, or it will cook unevenly.

4. Your hands, the work surface (preferably wood), and all the implements you will use should be scrupulously clean.

5. Wash the chicken under warm (not hot) running water and pat it dry with paper towels.

6. If the recipe requires you to skin the chicken, you can grasp and pull off most of the slippery skin effectively with a paper towel. Use a sharp knife to remove the skin from difficult areas.

7. Pull or cut off and discard all excess fat. A good pair of kitchen shears is very helpful and does the job neatly.

8. Use a very sharp boning knife or chef's knife to cut up the chicken as the recipe requires. Place the pieces on a plate. If you are not continuing the recipe at once, cover the chicken and refrigerate it.

9. Thoroughly wash everything you used in preparing the chicken, including your hands and the work surface, with hot water and soap and a disinfectant like Betadine.

You are now ready to use the prepped fowl in the recipe you have chosen.

I had a great time choosing the wonderful chicken and turkey stews for this section. I consider them old friends, and I envy you the pleasure you will have in discovering those that are new to you. Most of the recipes are easy, and, for stews, don't take long to prepare. All of them are tasty. I hope that many of them will become favorites with you, your family, and your guests.

Chicken and Dumplings

SERVES 6

Not so long ago, in many areas of the United States, chicken and dumplings was a well-known country stew served to hungry families, field hands, and unexpected guests. I remember the dish as a family favorite, deliciously rich in chicken fat and comfortingly filling. With the current emphasis on low-fat foods, chicken and dumplings has disappeared from family and restaurant menus. The great old American dish deserves to be rediscovered in this new, slimmed-down version.

FOR THE CHICKEN

8 to 10 chicken thighs
1¹/₂ teaspoons coarse salt
1 small onion, peeled
1 clove
1 rib celery
1 medium-size carrot, peeled
1 bay leaf (optional)

FOR THE DUMPLINGS

2 cups sifted flour
2 teaspoons baking powder
¹/₂ teaspoon coarse salt
3 tablespoons vegetable shortening
¹/₂ cup buttermilk
1 large egg, lightly beaten
3 to 4 teaspoons skim milk
Flour for rolling out
Freshly ground black pepper

1. Skin and defat the thighs. Wash them well under warm running water, and pat them dry. Sprinkle them with the salt.
2. Spike the onion with the clove. Tie the celery, carrot, and bay leaf together with cotton string.
3. Put the chicken, 2 quarts of cold water, the spiked onion, and the celery bundle in a heavy-bottomed kettle. Cover and simmer for 40 minutes.
4. Meanwhile, make the dumplings: Mix the flour, baking powder, and salt. With your fingers, pinch the shortening into the mixture until it resembles crumbs. Mix the buttermilk, egg, and skim milk together. Stir this mixture quickly into the flour to form a sticky ball. Sprinkle some of the extra flour on a board. Place the dough on it, then sprinkle more flour on top. With your knuckles, nudge the dough into a mass ¹/₂ inch thick. With a knife dipped in water, cut the dough into 1 × 2-inch rectangles.

5. Skim all the froth and fat from the broth. Discard the onion and the bundle of vegetables, and gently slide the dumplings, one by one, into the broth. (If you don't have enough broth to float the dumplings, add a little hot water.) Cover the kettle and simmer the dumplings for 15 minutes.

6. Turn off the heat. Allow the dumplings to puff in the covered kettle for 3 minutes. Sprinkle with freshly ground black pepper. Serve hot.

Brunswick Stew

SERVES 6

This stew, named for a county in Virginia, dates back to the days when Virginia and the Carolinas were British colonies. Once a hunters' stew, it was made from whatever the hunt and the summer vegetable garden provided. It was a must at plantation barbecues in the antebellum South. In fact, as you may recall, Brunswick stew was one of the dishes served at the big party at Tara in the opening chapter of Gone with the Wind. Brunswick stew is still esteemed in the South, but as a simpler dish made with chicken and vegetables. In Charleston and Savannah, many cooks give the stew a distinctive taste and texture by adding a little sugar, a cup of sliced okra, and a handful of rice—and they insist on not serving the stew the day it is made. Its flavor, I admit, does improve overnight.

4 to 5 pounds chicken backs and wings

1¹/₂ teaspoons coarse salt

1 bouquet garni made up of 2 sprigs fresh thyme, 2 sprigs fresh rosemary, 1 sprig fresh sage, and 2 bay leaves, all bound together with cotton string

3 medium-size potatoes, peeled and quartered

3 medium-size carrots, peeled and cut into 2-inch pieces

3 medium-size yellow onions, coarsely chopped

One 15-ounce can stewed tomatoes, coarsely chopped, with their juice

1¹/₂ cups fresh baby lima beans

3 medium-size yellow squash, cut into ¹/₂-inch rounds

1¹/₂ cups fresh whole-kernel corn

¹/₂ teaspoon freshly ground black pepper

¹/₂ teaspoon ground cayenne

Salt

1. Cut off and discard the excess fat, loose skin, and the wing tips from the chicken. Cut the chicken into manageable pieces.
2. Put the chicken, salt, 6 cups of cold water, bouquet garni, potatoes, carrots, and onions in a large heavy-bottomed kettle. Cover tightly and simmer for 50 minutes, or until the chicken is tender. During the first 15 minutes, skim off the rising fat and foam.

3. With a slotted spoon, remove the potatoes, carrots, and onions and run them through a food mill or coarse sieve back into the stew. Discard the bouquet garni.

4. Add the tomatoes and their juice, the lima beans, squash, corn, black pepper, and cayenne. Simmer for 10 minutes.

5. Salt to taste and serve hot in a large tureen.

Quick Chicken Gumbo

SERVES 4

M y quick chicken gumbo, I admit, is more akin to New York's bistro chic than to Louisana's bayou ya-ya; yet, on the strength of its own merits, I believe you will forgive its arrogant lack of genuine Cajun pedigree. The peanut butter, though not as assertive as the time-consuming dark roux, is a worthy stand-in, and it saves half an hour in cooking and cleanup time. Besides, this gumbo, as they say in Cajun-land, "Y'est binbon!"

1 small white onion, peeled

1 clove

2 medium-size chicken breasts

1 tablespoon fresh lemon juice

2 bay leaves

2 plump cloves garlic, peeled

1 tablespoon coarse salt

1 medium-size yellow onion, peeled

1 medium-size green bell pepper, cored and seeded

2 ribs celery

3 tablespoons vegetable oil

$^1/_2$ teaspoon ground allspice

$^1/_4$ teaspoon ground cayenne

1 teaspoon ground black pepper

One 14-ounce can stewed tomatoes, drained

1 teaspoon sugar

2 tablespoons smooth peanut butter

2 slices stale white bread, finely crumbled

One 10-ounce package frozen sliced okra, thawed

Salt and Tabasco

1. Spike the small onion with the clove. Poach the unskinned chicken breasts in 4 cups of cold water and the lemon juice, spiked onion, and bay leaves for 30 minutes. Allow the chicken to cool in the stock. Discard the skin and cube or coarsely shred the chicken. Defat and save the stock. Discard the spiked onion and bay leaves.

2. Using the flat side of a chef's knife or a mortar and pestle, crush the garlic with the salt to a smooth paste. Coarsely chop the yellow onion, bell pepper, and celery.

3. Heat the oil in a heavy-bottomed kettle and gently sauté the garlic paste, the chopped vegetables, and the spices until the vegetables have wilted.

4. Chop the tomatoes and add them to the kettle, along with the sugar, peanut butter, and bread crumbs. Increase the heat. With a wooden

spatula, scrape the ingredients back and forth until the tomato juice has disappeared.

5. Add 2 cups or more of the stock, the chicken, and the okra. Reduce the heat and simmer for at least 15 minutes.

6. Add salt and hot sauce to taste and serve on plain boiled rice.

NOTE: Fresh okra and fresh tomatoes should be used in season. Their canned counterparts have been called for here because they are always available and are good substitutes for those who have very little time. If you are on a low-salt diet, you may want to omit the salt, since canned tomatoes usually contain some salt.

Chicken and Gravy with
Hot Biscuit Topping

SERVES 4 TO 6

*I*n my sister's household on the Bosque River, "deep in the heart of Texas," this dish is a favorite for Sunday brunch.

8 pieces of chicken (2-2¼ pounds)
1 teaspoon coarse salt
1 cup flour
3 tablespoons vegetable oil
Two ¼-inch-thick strips lean smoked bacon, cut into ¼-inch pieces
1 cup milk

1½ cups unsalted chicken stock or water
½ teaspoon cracked black pepper
Salt
1 cylinder of 10 ready-to-bake buttermilk biscuits or 10 Bisquick drop biscuits
1 small egg, lightly beaten with ¼ cup cold water

1. Skin and defat the chicken pieces. Wash them well and blot them dry. Sprinkle with the teaspoon of salt. Dust lightly with half the flour. Brush off the excess.
2. Heat the oil in a deep, wide, heavy-bottomed skillet and sauté the bacon just until the pieces begin to blanch on the edges. Remove them and brown the chicken slowly and well on all sides until done. Remove the pieces.
3. Discard all but 2 tablespoons of the fat. With 3 tablespoons of the flour, make a white roux. Add the milk and stock and deglaze the pan. Add the pepper and simmer for 5 to 7 minutes. Salt to taste. The gravy should not be thicker than heavy cream. Add more milk if necessary.
4. Preheat the oven to 400°F. Place the chicken and bacon in a deep oven-to-table dish and cover with the gravy.
5. Dip one side of each biscuit in the egg wash and cover the surface of the dish completely with the biscuits.
6. Bake for about 15 minutes, or until the biscuits are golden brown. Serve very hot.

NOTE: In summer, round out the brunch with plates of sliced, chilled fresh fruit, including melon. In autumn and winter, I suggest serving an assortment of jellies and preserves and, of course, an extra pan of hot biscuits.

Chicken and Macaroni Stew

SERVES 5 TO 6

When we were children, we used to pester our dear mother with the question "What's for supper?" Once or twice a year, to our delight, she would answer, "Ees and knees and chickens' elbows," the derisive name she gave to a stew she concocted of chicken backs and wings, odds and ends, and elbow macaroni. We adored it. Nowadays I sometimes make it for kids and for grown-ups, too. They all seem to love it as much as we did.

4 to 5 pounds chicken backs and wings

1 teaspoon coarse salt

1/2 teaspoon ground white pepper

1/2 teaspoon ground sage

3 tablespoons vegetable oil

3 strips lean smoked breakfast bacon, cut into 1/4-inch pieces

1 medium-size onion, coarsely chopped

1/2 medium-size bell pepper, finely chopped

1 rib celery, finely chopped

1 large clove garlic, finely chopped

2 tablespoons finely chopped flat-leaf parsley

One 10-ounce can stewed tomatoes, drained and coarsely chopped

3 tablespoons tomato paste

1/4 teaspoon ground cinnamon

1 teaspoon sugar

1 cup unsalted chicken stock

1 tablespoon fine bread crumbs

1 pound elbow macaroni

1 tablespoon olive oil

1 cup grated mild Cheddar cheese

1. Pull off and discard all loose skin and excess fat from the chicken, and cut the chicken into manageable pieces. Cut off and discard the wing tips. Rub the chicken pieces with the salt, pepper, and sage.
2. Heat the oil in a large, deep, heavy-bottomed skillet or kettle over moderate heat. When it hazes, brown the chicken well on all sides. Remove it with a slotted spoon, and set it aside on a large platter.
3. Sauté the bacon in the oil until it begins to whiten around the edges. Remove the bacon before it browns, and place it with the chicken.
4. Remove all but 2 tablespoons of the fat from the skillet and sauté the onion, bell pepper, celery, garlic, and parsley for 5 to 7 minutes, or until soft, raking the vegetables back and forth with a wooden spatula.
5. Add the tomatoes, tomato paste, cinnamon, and sugar and stir all the

ingredients together well. Add the chicken and bacon, the stock, and the bread crumbs, and scrape the bottom of the pan briskly with a wooden spatula to deglaze it. Cover and simmer for 45 minutes, or until the chicken is tender.

6. Meanwhile, cook the macaroni for about 13 minutes in 4 quarts of boiling water. Drain quickly in a colander, then return to the empty kettle, adding the olive oil. Shake the kettle to coat the macaroni. Pour in the stew and toss together briefly with a wooden spatula. Sprinkle in the cheese and shake the kettle well to distribute it. Let the kettle sit, covered, for a few minutes, then turn the stew out onto a large, deep platter and serve immediately.

NOTE: I remember this stew as a one-dish supper. As children we ate it with thick slices of bread and butter. It was completely satisfying. If you are serving the stew to grown-ups, give them a stout California Merlot or Mountain Red to drink with it and a crisp salad of mixed greens sauced with a mustard vinaigrette to set it off. For dessert, try a generous selection of soft, hard, mild, and strong cheeses or a variety of fresh fruits.

Stuffed Cornish Hens with Summer Vegetables

SERVES 4

This is a very special dish for a festive occasion. Much like the French classic, poule au pot, it is equally impressive to serve and delightful to eat but far easier to make. Don't be put off by the long list of ingredients; they are all readily available. The steps are logical, and they call for only one pot! If you are looking for a recipe to dazzle guests, this may be your dish.

2 Cornish game hens
(about 1¹/₂ pounds each)

1 teaspoon coarse salt

¹/₂ teaspoon freshly ground black
pepper

¹/₂ teaspoon ground sage

3 strips breakfast bacon, cut into
¹/₄-inch pieces

3 plump cloves garlic, finely
chopped

2 plump shallots, thinly sliced

2 gizzards and 2 livers from the
hens, chopped

2 tablespoons finely chopped
flat-leaf parsley

2 medium-size yellow squash, cut
into ¹/₄-inch rounds

1 ear of corn, cooked, cut through
the cob into 1-inch rounds

1 cup cooked rice

¹/₂ cup soft bread crumbs

3 tablespoons grated Parmesan
cheese

1 egg, lightly beaten with
2 tablespoons water

One 8-ounce can stewed
tomatoes, with their juice

1 cup unsalted chicken stock or
water

1. With kitchen shears, halve the hens, cutting down each side of the backbone and through the breast. Save the backbones. Remove and discard the excess fat. Wash the halves well and blot them dry. Sprinkle the cavity sides with the salt, pepper, and sage. Stack the halves, skin sides up, on a plate.

2. Heat a large heavy-bottomed braising pan or skillet over moderate heat and sauté the bacon bits until they are limp and start to take on color. Remove them at once with a slotted spoon and set them aside.

3. Sauté the hen halves in the bacon fat until they are well browned on both sides. Remove them, placing them, cavity sides up, on the

plate. Tip the pan and discard all but 4 tablespoons of the fat (2 for the pan and 2 for the stuffing). Put the latter aside in a little cup.

4. In the 2 tablespoons of fat remaining in the pan, sauté the garlic, shallots, the chopped gizzards, and the parsley for 5 minutes, stirring often. Remove and reserve half the sauté. Add the squash and corn. Stir well and remove the pan from the heat.

5. Make the stuffing by mixing the rice, bread crumbs, Parmesan, the egg mixture, the reserved sauté, and the 2 tablespoons of fat you set aside. Pack the stuffing into the cavity side of each half hen. Place the halves, stuffing sides down, back in the pan, so they nestle in with the remaining sauté and vegetables. Add the tomatoes and their juice, the stock, and the backbones you cut out and saved. Sprinkle in the bacon. Simmer very gently, uncovered, for 30 minutes, taking care the heat is not strong enough to disturb the stuffing.

6. With a spatula, carefully remove the hen halves, stuffing sides down, to a serving platter. Arrange the braised vegetables around them and pour over them whatever sauce remains in the pan. Discard the backbones. Serve the dish warm.

NOTE: This beautiful dish, with its "corn blossom" rounds, needs only a simple green salad to accompany it. I sometimes serve it with halves of grilled radicchio, sauced with virgin olive oil and rice vinegar. *Bonne fête!*

French Country Chicken Stew

*T*his good old-fashioned dish reminds me of the French cooking typical of rural France when I was a young man living there in the fifties. Make this stew once, and you'll be persuaded that it's well worth making again and again.

4 pounds chicken pieces

1 teaspoon coarse salt

3 tablespoons flour

One $1/4$-inch-thick slice smoked
   bacon

$1/2$ cup vegetable oil

1 medium onion, finely chopped

1 teaspoon ground white pepper

$1/2$ teaspoon crumbled dried
   tarragon

One 8-ounce can stewed tomatoes

$1/2$ cup dry white wine

1 chicken bouillon cube, broken
   into pieces

One 8-ounce package frozen
   green peas, thawed

3 medium-size carrots, peeled and
   cut into 1-inch rounds

12 tiny red new potatoes

3 tablespoons finely chopped
   flat-leaf parsley

Salt

1. Prepare the chicken (see page 14) but do not skin it. Salt the pieces and dredge them lightly in the flour, brushing off and saving the excess.
2. Trim off and discard the bacon rind. Slice the bacon across the width into $1/4$-inch pieces.
3. Heat the oil in a large heavy-bottomed kettle and brown the bacon lightly. Remove and set aside. Brown the chicken pieces in batches, removing them as they finish browning.
4. Remove and discard all but 3 tablespoons of the frying fat. Add the onion, pepper, tarragon, and the remaining flour. Scrape these back and forth in the hot fat until the onion is transparent.
5. Add the tomatoes and their juice and continue the scraping action until most of the juice has evaporated. Then add $1^1/2$ cups of water, the wine, and the crumbled bouillon cube.
6. Add the bacon, chicken, peas, and carrots. Cover and simmer gently for 30 minutes.
7. Scrub the new potatoes under cold running water and pare off a 1-inch strip around the middle of each one, leaving the peel on the ends. Add them to the stew and simmer for 20 minutes.
8. Stir in the parsley. Salt to taste, and serve hot.

Provençal-Style Chicken Wings and Vegetables

SERVES 6 TO 8

*T*his stew will fill your kitchen with the perfumes of wild thyme, rosemary, and lavender and make you think that you are in the fields of Provence in high summer. The dish is delectable warm, straight from the pot. Yet, if you can bear to put off devouring it at once and allow it to mature overnight in the refrigerator, when you serve it chilled, the bouquet of tastes will be enhanced beyond belief! In this case, sprinkle the stew with finely chopped flat-leaf parsley, drained capers, and Niçois olives, and have plenty of lemon wedges available.

1 large eggplant, unpeeled, cut into 1¹/₂-inch cubes

3 tablespoons coarse salt

12 chicken wings (see Note)

1 tablespoon coarsely ground black pepper

¹/₂ teaspoon ground mace

3 tablespoons vegetable oil

3 large cloves garlic, finely chopped

1 large sweet onion, peeled, quartered, and separated

4 shallots, thinly sliced

3 large scallions, green and white parts, coarsely chopped

1 large bell pepper, cut into 2-inch squares

2 ribs celery, cut into ¹/₂-inch slices

1 medium-size carrot, peeled and thinly sliced

1 large bay leaf

1 teaspoon *herbes de Provence* (see Note)

One 8-ounce can whole peeled tomatoes with their juice

2 cups dry white wine

¹/₂ teaspoon finely grated orange peel

Salt

1. Salt the eggplant cubes with all but 1 teaspoon of the coarse salt and put them in a colander to drain for 30 minutes. Rinse, squeeze, and blot them dry.
2. Wash the chicken wings and blot them dry. Sprinkle them with the rest of the coarse salt, the pepper, and the mace.
3. Heat the oil in a deep 12-inch heavy-bottomed skillet or kettle and brown the wings well. Remove them and set them aside.
4. Increase the heat slightly and sauté the eggplant until all the surfaces look slightly melted, tossing the cubes lightly to coat them with the

fat. Add the remaining ingredients, including the chicken, and simmer, uncovered, for 40 minutes. Turn the top vegetables under from time to time. Don't overcook or overstir this rough country braise. It should be chunky.

5. Salt to taste. Discard the bay leaf. Serve at once with plain boiled rice.

NOTE: Chicken wings are packaged precut in most supermarkets, and many markets stock *herbes de Provence* in the spice section.

Chicken Wings with Yellow Squash and Fettuccine

SERVES 6

There is much to be said in praise of this tasty family dish: It is economical, low in fat, but savory, a fine pasta dish that contains no tomato sauce— and last, but certainly not least, it is wonderfully soothing to an ailing stomach.

12 chicken wings
1 teaspoon coarse salt
$1/2$ teaspoon freshly ground black pepper
$1/2$ teaspoon ground sage
3 tablespoons vegetable oil
1 bay leaf
1 medium-size onion, peeled, quartered, and separated
2 large scallions, green and white parts, coarsely chopped

2 medium-size yellow squash, cut into $1/8$-inch rounds
3 large white mushrooms, stems on, wiped clean and sliced lengthwise
1 medium-size carrot, peeled and sliced into very thin rounds
1 tablespoon chicken or vegetable concentrate (see Notes)
1 pound fettuccine
Salt

1. Wash and dry the wings and rub the salt, pepper, and sage into them well.
2. Heat the oil in a large deep heavy-bottomed kettle and brown the wings well. Remove them and blot with paper towels. Discard all but 2 tablespoons of the fat in the kettle.
3. Toss the bay leaf, onion, scallions, squash, mushrooms, and carrots in the hot fat and sauté until the onion wilts. Add the concentrate and 1 cup of cold water and deglaze the bottom of the kettle.
4. Return the wings to the kettle, cover, and simmer for 30 minutes.
5. Meanwhile, in another kettle, cook the fettuccine in 4 quarts of boiling water for 10 minutes. Drain and add to the wings and vegetables. Simmer for 5 minutes. Discard the bay leaf. Salt to taste and serve in bowls.

NOTES: I prefer granulated concentrates to bouillon cubes because the granules dissolve more quickly. Since they are practically interchangeable, use cubes instead if you prefer, but monitor their salt content.

This recipe makes a fine brothy dish that can be turned into an Oriental-style hot pot by adding 3 cups of unsalted chicken stock, more mushrooms, some cubed tofu, and sliced Oriental vegetables such as bok choy.

Tuscan Chicken Stew with Angel Hair Pasta

SERVES 4

Regardless of the season, this Tuscan ragout is an ideal one-dish meal. It is light-textured, yet the dried porcini impart a rich and trufflelike flavor. (Porcini are sold in supermarkets, Italian groceries, and gourmet food shops.)

¹/₂ cup dried porcini

2 cups unsalted chicken stock

One 3¹/₂- to 4-pound frying chicken, cut up

1 teaspoon coarse salt

¹/₄ cup olive oil

3 tablespoons unsalted butter

1 small white onion, finely grated

2 cloves garlic, crushed

1 teaspoon cracked black pepper

¹/₂ cup dry white wine

One 8-ounce can stewed tomatoes with their juice

Salt

1 pound angel hair pasta

1. Break each of the dried mushroom slices into three pieces. Soak them in 1 quart of warm water for 30 minutes. Discard the soaking water and place the mushroom pieces in a colander. Run plenty of warm water over them. Drain them well and put them in a glass bowl with 1 cup of the stock. Set aside.

2. Wash, dry, and salt the chicken.

3. Heat 3 tablespoons of the oil and all the butter in a deep heavy-bottomed frying pan and brown the chicken well in batches. Remove the pieces to a plate as they finish browning.

4. Sauté the onion, garlic, and cracked pepper in the same pan for 3 minutes, stirring. Add the wine and the tomatoes with their juice and increase the heat. Continue stirring and crushing the mixture against the bottom of the pan until the wine and juice have reduced and the vegetables form a loose paste.

5. Add the chicken, the mushrooms with their soaking liquid, and the remaining 1 cup of stock. Reduce the heat. Cover the pan well and simmer for 40 minutes, or until the chicken is fork-tender. Salt to taste and turn off the heat.

6. Cook the pasta in the boiling water until it is al dente. (Time the cooking of the pasta [5 minutes] so that the pasta and ragout finish at

about the same time.) Drain it well in a colander and immediately return it to the pot in which it cooked. Add the remaining 1 table-spoon oil and shake the pot until the pasta is lightly covered with the oil. Dump the pasta into the ragout and stir well with a wooden spoon. Cover and allow to sit for 1 minute.

7. Arrange attractively on a deep serving platter and serve hot.

NOTE: Don't be dismayed if there is not a lot of sauce. Although this is a Northern Italian dish, traditionally, most of the ragout is absorbed by the pasta, as it is in many Sicilian pasta dishes.

Manhattan Red *Mole*

SERVES 4 TO 5

All seven classic Mexican stews called moles are delectable. No wonder! A formidable set of ingredients and steps ensure their complex bouquets, colors, and consistencies. All that, I admit, is a little overpowering, even for a devoted cook. And not just for gringo cooks; many of my Mexican-American friends rely on a commercially produced powder for their moles. After returning from a stay in Oaxaca, the mole capital, I determined to make a simplified version of the coloradito, or red mole, in my Manhattan kitchen, using only supermarket ingredients and not the powder. Here's the recipe. Despite the shortcuts, it is amazingly good and very near the original in taste.

3^1/$_2$ to 4 pounds chicken thighs

1 cup orange juice

1 bay leaf

3 medium-size zucchini, yellow squash, or some of both, cut into ^{1}/$_2$-inch rounds

3 ribs celery, cut diagonally into ^{1}/$_2$-inch slices

3 ears fresh or thawed frozen green corn, cut through the cob into ^{1}/$_2$-inch rounds

^{1}/$_2$ pound fresh green beans, stemmed, tailed, and broken into 2-inch pieces

One 6-ounce jar pimientos

5 plump cloves garlic, peeled

1 teaspoon coarse salt

One 8-ounce can tomato sauce

3 tablespoons smooth peanut butter

^{1}/$_4$ teaspoon ground cloves

1 teaspoon ground cinnamon

1 teaspoon ground black pepper

1 envelope ham concentrate (see Note)

3 tablespoons vegetable oil

1 tablespoon grated orange peel

1^1/$_2$ ounces bittersweet chocolate

1 tablespoon dark brown sugar

1 tablespoon freshly squeezed lime or lemon juice

Salt

3 medium-size scallions, white parts only, finely chopped

^{1}/$_2$ cup finely chopped cilantro

1. Skin and defat the chicken. Simmer it in a heavy-bottomed kettle with 3 cups of water, the orange juice, and the bay leaf for 35 minutes. Skim off the fat and foam. Discard the bay leaf.
2. Add the squash, celery, corn, and green beans to the kettle and continue to simmer for 20 minutes.

3. Meanwhile, with a food processor, process the pimientos, garlic, salt, tomato sauce, peanut butter, spices, and ham concentrate to a smooth paste.

4. In a heavy-bottomed kettle, heat the oil and fry the paste for 3 minutes, stirring with a wooden spatula. Stir in the chicken, vegetables, and three quarters of their broth and simmer for 5 more minutes.

5. Add the orange peel, chocolate, brown sugar, and lime juice and stir them in well. The sauce should be as thick as cream. Add more of the broth if necessary. Turn off the heat and let the stew cool a bit. Salt to taste.

6. Spoon the warm (not boiling) *mole* onto a bed of plain boiled rice and sprinkle liberally with the chopped scallion and cilantro. Serve a hot salsa (see page 260) for those who wish it.

NOTE: Ham concentrate is sold in eight-envelope packages by Goya Food, Inc. A passable, though weaker, substitute for Goya's ham concentrate can be made by boiling 1 finely chopped strip of smoked bacon in 1 cup of water until the water is reduced to one quarter its volume. Strain the liquid through two thicknesses of moistened cheesecloth. Discard the solids and use the few tablespoons of liquid in place of the ham concentrate.

East African Spicy Chicken Stew

T*his is a peppery chicken stew with a beautiful orchestration of piquant fla-vors. It cries out for a salad accompaniment of chilled cucumbers and toma-toes, a platter of refreshing crudités, or sliced tropical fruits and melons.*

3 pounds chicken pieces

1 lemon, halved

1 teaspoon coarse salt

2 large yellow onions, finely grated (use a food processor if you can)

4 scallions, green and white parts, coarsely chopped

$^1/_2$ cup (1 stick) unsalted butter, melted

3 plump cloves garlic, finely crushed

$^1/_4$ teaspoon ground cloves

$^1/_2$ teaspoon ground cinnamon

$^1/_2$ teaspoon freshly grated nutmeg

1 tablespoon grated fresh ginger

$^1/_2$ teaspoon ground cardamom

1 teaspoon Madras curry powder (see Note)

2 tablespoons chili powder

$^1/_2$ teaspoon red pepper flakes

2 cups unsalted chicken stock

$^1/_2$ cup dry white wine

4 hard-boiled eggs, peeled

Salt

$^1/_2$ teaspoon freshly ground black pepper

1. Remove and discard the chicken skin. Rub all the chicken pieces with the lemon halves, making sure that each piece is covered with lemon juice. Salt all the pieces carefully and set them aside.
2. The next step must be done carefully. The object is to dry-cook the grated onion and chopped scallion without fat and not scorch them. Heat a large heavy-bottomed skillet over low heat. Add the onion and scallion and stir constantly for approximately 7 minutes, until their juices have disappeared and they have gone soft. Remove the skillet from the heat from time to time if it seems to be too hot.
3. Add the melted butter, garlic, and all the spices, tossing them with the sauté until the butter has disappeared.
4. Add the stock and wine and increase the heat. Boil for 5 minutes, then reduce the heat to very low.
5. Bury the chicken pieces in the sauté and simmer gently, covered, for 50 minutes.

6. Pierce the hard-boiled eggs in several places with a toothpick or the tines of a fork. Bury them in the sauce and continue to simmer the ingredients for 10 minutes, or until the chicken is quite tender.

7. Salt to taste. Sprinkle the black pepper over the stew, and serve immediately with boiled rice. Each diner gets an egg. It is customary to pass a large bowl of plain yogurt for those who wish to add a dollop. If East African flatbread is unavailable, warmed pita is an appropriate substitute.

NOTE: Sun brand curry powder, made by Merwanj Poomjiajee & Sons, is often sold in supermarkets.

Chicken and Green-Chili Stew

SERVES 4 TO 5

This Afrikaner stew is an ingenious admixture of Dutch and African cooking. The piquancy of the green chilies is subtly softened by the peanut butter and buttermilk. The flavors in the sauce are mysteriously balanced, savory, and unidentifiable, yet very appealing. I prefer using mild green chilies here, but use hotter ones if you like.

3 pounds chicken pieces
1/2 teaspoon freshly ground black pepper
1/2 teaspoon freshly grated nutmeg
1 teaspoon ground cardamom
1 teaspoon coarse salt
2 tablespoons vegetable oil
3 tablespoons unsalted butter
1 large yellow onion, sliced 1/8 inch thick
1/2 cup green pepper, coarsely chopped

2 tablespoons smooth peanut butter
1 cup unsalted chicken stock
3 medium-size potatoes, peeled and cut into 1/2-inch dice
1 tablespoon cornstarch
1 cup buttermilk
Two 4-ounce cans peeled green chilies, washed, drained, and coarsely chopped
Salt

1. Prepare the chicken (see page 14), but do not remove the skin. Rub the pieces well all over with the pepper, nutmeg, cardamom, and salt.
2. Heat a large heavy-bottomed skillet or braising pan. Add the oil and butter. When the butter is sizzling, brown the chicken gently until it is dark golden all over. Remove the pieces as they finish browning. Take your time. Thorough browning is crucial to the taste and color of the stew.
3. Add the onion, pepper, and peanut butter. Stir together well with a wooden spatula. While the vegetables are sautéing, stir them from time to time so that they do not scorch. When the onion has wilted, add the stock and deglaze completely.
4. Add the chicken and potatoes. Cover and simmer gently for 45 minutes, or until the chicken is fork-tender.
5. Mix the cornstarch with the buttermilk. Add this mixture and the chilies, stirring them in completely. Simmer for 5 minutes.
6. Salt to taste. Serve hot over large slices of fresh, crusty bread.

Apricot Chicken

SERVES 6

Turkish friends tell me this exotic dish is definitely Turkish. The recipe was given to me by an Egyptian friend, the late Azzis Izet. It had been given to him by a teacher of his, Georges Enescu, who said it was typically Romanian. Ethnic origins aside, I can attest to only one thing: The exotic combination of chicken and stewed fruit is wonderful. For the stew to be at its best, the dried fruits should be soaked overnight.

$^3/_4$ pound dried apricots

$^1/_2$ cup golden raisins

2 cups dry white wine

$^1/_4$ cup cider vinegar

2 tablespoons sugar

6 chicken legs (both joints)

2 teaspoons coarse salt

2 teaspoons ground cardamom

1 teaspoon ground white pepper

$^1/_2$ teaspoon ground cinnamon

3 tablespoons flour

$^1/_2$ cup vegetable oil

2 large leeks, white parts only, split, well washed, and coarsely chopped

2 plump cloves garlic, coarsely chopped

1 teaspoon finely grated orange peel

1 teaspoon finely grated lemon peel

1 teaspoon fennel seeds

$^1/_2$ cup orange juice

Salt

1. Wash the apricots and raisins in a colander under cold running water and drain. Mix 3 cups of water with the wine, vinegar, and sugar. Soak the fruit in this mixture overnight at room temperature in a noncorrosive bowl.
2. Rub the chicken legs with the salt and ground spices, then dredge them with the flour. Dust off the excess.
3. Heat the oil in a large heavy kettle and gently brown the chicken, a few pieces at a time. Set the pieces aside.
4. Remove and discard all but 2 tablespoons of the browning fat.
5. Toss the chopped leeks and garlic in the remaining fat and sauté them until they wilt. Place the chicken legs on top of the sautéed leeks and garlic. Add the soaked fruits and their liquid. Sprinkle in the orange and lemon peel, the fennel seeds, and the orange juice. Cover the kettle and simmer for 45 minutes, or until the chicken is tender.

6. Salt to taste. Turn off the heat and let the stew sit for 5 minutes before serving.

NOTE: Served warm, apricot chicken is excellent with steamed saffron rice. Well chilled, it is a perfect luncheon dish; sprinkle it with coarsely chopped cilantro, finely chopped pimiento, and tiny whole capers. A rice salad dressed with a light mustard vinaigrette is a good accompaniment.

Danubian Chicken Stew

*Z*eke was an old Czech friend of my mother's, who lived in the parish where I grew up. She was a fine cook, famous for her prune kolaches and this distinctively Danubian stew, which she herself referred to as "Zeke's Bohemian chicken stew." This is my modernized version of that much-loved stew.

4 to 5 pounds chicken thighs and wings

3 tablespoons cider vinegar

2 tablespoons sugar

2 teaspoons coarse salt

1 teaspoon ground black pepper

2 bay leaves

2 cloves

1 teaspoon caraway seeds

1 rib celery, finely chopped

2 medium-size carrots, peeled and cut into $1/4$-inch rounds

3 medium-size onions, cut into $1/4$-inch slices

3 Granny Smith apples, peeled, cored, and quartered

1 small head white cabbage, cored and torn into 2-inch squares

1 cup heavy cream

3 tablespoons soft bread crumbs

2 tablespoons Wondra flour

1 tablespoon paprika

1 tablespoon fresh or dried dill, finely chopped or crumbled

Salt and sugar

1. Defat the thighs, but do not skin them. Clip off and discard the wing tips. Mix the vinegar and the sugar and moisten the chicken pieces well. Sprinkle them with the salt and pepper and set them aside for 15 minutes.

2. Put the chicken, bay leaves, cloves, caraway seeds, celery, carrots, onions, and 5 cups of water in a large heavy-bottomed kettle and simmer, covered, for 40 minutes. During the first 15 minutes, skim off the fat and froth.

3. Discard the bay leaves. Add the apples and cabbage and simmer, uncovered, for 20 minutes.

4. Mix the cream, bread crumbs, flour, and paprika together and stir this mixture well into the stew. Add the dill and simmer for 10 minutes, stirring from time to time.

5. Salt and sugar to taste. Serve with boiled potatoes or spätzle, tossed with a little unsalted butter and sprinkled with a few caraway seeds.

NOTE: Most Middle Europeans like this stew both somewhat sweeter and more sour than this recipe indicates. Adjust the taste to your satisfaction. Thickly sliced fresh rye bread, plenty of sweet butter to spread on it, chilled Pilsener to wash it all down with, and Slavonic polkas to lighten the spirits and encourage hopping about are very appropriate accompaniments for this remarkable stew.

German Ginger Chicken

SERVES 4 TO 5

W*hen you've been cholesterol-conscious for a long, long time, and you feel that you can afford to indulge yourself with a one-shot excess, this is a great stew for the occasion.*

3 pounds chicken thighs
2 teaspoons coarse salt
$^1/_2$ teaspoon ground white pepper
$^1/_2$ teaspoon ground allspice
4 tablespoons ($^1/_2$ stick) unsalted butter
$^1/_2$ cup diced cooked ham
1 bay leaf
1 teaspoon caraway seeds
6 juniper berries, roughly crushed in 3 tablespoons gin

1 tablespoon cider vinegar
$^1/_2$ teaspoon sugar
1 cup unsalted chicken stock
One 8-ounce can tomato sauce (not purée)
$^1/_2$ teaspoon baking soda
3 tablespoons Wondra flour
1 cup heavy cream
6 gingersnaps, crushed to fine crumbs
Salt

1. Defat the chicken, but do not remove the skin. Rub the salt, pepper, and allspice into the thighs and set them aside.
2. Heat a large heavy-bottomed kettle over moderate heat. Add the butter. When it sizzles, reduce the heat and gently brown the chicken thighs well on all sides.
3. Add the ham, bay leaf, caraway seeds, and the juniper berries in gin, and toss well with the chicken. You may flame the gin if you wish, but it isn't necessary, since it will cook off anyway. Add the vinegar, sugar, and stock. Deglaze the bottom of the pan. Cover tightly and simmer gently for 50 minutes.
4. Add the tomato sauce and the baking soda and stir in very well, so that the soda can neutralize the acidity of the tomato before you add the cream.
5. Mix the flour and cream together. Slowly whisk this mixture and the gingersnap crumbs into the stew until smooth. Simmer, uncovered, for 5 minutes.

6. Salt to taste. Discard the bay leaf. Serve on lightly buttered spätzle, wide noodles, plain boiled rice, or boiled potatoes. If you dare to be truly Westphalian, serve the stew with potato dumplings, then "settle down for a long winter's nap."

Chicken Paprikash

SERVES 6

*I*n the current war on cholesterol, the great Hungarian classic, chicken paprikash, with its "shmaltzed" onions, sour cream, and heavy cream, has
beaten a hasty retreat. Here is my godmother's pre–World War I recipe (may
she forgive me!), slimmed of most of its fat and updated. The obligatory accompaniment is Hungarian dumplings (recipe follows).

3 to 4 pounds chicken thighs
1 teaspoon coarse salt
2 tablespoons vegetable oil
2 medium-size yellow onions,
  finely grated
One 8-ounce can stewed
  tomatoes, coarsely chopped,
  with their juice
3 cups unsalted chicken stock

2 tablespoons sweet Hungarian
  paprika (see Note)
1 medium-size green bell pepper,
  cut into $1/4$-inch strips
1 tablespoon flour
$1/2$ cup sour cream
Salt
2 tablespoons heavy cream
1 teaspoon finely scissored fresh
  dill (optional)

1. Defat and skin the chicken thighs. Salt them and set them aside.
2. In a heavy-bottomed braising pan or kettle, heat the oil over low
   heat. Toss the onion thoroughly in the oil. Cover the pan and simmer
   for 5 to 7 minutes. The onion should almost melt but not brown.
3. Add the chicken, tomatoes and their juice, the stock, paprika, and
   bell pepper. Toss together well. Simmer, covered, for 40 minutes.
4. Uncover the pot and let the stew reduce for 10 minutes, stirring to
   prevent scorching.
5. Whisk the flour and sour cream together. Stir the mixture into the
   stew and simmer gently for 10 minutes, or until the chicken is fork-
   tender.
6. Salt to taste. Stir in the heavy cream. Serve at once, sprinkled with
   the dill.

NOTE: Szèged and Noble Rose brands of sweet Hungarian paprika are
available in good supermarkets and gourmet food stores.

Hungarian Egg Dumplings

MAKES 12 TO 15

K nown as galuska *(gah-LOOSHKA-kah)*, these are the best known of the vast repertoire of Hungarian dumplings. In recent years dumplings seem to have lost out in popularity to pasta, but they are just as nutritious and deserve to be reinstated as trusty standbys with stews. They are considered a must with chicken paprikash, but they are also delicious with braised short ribs and with sauerkraut dishes. (See Note for other suggestions.)

3 tablespoons melted chicken fat
  or vegetable oil
1 egg, slightly beaten
1 tablespoon plus 1 teaspoon
  coarse salt

1 ¹/₂ cups flour
¹/₂ teaspoon caraway seeds
  (optional)

1. In a mixing bowl, briefly whisk together 1 teaspoon of the fat or oil, the slightly beaten egg, 1 teaspoon of salt and 3 tablespoons of water.
2. Add the flour and mix to a smooth dough. Do not stir any longer than necessary. Cover and refrigerate for 15 minutes.
3. Put 3 quarts of water and the remaining 1 tablespoon of salt in a large kettle and bring to a rolling boil. Using 2 tablespoons, dipped each time in the boiling water, spoon the dough by scant table-spoonfuls into the kettle. The dumplings are cooked when they rise to the surface.
4. With a slotted spoon, remove the dumplings to a colander and rinse them quickly with hot water.
5. Heat the remaining fat or oil in a large skillet and toss in the caraway seeds. When they start to pop, add the dumplings and shake them about until they are coated. Remove them and serve them at once.

NOTE: Most children, I have discovered, are very fond of *galuska* prepared in the following way (without the caraway seeds): Place the dumplings in a shallow baking dish with a little butter and milk. Sprinkle them liberally with grated Gruyère cheese and bake them at 375° until golden brown. Sometimes I substitute canned tomato sauce for the milk. Both versions are a success at my house.

Mexican Chicken Stew with Beer and Chick-Peas

SERVES 4

This stew, affectionately referred to by Mexicans as "drunken chicken" because it is braised in, among many other wonderful ingredients, an entire bottle of beer, combines at least three traditional Mexican cooking techniques. It is one of the tastiest, most distinctive chicken dishes I know, an excellent antidote to the culinary cynicism of those who believe that chicken is chicken regardless of how it's prepared.

One 3½- to 4-pound chicken, cut into serving pieces
1 teaspoon coarse salt
3 plump cloves garlic, peeled
1 tablespoon Dijon mustard
1 tablespoon honey or cane syrup
3 tablespoons Worcestershire sauce
2 tablespoons chili powder
1 cup *masa harina* (corn tortilla flour; see Note)
¾ cup vegetable oil
6 medium-size onions, peeled and quartered

1 teaspoon dried oregano, crumbled
1 teaspoon cumin seeds
One 14-ounce can stewed tomatoes, drained and coarsely chopped
3 tablespoons cider vinegar
1 teaspoon sugar
One 11-ounce bottle light beer
1 tablespoon chicken-stock granules
One 10½-ounce can chick-peas
Salt to taste

1. Wash the chicken pieces and pat them dry. Using a food processor, make a smooth paste (*adobo*) of the salt, garlic, mustard, honey, Worcestershire, and chili powder. Coat the chicken pieces well with this paste and marinate for at least 1 hour or even overnight.
2. With a dampened paper towel, blot off the excess marinade and dredge the chicken pieces lightly in the tortilla flour. Brush off the excess flour.
3. In a large braising pan or heavy-bottomed skillet, heat the oil and brown the chicken in batches. Set aside.
4. Discard all but 3 tablespoons of the frying oil. Gently sauté the onions, tossing them well with a wooden spoon so that all the pieces

are coated. Sprinkle in the crumbled oregano and the cumin seeds. Cover and steam until the onions are wilted but not browned.

5. Add the chopped tomatoes, vinegar, sugar, beer, chicken-stock granules, and 2 cups of water. Place all of the chicken pieces in a layer over the onions. Cover and simmer gently for 1 hour.

6. Rinse and drain the chick-peas and stir them in. Simmer for 3 minutes.

7. Salt to taste and serve with salsa (see page 260).

NOTE: *Masa harina* is sold in most supermarkets, in the flour section or among Latino foods. If you can't find any, coat the chicken lightly with yellow cornmeal.

Curried Chicken Stew

T*his is about the best curry you can make if you lack the time or the inclination to prepare your own garam masala. Several brands of garam
masala are now available in good supermarkets and Oriental groceries. In a
pinch, use Madras curry powder. Assorted chutneys, chopped scallions, chopped
hard-boiled egg, chopped cashews or peanuts, and the like are the traditional
trimmings for curries.*

6 large chicken legs, cut in two at
  the joint

2 tablespoons coarse salt

1 teaspoon freshly ground black
  pepper

2 tablespoons Madras curry
  powder (see Note, page 37)

1 cup freshly grated coconut

$^1/_4$ cup vegetable oil

1 teaspoon finely grated fresh
  ginger

3 plump cloves garlic, finely
  chopped

3 medium-size yellow onions,
  coarsely chopped

$^1/_2$ cup finely chopped cilantro

3 tablespoons flour

One 8-ounce can stewed
  tomatoes, coarsely chopped,
  with their juice

$^1/_2$ cup plain yogurt

Salt and red pepper flakes

1 tablespoon freshly squeezed lime
  or lemon juice

1. Skin and defat the chicken pieces. Wash them and pat them dry.
   Sprinkle them all over with the salt, black pepper, and 1 tablespoon
   of the curry powder, and set them aside on a plate for 15 minutes.

2. Steep the coconut in 2 cups of boiling water for 5 minutes. Strain,
   squeezing all the liquid out of the coconut. Discard all but 3 tablespoons of the coconut. Set it and the "milk" aside.

3. Heat the oil in a heavy-bottomed kettle and sear the chicken pieces
   on all sides, a few pieces at a time. Do not brown them. Remove
   them to a plate.

4. Discard all but 2 tablespoons of the oil. Toss the ginger, garlic,
   onions, and cilantro thoroughly in the oil and sauté gently until the
   onions are almost transparent.

5. Add the second tablespoon of curry powder and the flour, a little at a

time, stirring them well into the sauté. Stir in the juice from the tomatoes, then the tomatoes, the "milk" from the coconut, and the yogurt, combining them well.

6. Place the chicken in the kettle in one layer, along with any juice that has accumulated in the plate. Cover and simmer for 30 minutes, or until the chicken is fork-tender. Add the rest of the salt and some hot red pepper flakes, if you like the curry piquant.

7. Place the chicken on a deep platter and pour the sauce over it. Sprinkle with lime juice and serve at once.

NOTE: Boil the rice for this dish with the 3 tablespoons of coconut you saved. It makes a subtle, but appropriate, difference.

Chinese Swimming Chicken

SERVES 4 TO 5

This is one of the most delicious stewed chicken dishes you will ever find. It is so easy that once you have tried it, you'll find yourself preparing it again and again. Here is another reason for making the dish: It produces an abundance of exquisitely flavored sauce, the kind Chinese cooks call lo (as in lo mein)—enough, in fact, to make that famous noodle dish as a main course for another meal.

One 4-pound chicken	One 2-inch cinnamon stick
2 ribs celery	5 black peppercorns, crushed
3 medium-size carrots, peeled	3 small bay leaves
3 scallions, white parts only	1 cup soy sauce
2 tablespoons vegetable oil	$^1/_2$ cup honey
One 2-inch piece fresh ginger, peel left on	3 tablespoons distilled vinegar
	1 jigger ($1^1/_2$ ounces) dry sherry
3 plump cloves garlic	3 tablespoons cornstarch
2 pods star anise (see Notes)	Sesame oil (optional)

1. Wash, dry and truss the chicken.
2. Cut the celery, carrots, and scallions into $^1/_4$-inch diagonal slices. Poach them in 2 cups of gently boiling water for 7 minutes.
3. In a large wok or braising pan, heat the oil until it hazes. Cut the ginger in half lengthwise. Crush but do not peel the garlic. Toss the ginger, star anise, cinnamon, peppercorns, bay leaves, and garlic into the hot oil. Stir them quickly for 30 seconds.
4. Immediately add the soy sauce, honey, vinegar, and $2^1/_2$ cups of water. Rake the mixture back and forth with a wooden spoon or spatula until the honey is dissolved. Allow the liquid to boil for 5 minutes, then reduce the heat to a simmer.
5. Put the chicken in the wok, breast down, cover, and simmer for 35 minutes. Remove and discard the solid seasonings. Turn the chicken on its back and simmer it, covered, for another 20 minutes.
6. Remove the chicken. Untruss it. Cut it with a cleaver into serving-size pieces and set aside.

7. Remove and set aside all but $^1/_2$ cup of the liquid in which the chicken was cooked. Bring the $^1/_2$ cup liquid to a rapid boil. Add the vegetables and 1 cup of their poaching water. Mix the sherry and cornstarch and stir in. Boil for 3 minutes and turn off the heat.
8. Arrange the chicken and vegetables in a deep serving platter and ladle some of the thickened sauce over them. Sprinkle a little sesame oil over the dish if you like. Serve at once with plain boiled rice.

NOTES: Look for star anise in the spice section or Oriental foods section of your supermarket. A possible substitute is 1 tablespoon anise extract.

Purify the rest of the *lo* by filtering it through several thicknesses of dampened cheesecloth. Refrigerated in a tightly closed glass jar or bottle, the *lo* will keep for at least 10 days. Use it as a base for soups and sauces or as a dressing for noodles. There will be enough for about 4 servings of lo mein.

Caribbean Sweet-and-Sour Chicken Stew

SERVES 6

This savory red stew is an old Castilian favorite that came to the New World with the earliest Spanish colonists. It is a dish that is greatly appreciated in the Spanish-speaking islands of the Caribbean. Despite the many ingredients, this version is easy and quick to prepare. ¡Buen proveche!

3 plump cloves garlic, finely chopped

1 teaspoon coarse salt

12 black peppercorns

1 teaspoon dried oregano

3 tablespoons freshly squeezed lime juice

$^1/_3$ cup olive oil

$^3/_4$ cup cider vinegar

One 4-pound chicken

2 links (3 ounces) chorizo sausage (see Notes)

1 cup unsalted chicken stock

$^1/_2$ cup dark brown sugar

1 cup diced boiled ham

1 tablespoon cornstarch

1 jigger ($1^1/_2$ ounces) rum (optional)

2 tablespoons pickled capers

10 to 12 stuffed olives

2 tablespoons finely chopped sweet gherkins

3 slices pineapple from an 8-ounce can, with all the juice

1. In a food processor reduce the garlic, salt, peppercorns, oregano, and lime juice to a loose paste. Add $^1/_4$ cup of the olive oil and 1 tablespoon of the vinegar and process to a thick paste (*adobo*).
2. Cut up the chicken into serving pieces. Wash and pat the pieces dry. Coat the pieces well with the paste. (This part of the recipe can be done the night before, and the chicken covered and refrigerated, provided you have the time. If you're in a hurry, let the chicken marinate for 15 minutes while you do the next step.)
3. Slice the chorizo into $^1/_4$-inch rounds. Peel off and discard the outer skin. Set aside.
4. Blot the chicken pieces well with paper towels. Discard the remaining *adobo*.
5. Heat the remaining 2 tablespoons of oil in a large heavy skillet. Gently brown the chorizo and then the chicken pieces, a few at a time. Remove the sausage and chicken pieces as they finish browning.

6. Wipe out the skillet with a paper towel, but do not wash it. Return the pan to the heat and deglaze the bottom with the chicken stock. Add the brown sugar, the remaining vinegar, the chicken, chorizo, and ham. Simmer very gently for 30 to 40 minutes.

7. Remove all the meats to a serving platter, using tongs and a slotted spoon.

8. Bring the liquid in the skillet to a rolling boil. Mix the cornstarch with 3 tablespoons of water and stir it into the boiling liquid. When it has thickened slightly, add the rum. Lower the heat and add the capers, olives, chopped gherkins, the quartered pineapple slices, and their juice. Turn off the heat, ladle the sweet-and-sour sauce and its ingredients over the meats in the platter, and serve.

NOTES: Goya packages chorizo in pairs. Look for them among the packaged cold cuts in your market.

This dish can be made more festive by serving it on a bed of chopped iceberg lettuce and garnishing it with quartered hard-boiled eggs and sliced bottled pimientos. It is often served with baked or boiled sweet potatoes, fried plantains, and yellow rice.

Brazilian-Style Chicken with Black Beans and Rice

SERVES 6 TO 8

A traditional feijoada *calls for many fresh and smoked meats and hours (or days!) of preparation. This is a simpler version of that Brazilian dish, with fewer ingredients, and it takes only an hour to make. The trick lies in not hurrying the simple steps. You make it all in one pot. The result is a delightful, heartwarming meal for those who love Latino food and have hefty appetites. The Tabasco peppers, canned black beans, and short-grain rice can be found in the Latino section of most supermarkets.*

8 chicken thighs

2 teaspoons coarse salt

1¹/₂ teaspoons freshly ground black pepper

3 tablespoons vegetable oil

1 link chorizo sausage, cut into ¹/₄-inch rounds (see Notes, page 54)

¹/₂ pound sweet Italian sausage

¹/₂ teaspoon cumin seeds

¹/₂ teaspoon red pepper flakes

2 bottled Tabasco peppers, finely chopped (wash your hands well after touching them)

1 cup short-grain rice

2 medium-size onions, coarsely chopped

2 plump cloves garlic, finely chopped

One 8-ounce can stewed tomatoes, coarsely chopped, with their juice

2 cups coarsely chopped white cabbage

3 cups unsalted chicken stock or water

1 envelope ham concentrate (see Note, page 35)

One 16-ounce can black beans, rinsed and drained

1. Skin and defat the chicken thighs. Rinse them well under warm running water and blot dry. Sprinkle liberally with salt and black pepper and stack on a plate to drain further. You may do this step several hours ahead.

2. Heat the oil in a deep, 12-inch, heavy-bottomed skillet. Peel off and discard the chorizo skin and slowly brown the sausage. Remove the pieces and set them aside. Brown the chicken slowly on both sides and remove. Prick the Italian sausage all over and brown it. Remove and cut it into 1-inch pieces.

3. Tip the pan and discard all but 1 tablespoon of the fat. Add the cumin seeds, pepper flakes, chopped peppers, and rice. Stir with a wooden spatula until the rice whitens evenly. Throw in the onions, garlic, cabbage, the tomatoes and their juice, the stock, and the ham concentrate. Toss well. Fit the chicken, chorizo, and Italian sausage in snugly, then add the beans. Increase the heat. Bring to a boil, then reduce to a simmer.
4. Simmer for 15 to 20 minutes, or until the rice "blooms" and the liquid has disappeared except for the tiny bubbles that come up through the rice. Turn off the heat. Cover tightly and let sit for 5 minutes.
5. Place the skillet in the middle of the table like a paella pan and serve your guests from it. Pass a bowl of Brazilian *molho* (recipe follows) for those who like the dish more piquant.

NOTES: Ham concentrate is sold in eight-envelope packages by Goya Food, Inc. If you can't obtain it, make the substitute on page 35.

Side dishes of chilled avocado, mango, melon, or greens are perfect foils for the delectable warmth this dish kindles in your mouth and soul.

Brazilian Uncooked Hot Sauce

MAKES 1 CUP

T his is the Brazilian equivalent of salsa cruda, though it is much more so-phisticated in taste and many times more piquant. In Brazil, this sauce, known as molho, is made with malagueta peppers. It is difficult to find those blazing African peppers in the States, so I have substituted pickled Tabasco pep-pers. Suit yourself as to just how hot you like the sauce by increasing or decreas-ing the amount of peppers accordingly.

$^{1}/_{2}$ cup light olive oil

2 scallions, green and white parts, finely chopped

3 bottled Tabasco peppers, finely chopped

$^{1}/_{2}$ clove garlic, finely chopped

$^{1}/_{2}$ teaspoon coarse salt

3 tablespoons finely chopped cilantro

1 medium-size ripe red tomato, skinned, seeded, and coarsely chopped, or an equal amount of canned tomatoes

3 tablespoons freshly squeezed lime or lemon juice

1. Mix all of the ingredients together well in a noncorrosive bowl. Cover and refrigerate for at least 2 hours.
2. Allow the sauce to return to room temperature before serving.

NOTE: Warn your guests about the piquancy of this lively sauce. Be aware, too, that the sauce's wonderful tastes begin to deteriorate after a few hours at room temperature, so discard any leftover sauce.

Brazilian Dill-Flavored Hot Pot

SERVES 5 OR 6

S*ome of the most venerable family stews in the international repertoire are "bread soups," in which hefty slices of toast, anointed with aromatic oil, are steeped in hot, savory broth. Notable examples are Burgundian onion soup, the açordas and migas of Portugal, and the sopas secas of Brazil. Here is a robust, peppery sopa seca whose mandate seems to be "Heal the ailing and raise the dead!" I can swear to its restorative powers. My thanks to Sandra Allen, a good friend and fine cook, for this spirit-warming recipe from her native Brazil. Look for Angolan piri-piri peppers in Portuguese and Brazilian food shops. If you can't find them, use Tabascos (see headnote, page 55).*

4 pounds chicken pieces (wings are a good choice)

1 teaspoon coarse salt

1/2 cup flour

1/2 cup vegetable oil

2 cups coarsely chopped scallions, white and green parts

3/4 cup finely chopped fresh dill

4 medium-size potatoes, peeled, quartered, and cut into 1/4-inch slices

2 medium-size carrots, peeled and sliced into 1/8-inch rounds

8 cups unsalted chicken stock, or 4 tablespoons chicken-concentrate granules dissolved in 8 cups water

2 or 3 pickled *piri-piri* or Tabasco peppers, finely chopped (wash your hands well after touching them)

Salt

Twelve 1/2-inch slices French bread

6 plump cloves garlic, coarsely chopped

1. Skin and defat the chicken pieces. Wash them well and dry them. Salt them and dredge them lightly in the flour.
2. In a heavy-bottomed, 4-quart kettle, heat half the oil and gently brown the chicken pieces on all sides. Remove the pieces and blot them well.
3. Remove and set aside all but 2 tablespoons of the frying oil. Add the scallions and dill. Toss well with a wooden spatula and sauté until wilted. Add the potatoes and carrots and toss them thoroughly. Return the chicken to the kettle. Add the stock and peppers. Bring to a boil and deglaze the kettle. Reduce the heat, cover, and simmer

gently for $1^1/_2$ hours. Salt to taste. These steps may be done a day ahead, if you like.

4. Oven-toast the bread to a golden brown.

5. In a small frying pan, heat the oil you set aside and the remaining $^1/_4$ cup of oil and very slowly sauté the garlic until it begins to take on a golden color. Remove the pan immediately from the heat. Skim out all the garlic bits and blot them on a paper towel.

6. Lay out six of the toasts in the bottom of a large bowl. Drizzle them with some of the garlic oil. Ladle the boiling-hot soup over them, distributing the chicken and vegetables in equal portions over each piece of toast. Cover each portion with another toast. Sprinkle some of the garlic oil on each "lid" and add some of the crisped garlic bits. Serve steaming hot in individual bowls.

NOTES: The toasts drink up most of the broth, hence "dry soup." Use a skimmer to lift out each portion intact.

Instead of poaching an egg in the broth for each person and serving it up as part of each person's portion, as is often done, I suggest rounding out the meal with coleslaw, a salad of beets, and a selection of low-fat cheeses. Dill, like asparagus, doesn't wed well with wine, but it does with light beer, and it is a pleasant foil to the peppery broth.

Cajun-Style Turkey Stew

SERVES 6

*I*f you are looking for a different way to deal with your postholiday turkey leftovers, here is a delightful suggestion. This Cajun stew is almost a meal in itself.

3 tablespoons unsalted butter

1 large leek, white part only, split, well washed, and coarsely chopped

1 small green bell pepper, finely chopped

1 medium-size onion, finely grated

3 ribs celery, with their leaves, finely chopped

2 medium-size carrots, peeled and coarsely chopped

1 medium-size ripe red tomato, skinned, seeded, and finely chopped

2 tablespoons finely chopped flat-leaf parsley

1 cup ¼-inch fresh okra slices (thawed frozen okra may be substituted)

1 bay leaf

⅛ teaspoon dried thyme

⅛ teaspoon red pepper flakes

2 tablespoons Wondra flour

The leftover carcass, wing, and leg bones of 1 large turkey

Salt

Freshly ground black pepper

1½ cups coarsely shredded skinless leftover turkey flesh

3 tablespoons gumbo filé (see Note)

3 cups steamed rice

1. Heat the butter in a large heavy-bottomed kettle until it sizzles. Add the leek, green pepper, onion, celery, carrots, tomato, parsley, okra, bay leaf, thyme, and pepper flakes and toss thoroughly. Sauté over moderate heat, tossing constantly, for 7 minutes. Remove from the heat, stir in the flour until it disappears, cover tightly, and let sit for 5 minutes.

2. Break up the carcass into five or six pieces and crack the bones. Make a loose bundle of the carcass pieces and the bones and bind them together with cotton string.

3. Place this bundle among the sautéed vegetables. Add 2 quarts of cold water and bring to a rolling boil. Reduce the heat immediately and simmer the stew, covered, for 1½ hours.

4. Salt and pepper to taste. Discard the bundle of bones and the bay leaf. Stir in the shredded turkey. When the stew begins to boil again, remove the kettle from the heat and stir in the gumbo filé. (If you have any leftover giblet gravy, stir it in, as well.)

5. Serve the stew boiling hot in large, individual bowls. Let each guest add the amount of rice he or she wishes to the stew. Proper Cajuns, I am told, never cook the rice with the stew and never boil the stew after adding the gumbo filé.

NOTE: Look for gumbo filé (ground dried sassafras leaves) in the Cajun section of food speciality shops. Zatarain's is a popular brand. A $1^{1}/_{4}$-ounce jar (the smallest) will suffice for preparing four to five gumbo stews.

Middle Eastern Turkey Stew

SERVES 4

The packaged, thinly sliced raw turkey breasts sold in most markets these days may be the answer to a dieter's prayer; however, even with very little grilling they become dry, tasteless, and unappetizing. Here is a recipe that helps the turkey remain juicy and delicious in an exotic braise of Middle Eastern vegetables and aromatics. Appropriate accompaniments are a Turkish pilaf or a plain steamed couscous.

1 medium-size eggplant, stemmed, quartered lengthwise, and cut into 12 chunks

2 tablespoons coarse salt

3 tablespoons flour

4 to 5 slices raw turkey breast, cut into bite-size pieces

1 teaspoon ground cardamom

$1/2$ teaspoon ground white pepper

3 tablespoons freshly squeezed lemon juice

$1/4$ cup vegetable oil

3 plump cloves garlic, peeled and quartered lengthwise

One 2-ounce jar pimientos, drained and coarsely chopped

One $11^1/2$-ounce can Contadino peeled tomato wedges, with their juice

$1/4$ cup golden raisins

One 2-inch cinnamon stick

4 cloves

2 small bay leaves

2 cups unsalted chicken stock

3 tablespoons cornstarch

12 to 16 pearl onions, peeled

3 tablespoons toasted pine nuts (optional)

1 tablespoon sugar

Salt

1. Salt the eggplant chunks and put them in a bowl. Cover them with cold water and let them soak for 20 minutes. Rinse the chunks well under cold running water and squeeze them out well. Dredge them in the flour and set them aside to dry a bit.
2. In a glass or ceramic bowl, thoroughly combine the turkey pieces, cardamom, white pepper, and lemon juice. Cover and set aside in a cool place to marinate while proceeding.
3. Heat half of the oil in a large heavy-bottomed kettle and brown the eggplant on all the cut surfaces. Add the garlic and sauté briefly without browning it.

4. Add the pimientos, the tomatoes and their juice, the raisins, cinnamon, cloves, bay leaves, and stock. Stir well and simmer gently, covered, for 45 minutes.

5. Blot the turkey pieces almost dry and dredge them in the cornstarch, patting it into the pieces.

6. Heat the remaining oil (about 3 tablespoons) in a frying pan until it hazes and sauté the turkey and pearl onions for 5 minutes, tossing them constantly with a wooden spatula.

7. Stir the turkey and onions into the stew and continue simmering, uncovered, for 10 minutes. Meanwhile, toast the pine nuts by shaking them briefly in a dry frying pan over low heat.

8. Add the sugar, and salt the stew to taste. Discard the cinnamon and bay leaves. Serve the stew hot with the pine nuts scattered over the surface.

NOTE: Served chilled, this stew is an excellent main course for a summer luncheon. Sprinkle each serving with a little finely chopped cilantro and grated orange peel.

Turkey Cacciatore with Rigatoni

SERVES 6

This is one of the heartiest of pasta dishes. It is also one of the most festive, so save it for a special occasion. Traditionally, cacciatore is made with chicken; however, I find the dish assumes a different character with turkey. The turkey wings become pheasantlike, taking on the dark, savory taste of the wild mushrooms, smoked bacon, anchovy, herbs, and spices. The large, ridged pasta absorbs almost all of the ragù, like a Sicilian pasta al forno.

1 ounce dried porcini

3 medium-size turkey wings, cut in two at the joint

1 tablespoon coarse salt

1 teaspoon cracked black pepper

1/2 cup flour

1/4 cup vegetable oil

3 thick slices smoked bacon, cut into 1/4-inch pieces

2 bay leaves

6 to 8 fresh rosemary leaves

1 teaspoon finely crumbled dried sage

1/2 teaspoon fennel seeds

2 plump cloves garlic, finely chopped

1 small onion, coarsely chopped

1 medium-size carrot, peeled and coarsely chopped

3 flat anchovy fillets, finely chopped

1/2 teaspoon ground cinnamon

1 cup unsalted chicken stock or water

1 cup dry white wine

6 to 8 medium-size fresh white or brown mushrooms, wiped clean and sliced lengthwise

One 14 1/2-ounce can stewed tomatoes, coarsely chopped, with their juice

1 pound rigatoni

1 tablespoon olive oil

Salt and pepper

3 tablespoons pine nuts

2 tablespoons finely chopped flat-leaf parsley

Freshly grated Parmesan cheese

1. Rinse the dried mushrooms well under running water to remove any sand. Soak them for 30 minutes in 2 cups of warm water, then squeeze them out and chop them coarsely.

2. Wash and dry the turkey pieces. Sprinkle them with the salt and cracked pepper and dredge them in the flour, brushing off the excess.

3. In a large heavy-bottomed kettle, heat the vegetable oil and brown the turkey pieces well, a few at a time. Remove them and blot with paper towels.

4. Sauté the bacon. When it begins to take on color, add the bay leaves, rosemary, sage, fennel seeds, garlic, onion, carrot, anchovies, porcini, and cinnamon. Sauté until light brown, tossing often with a wooden spoon. Tip the kettle and discard as much of the fat as you can spoon out.

5. Add the stock, wine, fresh mushrooms, tomatoes and their juice, and the turkey pieces. Simmer, covered, for 50 minutes, or until the turkey is fork-tender.

6. Meanwhile, cook the pasta until al dente in 3 quarts of rapidly boiling water. Drain it. Toss it with the olive oil, then empty it into the stew. Turn off the heat. Toss the pasta well with the stew. Salt and pepper to taste. Cover and let sit for 3 minutes while you toast the pine nuts by shaking them very briefly in a dry frying pan over low heat.

7. Discard the bay leaves. Transfer the cacciatore to a large serving platter. Sprinkle with the chopped parsley and pine nuts and serve at once. Pass a dish of freshly grated Parmesan for those who wish it.

Turkey and Vegetable Couscous

SERVES 6

A traditional North African couscous, prepared from scratch, takes hours, so I used to make it only for special occasions. Fortunately, with the new precooked couscous available in most supermarkets, you can now turn out a very acceptable family couscous in about an hour. Try this recipe; it may become a favorite. It is an ample, nutritious, economical one-dish meal. Don't be daunted by the number of ingredients. Most of them are familiar vegetables. You may make the stew with fewer vegetables, if you like.

4 medium-size turkey wings, cut in two at the joint

1 tablespoon coarse salt

1 tablespoon hot paprika (see Notes)

4 plump cloves garlic, peeled

6 tablespoons vegetable oil

3 bay leaves

One 2-inch cinnamon stick

1 teaspoon cumin seeds

8 cups unsalted chicken stock

1 teaspoon sugar

4 medium-size turnips, peeled and quartered

2 medium-size potatoes, peeled and quartered

3 medium-size carrots, peeled and sliced into 2-inch rounds

2 medium-size onions, peeled and quartered

1/4 head white cabbage, cored and cut into chunks

1/4 cup golden raisins

One 8-ounce can stewed tomatoes, with their juice

2 medium-size yellow squash or zucchini, cut into 1-inch pieces

One 10-ounce can chick-peas, rinsed and drained

1 tablespoon olive oil

1 teaspoon finely grated lemon peel

1 cup precooked couscous

Salt and Tabasco

3 or 4 sprigs cilantro (optional)

1. Wash and dry the disjointed wings. With a miniprocessor or a mortar and pestle, grind the salt, paprika, and garlic to a paste and rub it well into the turkey pieces. (Be sure to wash this hot mixture off your fingers with soap and water when you've finished this step.)

2. Heat the oil in a large heavy-bottomed kettle. When it hazes, toss in the bay leaves, cinnamon, and cumin seeds. Rake them about in the

hot oil for 15 seconds. Brown the turkey pieces well in the oil. Once finished, discard the oil.

3. Add the stock, sugar, turnips, potatoes, carrots, onions, cabbage, raisins, and the tomatoes and their juice. Simmer, covered, for 50 minutes, or until the turkey is fork-tender. Then add the squash and chick-peas and simmer for 10 minutes more.

4. Meanwhile, in a 2-quart stew pan, bring 1 cup of hot water, the olive oil, and the lemon peel to a rolling boil. Stir in the couscous, cover, remove from the heat, and allow to sit for 5 minutes.

5. Fluff the conscous with two forks. Spoon it around the edge of a large, deep serving platter. Discard the bay leaves and cinnamon stick. Pile the turkey and vegetables in the center of the platter. Season the broth to taste and ladle it over the mound. Garnish with cilantro, if you wish, and serve steaming hot in soup plates.

NOTES: Hot paprika can usually be found in the spice section of your supermarket, Pride of Szèged being one well-distributed brand. If you can't locate it, mix 5 parts sweet paprika with 1 part ground cayenne pepper to substitute.

If there are leftovers, refrigerate them and use them the next day with some fresh ingredients to create a salad. This North African favorite makes an unusual and very tasty light lunch.

CHAPTER TWO

Beef and Veal Stews

Introduction to Beef and Veal Stews

Despite the efforts of nutritionists to convince Americans that eating too much beef is bad for their health, it continues to be the favorite meat of most diners in the United States. This predilection is of long standing and probably dates back, according to the great historian, Braudel, to our fifteenth-century guild-member forebears in Europe, who survived the Black Death and were granted by public ordinance the privilege of eating two dishes of beef at the noon meal. Be that as it may, beef undoubtedly enjoys a privileged place in our esteem, along with all its macho lore and mythology. For those who are interested in knowing more about beef's sway over us, I recommend Jeremy Rifkin's excellent book, *Beyond Beef*; it explains very well why giving up beef is a rather complex problem for many Americans. It becomes much less of a problem if one remembers that no one should be obliged to give up beef entirely; rather, it is a matter of eating less of it.

In accordance with the great American bias for beef, many Americans think of stew as beef stew: a pot of beef, potatoes, carrots, onion, and sometimes tomato. Not only do the majority not know other stews, they don't know any of the hundreds of other beef stews. For that reason I have found and presented here a good sampling of lesser-known delicious beef and veal stews that deserve to be better known in the States.

Here are a few of the more important things to remember in shopping for stewing beef and veal and some timeworn tips for stewing and braising them well: The best stewing beef is usually from cuts called round, chuck, and flank; the best stewing veal is ordinarily cut from the shoulder, breast, hock, or shin. I heartily recommend getting to know a reliable butcher and staying with him. That way you can exact almost absolute accountability. Short of that, you are going to have to rely on your supermarket, where accountability can always be requested, but not exacted. Since many of you will find yourselves having to deal with supermarkets, I can only say, examine well what you buy. Most good stewing beef today, since it is not aged, should be bright red and should be purchased and used within three days of its packaging. Veal should be a rosy pink, without the faintest greenish tinge. It also should be used within three days of its packaging. Once you have broken the seal on the package, the meat should be smelled. Fresh beef, like fresh veal, has no decided smell. The meat should then be washed and blotted dry with paper towels. James Beard would have disagreed with me about washing the meat, but he knew his butcher very well. Most of us are not on such good terms with the backstage of a supermarket, so *do* wash the meat, not only because of what it may have touched but because power saws are generally used to cut meat in a supermarket, and they leave a lot of bone dust on much of the meat.

It is very important that beef and veal be stewed with a certain amount of fat, or they will turn out dry, tough, and stringy. Some cooks say that one quarter of the volume of the meat should be fat. I find good results can be obtained with less—one sixth, for instance. I judge the ratio by eye, but you may wish to do it by weight. This does not really fly in the face of the nutritionists who tell us to cut down on fat, because most of the fat can and should be discarded late in the stewing, when it has risen to the surface of the stew. The Burgundians are so insistent on stewing with a good amount of fat that they habitually add salt pork or bacon *en lardons* to all their beef and chicken stews and sweet butter to the veal ones.

The heat is as crucial to the texture of the beef and veal as the fat. Just remember that at 212°F, the boiling point of water, beef or veal will dry out and toughen. Beef and veal should be heated gently in cold water, stock, or an appropriate combination of liquids so that the albumen in the meat will not heat too quickly and toughen. When a rolling boil has been reached, the heat should be reduced to 175°F, so that the meat will poach instead of boil.

I have indicated in each recipe the techniques I felt appropriate and minimized the bother of too much cross-referencing to other recipes, preferring sometimes to repeat a technique rather than refer to another page, something of a bore in the midst of cooking. I hope you will enjoy the delicious beef and veal stews in this section half as much as I enjoyed choosing them for you.

O. Henry's Beef Stew

SERVES 4

*I*n his 1917 short story, "The Third Ingredient," O. Henry praises beef stew and its ability to draw people together, nourish them, and soothe their anxieties. In the guise of his protagonist, Hetty Pepper, O. Henry tells us, "You can't make beef stew without potatoes and onions." Hetty even goes on to affirm that "onion is the soul" of beef stew. Using her guidelines, I have put together the recipe for Hetty's stew. It is a simple model recipe for beginners.

2 pounds lean short ribs of beef, cut into serving-size pieces

1 teaspoon coarse salt

2 large yellow potatoes, peeled and cut into bite-size chunks

1 large yellow onion, peeled and cut lengthwise into 8 pieces

Salt and pepper

1. Wash the beef under cold running water and pat it dry with paper towels. Put it in a large heavy-bottomed kettle with the coarse salt and 6 cups of cold water. Bring slowly to a boil, then reduce the heat to a low simmer. For the first 15 minutes, skim off and discard the froth and fat that rise to the surface. Then cover the kettle tightly and simmer for 2 hours.
2. Skim off and discard all the liquid fat that has risen to the surface. Add the potatoes and onions. Cover the kettle and simmer again for $^1/_2$ hour.
3. Salt and pepper to taste and serve in deep soup plates.

NOTE: This stew may be used as a base for standard variations. You may brown the beef in oil before simmering it; you may substitute dry white or red wine for one third of the water; you may add other vegetables, a bouquet garni, and so on; and you may thicken the stew by stirring in 3 tablespoons cornstarch or flour dissolved in $^1/_2$ cup cold water, then simmering for 5 minutes. It won't be Hetty's simple stew, but it will be good, and you will have learned most of the techniques used in stew making.

Corned Beef and Cabbage Dinner

SERVES 6

*I*n the States, a version of corned beef and cabbage, sometimes dyed green with vegetable coloring and often stewed to "rags," traditionally appears on St. Patrick's Day menus. Not so this recipe, which is, I'm assured, the "really O'Reilly," an old-country version of that grand old Irish dish.

One 3-pound lean brisket of
  corned beef
12 peppercorns
2 plump cloves garlic, unpeeled,
  pierced in two or three places
6 medium-size carrots, peeled and
  cut into 1-inch pieces
3 medium-size waxy potatoes,
  peeled and quartered

1 large white cabbage, cored and
  cut into six wedges
12 pearl onions, peeled, a cross
  cut in each end
$^1/_2$ teaspoon caraway seeds
  (optional)
Salt

1. Soak the brisket for at least $^1/_2$ hour in cold water to cover, then wash it well under cold running water. Place the brisket in a heavy-bottomed kettle large enough to accommodate the meat without bending it. Add 6 cups of cold water, the peppercorns, and the garlic. Heat slowly to the boiling point, cover, reduce the heat, and simmer gently for 2 hours, or until the corned beef is fork-tender.
2. Skim off all the foam and fat that have risen during the simmering. Discard the garlic cloves. Add the carrots and potatoes. Cover and continue simmering for $^1/_2$ hour.
3. Add the cabbage and pearl onions. Scatter the caraway seeds over the stew. Cover and simmer for 15 minutes.
4. Remove the brisket to a carving board and blot it with paper towels. Carve into neat, diagonal slices.
5. Arrange the components on a large deep platter with the slices of corned beef in front, the steaming vegetables piled high in back. Salt the broth to taste and serve it in a tureen so that your guests may moisten the meat and vegetables as they like.

NOTE: Irish soda bread goes well with this dish, as does a sauce of lightly salted whipped cream laced with grated horseradish, a little Dijon mustard, and a speck of garlic crushed with salt. Place a saltcellar of coarse salt and a peppermill loaded with fresh peppercorns within easy reach of your guests.

Dublin Beef Stew

SERVES 4 OR 5

Dubliners invented this robust stew to fortify themselves against the damp, bone-chilling fog that often invades their fair city. The beef is braised to melting goodness in rich, dark Guinness stout. The slightly bitter bouquet of the stout is delicately balanced by the sweetness of the vegetables. For lovers of beef stew, this one is a winner.

5 tablespoons vegetable oil

2 strips Irish bacon, coarsely chopped

2 pounds $3/4$-inch-thick chuck steak, cut into bite-size pieces

$1/4$ teaspoon freshly ground black pepper

1 tablespoon coarse salt

3 tablespoons all-purpose flour

3 medium-size yellow onions, sliced $1/4$ inch thick

4 plump cloves garlic, peeled

3 medium-size carrots, peeled and cut into $1/4$-inch rounds

1 medium-size parsnip, peeled and cut into $1/4$-inch rounds

3 small white turnips, peeled, halved, and sliced $1/4$ inch thick

6 to 8 small white mushrooms, wiped clean and sliced $1/4$ inch thick

1 bouquet garni made up of 6 sprigs flat-leaf parsley, 2 fresh sage leaves, and 1 sprig fresh thyme, all bound together with cotton string

$2^{1}/2$ cups beef stock

2 cups Guinness stout

$1/2$ cup soft white bread crumbs

1 to 2 freshly shucked oysters for each diner (optional)

Salt

1. Heat the oil in a deep heavy-bottomed braising pan and gently fry the bacon bits just until they begin to brown on the edges. Remove them with a slotted spoon and set them aside.

2. Rub the pepper, salt, and flour into the pieces of steak, and, without crowding them, brown the pieces of steak in the oil and bacon dripping. Remove them as they finish browning and place them with the bacon bits.

3. Sauté the onions and garlic until limp. Add the carrots, parsnip, turnips, mushrooms, bouquet garni, and beef stock. Deglaze the bottom of the pan well, scraping loose all the browned bits. Return the

browned steak and bacon bits to the pan. Cover tightly and simmer over the lowest possible heat for $1^1/_2$ hours, or until the beef is fork-tender.

4. Add the Guinness and bread crumbs and simmer, covered, for another $^1/_2$ hour.

5. Discard the bouquet garni and add the oysters. Salt the stew to taste and serve at once, ladled over thick slices of crusty white bread. If you prefer, serve the stew with boiled potatoes tossed with chopped parsley, scallion, and olive oil. Provide plenty of crusty, fine-textured bread to mop up the copious sauce.

New England Boiled Dinner

A lmost every ethnic or regional cuisine has its own version of boiled beef and vegetables. The New England version is very similar to the French pot au feu in that it is so easy, almost anyone can prepare it. If you want to become a master of the dish, however, you must answer to the mavens of boiled beef who require that the broth be unclouded, without a single lunette of fat floating on the surface. That means boiling the potatoes separately, since they are the culprits that cloud the broth, and skimming away every trace of fat and heat-hardened froth that rises to the surface while the beef is poaching. Today we are far more demanding about removing the fat than our ancestors were. To learn many of the techniques for degreasing soups and sauces, see what I have to say on page 9.

One 4-pound beef brisket
(corned beef may be used)
1 tablespoon coarse salt (optional
if using corned beef)
1 bay leaf
6 peppercorns, bruised
1 small onion, unpeeled, spiked
with 2 cloves
1 tablespoon cider vinegar
3 medium-size yellow onions,
peeled, and quartered

3 large carrots, peeled and cut
into 1-inch rounds
2 large parsnips, peeled and cut
into $1/2$-inch rounds
3 medium-size turnips, peeled,
halved, and sliced $1/4$ inch thick
1 small white cabbage, core left
in, cut into six to eight wedges
3 medium-size waxy potatoes,
peeled and quartered
Salt

1. Wash the brisket well under cold running water. If using corned beef, soak it for at least 30 minutes in cold water to cover, then rinse it well under running water. Place the beef in a heavy-bottomed kettle large enough to accommodate the piece without bending it. Add 6 cups of cold water, the coarse salt, bay leaf, peppercorns, spiked onion, and vinegar. Heat these ingredients very slowly so that the meat will not toughen. Simmer the beef gently for 15 minutes, skimming off all the froth and fat that rise to the surface. Then cover tightly and simmer over the lowest possible heat for $2^1/2$ hours.

2. Remove the meat to a flat surface and cover it. Skim off and discard all the fat and solidified bits of albumen that have risen to the surface.

Discard the bay leaf and the spiked onion. Add all the vegetables except the cabbage and potatoes. Cover and simmer for 20 minutes.

3. In another pot, boil the potatoes in cold, slightly salted water until barely tender. Leave them in the water until you're ready to use them.

4. Add the cabbage to the vegetables in the kettle and simmer for 15 minutes.

5. Return the meat to the kettle briefly to heat it through. When warm, carve it into neat, thin, diagonal slices. Arrange the slices down the middle of a large serving platter, and surround them with the steaming vegetables and potatoes.

6. Salt the broth to taste. Serve it first, in deep soup plates. Change the plates, if you wish, and serve the meat and vegetables at once, while they are hot.

NOTE: It is customary to provide coarse salt, black pepper, Dijon mustard, grated horseradish, and pickles, so that your diners may heighten the seasoning as they wish.

London Broil Stewed in Stout

*L*ondon broil is a good, economical cut of beef that is usually grilled, sliced, and served au jus. The cut can be prepared many ways, however; it is really fine pot-roasted, braised, or "swissed" (floured, browned, and braised until tender). Here is a simple way of pot-roasting it suggested by those incomparable English cooks, the late Elizabeth David and Jane Grigson. Aside from transforming the sometimes tough, intractable London broil into a perfectly tender, daubelike dish, this way of preparing it is very easy. Once sealed up and put in the oven, the dish requires no attention for 3 hours, and it produces plenty of natural rich gravy.

One 2-pound piece of London broil, cut at least 1 inch thick

$1/2$ teaspoon coarse salt

1 teaspoon freshly ground black pepper

3 tablespoons cornstarch

$1/4$ teaspoon dried thyme

$1/4$ strip breakfast bacon, cut into $1/4$-inch pieces

1 plump clove garlic, peeled and cut lengthwise into small spikes

1 bay leaf

1 large onion, sliced $1/4$ inch thick

1 cup stout or dark ale

1 tablespoon honey

2 tablespoons red wine vinegar

1 tablespoon Worcestershire sauce

1. Preheat the oven to 275°F.
2. To prevent the meat from curling, trim off and discard the integument that surrounds it.
3. Pat the meat dry with paper towels and sprinkle it all over with half the salt and pepper. Dredge with the cornstarch, patting it well into the meat.
4. Pierce the beef through in half a dozen places. Press the thyme leaves into the bacon pieces and force a piece of bacon and a garlic spike into each of the holes in the meat.
5. Lightly oil a heavy-bottomed braising pan. Place the bay leaf in the center of the pan and the meat on top of it. Pile the onion slices on top of the meat.
6. Mix the stout, honey, vinegar, and Worcestershire sauce and pour over the onions. Sprinkle on the rest of the salt and pepper.

7. Cover the mound of meat and onions with a sheet of waxed paper. Seal the pot with two thicknesses of foil and press the lid down firmly.
8. Put the pot in the oven and bake, undisturbed, for 3 hours.
9. Serve the beef hot, with the thin sauce poured over it. Carve it at the table.

NOTE: The natural sauce from the beef will be full-bodied but thin. I sometimes "finish" it by adding 2 tablespoons of tomato sauce and a thickening of 3 tablespoons of cornstarch dissolved in 3 tablespoons of cold water. When the sauce has cooked and thickened sufficiently, salt it to taste and pour it over the meat. Jane Grigson suggested that the best accompaniment to this dish is creamy mashed potatoes. I agree. Other fine complements are puréed turnips or buttered noodles.

Old-Fashioned Oxtail Stew

SERVES 6 TO 8

*O*xtails, once prized by budget-conscious householders and gourmet diners alike, disappeared for years from most U.S. meat markets. They are back frozen, cut into 2-inch lengths, in 1¹/₂-pound packages but at three times their former price. If, however, you can find 4 hours to simmer them while doing other tasks, this copious, delicately spiced, satiny-sauced stew is well worth the price and your time. Here is my great granny Abbott's Edwardian recipe for this Lucullan delight, adapted to our times. It is a substantial family-and-friends dish to be eaten slowly, with lots of fun, conversation, and bone-picking.

3 pounds oxtails (well thawed, if frozen), cut into 2-inch pieces

3 tablespoons coarse salt

1 pound smoked pork neck bones

6 tablespoons vegetable oil

2 cups dry red wine

2 cups unsalted beef stock

One 8-ounce can tomato sauce

1 bouquet garni made up of 2 bay leaves, 6 sprigs fresh thyme, 2 sprigs fresh rosemary, and 8 cloves, all bound together with cotton string

1 tablespoon cracked pepper

2 medium-size turnips, peeled, halved, and cut into ¹/₄-inch pieces

6 medium-size onions, peeled and quartered

6 medium-size carrots, peeled and sliced into ¹/₄-inch rounds

2 large leeks, white parts only, well washed, cut into 2-inch pieces

6 ribs celery, cut into 2-inch pieces

Salt

1. Wash the oxtail pieces under cold running water. Sprinkle 2 tablespoons of the coarse salt over them and let them sit for 5 minutes, then rinse them again and pat them dry with paper towels. Set them aside.

2. Wash and dry the neck bones. Set them aside.

3. Heat the oil in a large heavy-bottomed kettle and brown the oxtail pieces until they are dark brown all over. (They spatter wildly, so beware!) When they are well browned, remove them and discard the browning oil. Wipe out the kettle with paper towels and return the browned pieces to it.

4. Add the neck bones, the remaining 1 tablespoon of coarse salt, the wine, 8 cups of cold water, the stock, tomato sauce, bouquet garni, and cracked pepper. Slowly heat to a rolling boil. Reduce the heat to a low simmer. During the first 15 minutes of simmering, skim off and discard the rising foam, then cover the kettle tightly and simmer for 3 hours.
5. Skim off and discard all the liquid fat that has risen to the surface. Add the turnips, onions, carrots, leeks, and celery. Cover and simmer over the lowest possible heat for 1 hour.
6. Discard the bouquet garni and salt the stew to taste. Take the kettle to the table and ladle the stew into deep soup plates, giving each diner plenty of sauce, meat, and vegetables. And, of course, provide each with a soup spoon, fork, and knife; all will be needed.

NOTES: This satisfying stew is a meal in itself and needs only pickles, hot mustard, and assorted relishes to accompany it. I suggest a simple green salad dressed with a tart vinaigrette to follow.

This stew will jelly firmly if refrigerated overnight. It reheats beautifully, but it is even better than jellied daube when served cold with chopped parsley and scallions and a lean lemon-juice vinaigrette made with only 2 tablespoons of oil.

Java Beef Stew

SERVES 6

Early Anglo settlers in Texas, where I grew up, always called coffee "java"; hence the name for this dark, richly flavored beef stew in which the browned beef is braised in strong black coffee. This great stew, Texas foodlore enthusiasts believe, was invented by an anonymous chuck-wagon cook who, unwilling to throw away the leftover breakfast coffee, used a cup of it to braise the beef for a stew. This unorthodox addition proved to be a felicitous one; the stew, as you will find, is hearty and delicious. Other versions of the stew are sometimes called "son-of-a-gun stew," "red-eye stew," or "cowpunchers' stew," but I prefer the name by which I first knew it: java stew.

2 pounds lean beef chuck, cut into 1 × 2-inch pieces

1 teaspoon coarse salt

1 teaspoon cracked black pepper

$^1/_2$ teaspoon ground allspice

$^1/_2$ teaspoon ground ginger

3 tablespoons flour

$^1/_4$ cup vegetable oil

1 cup strong black coffee

1 tablespoon cider vinegar

2 tablespoons brown sugar

3 plump cloves garlic, crushed

2 tablespoons Worcestershire sauce

$^1/_2$ teaspoon finely crumbled dried oregano

$^1/_4$ teaspoon red pepper flakes (optional)

1 tablespoon beef concentrate

1 teaspoon ground cumin

3 tablespoons tomato sauce

$1^1/_2$ cups onions, coarsely chopped

2 cups carrots in $^1/_4$-inch rounds.

2 cups potatoes in 1-inch dice

$^1/_2$ cup bread crumbs

Salt

1. Rub the coarse salt, cracked pepper, allspice, ginger, and flour into the pieces of beef.
2. Heat the oil in a large heavy-bottomed kettle and gently brown the beef in batches. Remove and set aside as the pieces finish browning.
3. Discard the remaining oil in the kettle and quickly wipe out the bottom with paper towels.
4. Mix the coffee, vinegar, sugar, and 1 cup of warm water. Over high heat, deglaze the kettle with this mixture.

5. Reduce the heat to very low. Add the browned beef, garlic, Worcestershire, oregano, and pepper flakes. Cover the kettle and simmer gently for 1 1/2 hours, or until the beef is fork-tender.
6. Stir in 2 1/2 cups of warm water, the beef concentrate, cumin, tomato sauce, onions, carrots, and potatoes. Simmer, uncovered, for 1 hour.
7. Stir in the bread crumbs and allow the stew to thicken for 5 to 10 minutes.
8. Salt to taste and serve hot.

NOTE: This stew may be served over plain boiled rice. However, for a real Western treat, serve it generously ladled over halved oversized buttermilk biscuits, still hot from the oven!

Texas Chili

SERVES 4 TO 6

*I*n the States, chili con carne is a well-known red-pepper stew. According to one Mexican lexicographer, it is "a detestable gringo dish, with a pseudo-Mexican name." The stew was, in fact, invented by early Texas settlers and was so much liked by non-Latinos that it is now, perhaps, the most popular dish in the United States. When I was a child in Texas sixty-odd years ago, chili was made every two to three weeks by local butchers from beef and pork scraps and sold in solid 1-pound bricks. When heated, this "Texas confit" turned into a highly spiced, chunky stew with a substantial layer of vermilion fat floating on its surface. It was served in thick, deep "chili bowls," into which saltines were crumbled. In those precholesterol days, we considered it a genuine treat. Here is my simple recipe for that incomparable dish, updated and defatted, but just as delicious as I remember it.

3 tablespoons vegetable oil

1¹/₂ pounds lean beef chuck, cut into bite-size pieces

2 plump cloves garlic, finely chopped

1 small onion, finely chopped

3 tablespoons chili powder

¹/₂ teaspoon cracked black pepper

1 teaspoon ground cumin

¹/₄ teaspoon cumin seeds

¹/₄ teaspoon crumbled dried oregano

2 cups unsalted beef stock

1 tablespoon cornmeal or *masa harina* (tortilla flour)

Salt

1. Heat the oil in a medium-size heavy-bottomed kettle and sear the beef quickly on all sides. Toss in the garlic and onion. Immediately reduce the heat to very low and sauté the garlic and onion until transparent.
2. Stir in the chili powder, black pepper, ground cumin, cumin seeds, oregano, stock, and 2 cups of cold water. Cover and simmer for 1¹/₂ hours. Uncover and continue simmering for 20 minutes.
3. Skim off and discard the floating fat. Sprinkle in the cornmeal and stir it in well. Continue to simmer for 5 minutes.
4. Salt to taste and serve immediately in deep bowls.

NOTE: Serve with plain boiled pinto beans or drained hominy. For those who like their chili hotter, provide Tabasco sauce or hot pickled peppers. The usual bread accompaniment is soda crackers.

Caterers' Party Chili

This recipe was given to me by a friend who caters in Manhattan. She tells me it is her most requested party dish. It is very tasty, very easy, and feeds more than a dozen guests.

²/₃ cup vegetable oil

2 large green bell peppers, coarsely chopped

4 large onions, coarsely chopped

3 plump cloves garlic, crushed

1 cup finely chopped flat-leaf parsley

3 pounds ground beef chuck

1 pound lean ground pork

¹/₂ cup chili powder

One 28-ounce can peeled tomatoes, coarsely chopped, with their juice

2 cups unsalted beef stock

Two 16-ounce cans pinto beans

1¹/₂ teaspoons freshly ground black pepper

1¹/₂ teaspoons cumin seeds

¹/₂ cup cornmeal or *masa harina* (tortilla flour)

Salt

1. Heat 2 tablespoons of the oil in a large frying pan and gently sauté the peppers, onions, garlic, and parsley, tossing often with a wooden spatula, until the onions and peppers are wilted. Set aside.
2. In a very large heavy-bottomed kettle, heat the rest of the oil and sauté the beef and pork for at least 15 minutes, tossing the meat and forcing it apart to break it up.
3. Add the sautéed vegetables to the meat. Stir in the chili powder, tomatoes and their juice, the stock, and 2 cups of cold water. Mix well and bring to a boil.
4. Reduce the heat to very low. Cover tightly and simmer for 1 hour.
5. Stir in the beans, black pepper, and cumin seeds. Continue simmering, uncovered, for ¹/₂ hour.
6. Sift in the cornmeal, a little at a time, stirring it in well. Simmer for another 15 minutes. Salt to taste and serve hot in deep bowls.

NOTE: This chili may be made as much as a day in advance and refrigerated. If you wish to freeze it to have in store as a quick resource, do so after step 4. Finish the steps after thawing it. It is a good central dish for a party or gathering. Provide grated Monterey Jack cheese for those who like to sprinkle it over their chili. Tabasco sauce for those who like their chili torrid, and lots of nacho chips for everyone. Guacamole and mixed green salad are nice cool foils for this dish.

Argentinian *Gaucho Puchero*

SERVES 6

This much-loved South American stew, like so many of its European predecessors, is customarily served in three courses: first the clear broth, then the beef, and finally the vegetables and hard-boiled eggs. It is a substantial meal that can easily become festive with a plethora of your own condiments and relishes. If you are a salsa maker, this meal will provide you with the occasion to show your mettle.

3 pounds beef shanks or lean short ribs, cut into serving-size pieces

1/2 lemon

1 tablespoon coarse salt

16 peppercorns, crushed

2 medium-size onions, peeled and quartered

2 large carrots, peeled, split, and cut into 2-inch pieces

2 large leeks, white parts only, trimmed and well washed, cut into 2-inch pieces

2 ribs celery, cut into 1-inch pieces

1 bay leaf

6 sprigs flat-leaf parsley, loosely bound with cotton string

3 ears corn on the cob, husked and cut across the cob into 1-inch pieces

2 medium-size sweet potatoes, peeled and cut into 1 1/2-inch chunks

3 large waxy potatoes, peeled and cut into 1 1/2-inch chunks

6 large eggs

1 small head white cabbage, cut into six pieces, core left in

Salt

1. Wipe the meat with a damp cloth, then rub the pieces all over with the lemon half. Put the meat in a heavy-bottomed kettle with the salt, peppercorns, and 2 quarts of cold water. Cover and simmer over low heat for 2 hours, skimming off all the fat and froth that rise to the surface.

2. Add the onions, carrots, leeks, celery, bay leaf, parsley, corn, sweet potatoes, and white potatoes. Cover tightly and simmer over the lowest possible heat for 40 minutes, or until the carrots are tender.

3. With a darning needle, barely pierce the shell of each egg at the rounder end to prevent its cracking.

4. Add the eggs and the cabbage to the kettle and simmer, uncovered, for 15 minutes.

5. Remove the eggs, and shell and peel them under cold running water. Halve them and set them aside.
6. Salt the stew to taste. Discard the bay leaf and parsley.
7. Strain the broth through three thicknesses of dampened cheesecloth and serve it first. It is customary to add a few cooked pasta shells to each plate of broth.
8. Arrange the meat on one platter, the vegetables and halved eggs on another. A dish of coarse salt, a pepper grinder loaded with black pepper, cruets of fine olive oil and wine vinegar, a pot of Dijon or Düsseldorf mustard, a jar of freshly grated horseradish, and a bottle of Tabasco peppers in vinegar are *de rigueur* with this meal.

Burgundian Beef and Onion Gratinée

SERVES 6

Forty years ago in Paris I used to see the night-shift butchers and porters of the former Les Halles wolfing down this strength-restoring dish at 4:00 A.M. Today, the dish is universally known outside France as French onion soup. Almost no one makes it from scratch, and what you are served nowadays in its stead is a ghost of its former self. Here is a recipe as near the original gratinée bourguignonne as you are likely to find. Serve it to hungry diners on a bone-chilling night, and you will win their hearts forever—but they will expect you to make it for them again and again.

3 pounds beef chuck neck bones, cut into approximately 1 × 2-inch pieces

12 peppercorns

1 tablespoon red wine vinegar

1 tablespoon coarse salt

1 bouquet garni made up of 2 bay leaves, 3 sprigs dried thyme, 1 sprig dried rosemary, 6 sprigs fresh flat-leaf parsley, and 3 cloves, bound together with cotton string

2 medium-size carrots, peeled and cut into 1-inch rounds

2 large leeks, well washed and trimmed, the green leaves bent back over the white shafts and bound together with cotton string

2 small turnips, peeled and cut into $1/4$-inch rounds

4 ribs celery, cut into 2-inch pieces

1 medium-size tomato, skinned, seeded, and coarsely chopped

$1/4$ teaspoon red pepper flakes

One $1/4$-inch-thick slice smoked slab bacon, cut into $1/4$-inch strips

6 large yellow onions, thinly sliced

6 plump cloves garlic, thinly sliced

1 teaspoon sugar

Salt

6 thick slices French bread

2 cups grated Gruyère cheese

1 jigger ($1^1/2$ ounces) port (optional)

1. Wash the beef bones well under warm running water. Place them, with 10 cups of cold water, the peppercorns, vinegar, and salt, in a large heavy-bottomed kettle that will fit under your broiler. Very slowly bring the ingredients to a boil, then simmer gently for 15 minutes, skimming off and discarding the foam and fat that rise to the surface.

2. Add the bouquet garni, carrots, leeks, turnips, celery, tomato, and pepper flakes. Cover and simmer for 2 hours.

3. Meanwhile, sauté the bacon in a large kettle until it begins to brown. Remove the bacon and discard the dripping. Return the bacon to the kettle, add the onions and garlic, and toss together thoroughly. Cover and cook over very low heat for 15 minutes, stirring occasionally with a wooden spatula to prevent scorching. Dissolve the sugar in $1/2$ cup of warm water and stir it in. Continue to sauté gently for $1/2$ hour, or until the onions are completely soft. They must not brown.

4. Salt the broth to taste, and strain it into the onion mixture. Simmer for 15 minutes. Discard the bouquet garni. Save the bones and vegetables (see Note).

5. Preheat the broiler and oven-dry the bread without toasting it. Float the slices on the broth and sprinkle them evenly with the grated cheese. Put the pot under the broiler. When the melting cheese is bubbling and golden brown, remove the pot immediately. Lift the cheese crust in several places and pour in the port.

6. Serve steaming hot in deep bowls. Give each diner plenty of broth and onions and a generous portion of the crust.

NOTE: Refrigerate the bones and vegetables overnight. Strip the meat from the bones and discard them. Untie and cut the leeks into $1/2$-inch slices. Dress the bits of meat, the leeks, and the other vegetables with a garlic-and-mustard vinaigrette and garnish this *saladier bourguigon* with finely chopped parsley and hard-boiled eggs. *Et voici:* you have a second regional favorite for taking the time and trouble to make the Burgundian gratinée from scratch.

Hungarian *Gulyàs* with Dumplings

SERVES 6

A t corner diners in the States, "goulash" is an orange-hued, fat-laden, catchall beef stew known more for its ability to bludgeon your hunger than delight your palate. Not so the true Hungarian gulyàs, from which the diner stew derives its name. An authentic gulyàs is a full-bodied stew of beef, onions, and potatoes, with lots of spicy broth and tiny dumplings; it may or may not contain paprika. Here is my slimmed-down version of the real article my godmother, Gusti Matzner, used to make for us.

FOR THE *GULYÀS*

3 tablespoons vegetable oil

2 cups peeled and thinly sliced yellow onions

3 pounds lean stewing beef, cut into 1-inch dice

2 plump cloves garlic, peeled

$^1/_2$ teaspoon caraway seeds

$^1/_4$ teaspoon dried marjoram

$^1/_2$ teaspoon coarse salt

2 tablespoons genuine Hungarian paprika (optional)

$^1/_2$ teaspoon freshly ground black pepper

2 tablespoons beef concentrate

1 envelope ham concentrate (see Notes)

One 8-ounce can stewed tomatoes, drained and coarsely chopped

2 large bell peppers, cut lengthwise into $^1/_2$-inch strips

2 cups coarsely chopped potatoes

Salt and pepper

FOR THE DUMPLINGS

$^1/_2$ cup flour

1 large egg

3 tablespoons cold water

$^1/_2$ teaspoon coarse salt

1 teaspoon vegetable oil

1. Heat the oil in a large heavy-bottomed kettle and gently sauté the onions until transparent. Add the beef cubes and brown them slowly, tossing the beef and onions together often to prevent scorching. This should take about 10 minutes.

2. In a miniprocessor or with a mortar and pestle, crush the garlic, caraway seeds, marjoram, and coarse salt together. Add this mixture, the paprika, the black pepper, and the beef and ham concentrates to the beef and onions. Then add 7 cups of warm water and stir everything

together well. Cover the kettle and simmer for $1^1/_4$ hours over low heat. Remove and discard any liquid fat that rises to the surface.

3. Add the tomatoes, bell peppers, and potatoes. Gently simmer the *gulyàs*, uncovered, for another hour, or until the beef is fork-tender but not falling apart.

4. Stir the ingredients for the dumplings together well and set aside for 5 minutes in the freezer.

5. Using two oiled spoons, drop the dumpling batter by scant teaspoonfuls onto the surface of the simmering *gulyàs*. Allow the dumplings to cook for 5 minutes.

6. Salt and pepper the *gulyàs* to taste. Turn off the heat and allow the stew to sit, covered, for 5 minutes.

7. Serve the stew and dumplings very hot directly from the kettle in large, shallow soup plates.

NOTES: Ham concentrate is sold in eight-envelope packages by Goya Food, Inc. If you can't obtain it, make the substitute on page 35.

Most Hungarians prefer their *gulyàs* very spicy. Rather than peppering up the entire stew, I suggest you place a bottle of pepper sauce on the table for those who like it spicy.

Assorted pickled peppers and cucumbers, a green salad, fresh raisin-pumpernickel bread, and sweet butter are appropriate accompaniments for this great stew.

Spanish Beef Stew

*I*t is said that this stew was brought back from the Low Countries by soldiers returning to Spain after the occupation. As you can see, this dish has nothing in common with a Flemish carbonnade except for the beef and the beer. Yet it is a wonderful stew with a distinctive Andalusian taste.

2 pounds lean stewing chuck, cut into bite-size pieces

1/4 cup light olive oil

1 teaspoon coarse salt

2 tablespoons flour

2 medium-size yellow onions, peeled and quartered

1 whole head garlic, cut in half across the cloves, peel left on

1 large green bell pepper, coarsely chopped

3 bay leaves

One 16-ounce can stewed tomatoes, with their juice, coarsely chopped

1 cup light beer

1 cup unsalted beef stock

5 medium-size potatoes, peeled and quartered

1/8 teaspoon red pepper flakes (optional)

12 saffron threads, briefly toasted and finely crumbled (see Note)

One 10-ounce package frozen green peas, thawed

Salt

1. Wash the meat under cold running water and dry it well with paper towels. Heat the oil in a large heavy-bottomed kettle and brown the meat over medium heat. Sprinkle the salt and flour over the meat and toss well until the flour is absorbed.

2. Add in the onions, the garlic "bouquets," green pepper, bay leaves, and tomatoes, with their juice. Stir in well.

3. Add the beer, stock, and 2 cups of cold water. Cover and simmer over the lowest possible heat for 1 1/2 hours.

4. Add the potatoes, pepper flakes, and saffron. Cover and simmer for 20 minutes, or until the potatoes are tender. Add the peas, discard the bay leaves, and salt to taste. (Normally the garlic "bouquets" are left in because they are considered prizes. Garlic lovers like to pick the savory bits of braised garlic out of their peel.)

5. Set the kettle on the table and serve the stew from it. It is a one-dish meal.

NOTE: Saffron stamens or threads are not only the most expensive spice but also the most fragile. Enhance their flavor by toasting them very briefly in a dry, already heated frying pan which has been removed from the stove. Toss the saffron for five seconds, then quickly turn it out onto a paper towel. Toasted saffron crumbles easily to powder.

Winter Pot Roast and Vegetables in Red Wine Sauce

SERVES 6 TO 8

*I*n the craggy, mountainous area of southern France near Foix, just north of Andorra, the favorite seasoning is a mélange of finely chopped vegetables, bacon, and aromatics, sautéed and cooked down to its essence. This mirepoix, like the famous graisse normande, is added to soups and stews to give them the particular flavor of the cuisine of the area and accounts for the distinctive taste of this stew. Don't be daunted by the number of ingredients listed below; the recipe is really easy. Once you have made the mirepoix, put in the meat, and sealed up the kettle, you simply leave it to simmer for 1¹/₂ hours. The result is a beautiful reddish amber–colored stew with a bounty of richly flavored sauce.

¹/₄ cup vegetable oil

One ¹/₄-inch slice smoked bacon, half finely chopped, half cut into ¹/₄-inch pieces and set aside

1 cup finely chopped white mushrooms

1 cup finely chopped onions

1 cup finely chopped carrots

1 cup finely chopped celery

1 cup finely chopped bell pepper

3 plump cloves garlic, peeled, crushed with the flat side of a chef's knife, and ground to a paste with 1 teaspoon coarse salt

3 tablespoons finely chopped flat-leaf parsley

¹/₄ teaspoon finely crumbled dried marjoram

¹/₄ teaspoon dried thyme

¹/₂ teaspoon cracked black pepper

¹/₂ teaspoon ground allspice

3 tablespoons flour

2 tablespoons beef concentrate

2 tablespoons tomato purée

1 cup dry red wine

3 tablespoons brandy (optional, but highly recommended)

1 teaspoon sugar

1 tablespoon red wine vinegar

¹/₂ teaspoon ground sage

One 3-pound beef chuck roast

2 bay leaves

2 cups potatoes in ¹/₂-inch dice

2 cups carrots in 1-inch pieces

1 cup cauliflower florets

Salt

1. Heat the oil in a large heavy-bottomed kettle and fry the chopped bacon until the bits begin to brown along the edges.
2. Reduce the heat to low. Add the mushrooms, onions, carrots, celery,

bell pepper, crushed garlic, parsley, marjoram, thyme, black pepper, allspice, and flour. Toss well with the browned bacon and fat. Sauté for 10 minutes, stirring frequently.

3. Stir in 2 cups of warm water, the beef concentrate, tomato purée, wine, brandy, and sugar.

4. Moisten the bacon pieces you have set aside with the vinegar and sprinkle them with the sage. Pierce holes in six to eight places in the roast and force the bacon pieces into the holes.

5. Bury the roast in the simmering ingredients in the kettle, with two bay leaves under it.

6. Place a double sheet of foil over the top of the kettle and force the lid down on top of it to seal the stew. Simmer over the lowest possible heat for 1$^1/_2$ hours.

7. Carefully skim off and discard all the fat that has risen to the surface of the stew. Add the potatoes, the other carrots, and the cauliflower, burying them in the sauce. Cover again tightly and simmer over very low heat for an hour.

8. Discard the bay leaves, salt to taste, and place the roast on a deep serving platter. Cut it into serving-size pieces. Heap the vegetables around the meat and ladle the sauce over them. Serve hot.

NOTE: This remarkable stew produces lots of full-bodied sauce. I sometimes toss cooked cavatelli or broad noodles in the sauce and serve it along with the meat and vegetables. The pasta, meat, and vegetables make a very festive meal for a cold, wintry evening.

Trastevere Beef Stew

SERVES 6

The thick stew called ragù, of which hundreds exist in Italian regional cooking, originated in Italy centuries ago. Catherine de Medici is credited with introducing it to France, where it was dubbed ragoût and considered sui generis a French invention. Here is a genuine Italian ragù of beef and vegetables that deserves to be better known. It is from the Trastevere district of Rome.

1 strip streaky breakfast bacon, finely chopped

One 2-pound piece beef chuck or rump

1 small onion, finely grated

1 plump clove garlic, crushed

1 rib celery, coarsely chopped

1½ cups dry white wine

1 tablespoon tomato paste

¼ teaspoon finely crushed dried marjoram

1 teaspoon coarse salt

2 cups hot unsalted beef stock

Salt

2 large trimmed fennel bulbs, cored and quartered lengthwise

One 4-ounce package frozen artichoke hearts, thawed

¼ cup soft bread crumbs

2 tablespoons finely chopped flat-leaf parsley

1. Choose a deep heavy-bottomed braising pan just wide enough to accommodate the meat and vegetables. Heat the pan gently and sauté the bacon until the edges begin to take on color. Remove the bacon bits with a slotted spoon and set them aside.
2. Bind up the beef securely with cotton string so that it will keep its shape while stewing. Brown well on both sides in the drippings. Remove the beef and set it aside.
3. Add the onion, garlic, and celery to the pan. Rake them about in the drippings until they start to take on color.
4. Combine the wine and tomato paste, add them to the sautéed vegetables, and increase the heat. Deglaze the bottom of the pan thoroughly and allow the liquid to boil rapidly until it has reduced to one-third of its volume. Add the marjoram, coarse salt, and hot stock.
5. Return the meat to the pan and reduce the heat to the lowest level. Seal the kettle by placing a sheet of aluminum foil over the top and

pressing the lid down firmly. Simmer for $2^1/_2$ hours, or until the beef is fork-tender. Salt the sauce to taste.

6. Meanwhile, poach the fennel gently in 3 cups of boiling water and a few drops of lemon juice or vinegar for 20 minutes and drain well.

7. Place the fennel and artichoke hearts in the pan with the beef. Sprinkle the bread crumbs over the surface and reseal the pan. Simmer for 20 minutes.

8. Remove the trussing strings from the beef and slice the meat into serving-size pieces. Place the slices in the middle of a deep serving platter and heap the fennel, artichoke hearts, and sauce around them. Sprinkle with chopped parsley and serve at once.

NOTE: Plain boiled potatoes go well with this dish, though it is quite satisfying served alone. You may want to provide freshly grated Parmesan cheese for those who wish to sprinkle it over the vegetables.

Deviled Short Ribs with Noodles

SERVES 4 OR 5

There was a time when versions of this Bavarian dish could be found in all the German restaurants of the Yorkville section of New York City. Unfortunately, not only have most of those popular restaurants disappeared, so have many of their specialties, among them deviled short ribs of beef. Here is my version of that great dish—with noodles, a bit spicy, and oh so delicious!

3 pounds lean short ribs of beef, cut into serving-size pieces

1 teaspoon coarse salt

1 teaspoon cracked black pepper

3 tablespoons flour

$^1/_4$ cup vegetable oil

1 cup dry white wine

2 cups unsalted beef stock

2 tablespoons cider vinegar

1 tablespoon honey

1 small onion, peeled and spiked with 2 cloves

4 allspice berries

1 bay leaf

$^1/_4$ cup Dijon mustard

$^1/_2$ cup soft bread crumbs

Salt

1 pound spätzle or broad noodles, cooked al dente and drained

$^1/_2$ teaspoon griddle-toasted cumin seeds (see Note)

1. Wipe the ribs with a damp cloth, and work the salt, cracked pepper, and flour well into the pieces.
2. Heat the oil in a large heavy-bottomed kettle and gently brown the ribs, without crowding them, until they are quite brown on all sides. Remove them as they finish browning and set them aside.
3. Discard all the browning fat. Wipe the kettle out quickly with a paper towel, removing as much fat as you can. Add the wine, stock, vinegar, and honey and deglaze the bottom of the kettle thoroughly.
4. Place the browned ribs evenly over the bottom of the kettle in the braising liquid. Add the spiked onion, allspice, and bay leaf. Place a sheet of aluminum foil over the top of the kettle and press the lid down securely over it to seal the kettle. Simmer the ribs over the lowest possible heat for 2 to 2$^1/_2$ hours, or until fork-tender.
5. Preheat the oven to 375°F.
6. Remove the ribs and drain them. Using a brush, coat the ribs all

over with mustard and sprinkle them with bread crumbs. Bake them on an oiled baking pan for 20 minutes or until they are golden brown.

7. Meanwhile, cook and drain the noodles.

8. Strain the sauce, discarding the spiked onion, bay leaf, and allspice berries, and salt to taste.

9. Toss the noodles in the braising sauce. Serve them in a deep serving platter with the browned ribs nestling in them. Sprinkle the toasted cumin seeds over the platter and serve at once.

NOTE: Toasting spices to enhance their flavor is a technique common to the cooking of many countries. The knack is to toast—but not burn—the seeds, nuts, or aromatics on the dry, heated surface of a griddle or frying pan. Like pine nuts, dill seeds, and saffron threads, cumin seeds burn very quickly. The best way is to heat the griddle or pan until a drop of water dances on it, then remove it from the fire. Add the seeds and carefully stir them with a spatula for about five seconds, then remove them to a dish or paper towel. Once cooled, the seeds crush easily. For this recipe you may use them whole or crushed.

Beef with Olives, Peppers, and Peas

SERVES 6

*F*riuli lies between Venice and Trieste. In winter it is buffeted between the icy winds of the Dolomites and the damp drafts that blow in off the Bay of Venice. You can understand why the Frolani (as the inhabitants of this region are known) came up with this delightfully bracing stew. It is a beef stew with a difference or two from most other Italian ragùs.

2 pounds lean chuck, cut into
   1 × 1 × 2-inch pieces
1 teaspoon coarse salt
1/4 teaspoon *each* ground black
   pepper, nutmeg, cloves, and
   allspice
3 tablespoons all-purpose flour
6 tablespoons olive oil
2 large leeks, white parts only,
   slit, well washed, and coarsely
   chopped
2 plump cloves garlic, crushed
2 ribs celery, coarsely chopped
10 small white mushrooms, wiped
   clean and cut into 1/4-inch
   slices
1 1/2 cups dry white wine
2 cups unsalted beef stock

1 bouquet garni made up of 2 bay
   leaves, 12 fresh rosemary
   leaves, and one 2-inch piece
   orange peel, all wrapped in a
   green leek leaf and secured
   with cotton string
2 large green bell peppers, cut
   into 1/2-inch strips
12 black Italian olives, pitted and
   coarsely chopped
One 10-ounce package frozen
   peas, thawed
One 8-ounce can tomato sauce
3 tablespoons finely chopped
   flat-leaf parsley
1 tablespoon yellow cornmeal or
   semolina flour
Salt
1 cup coarsely grated Fontina
   cheese

1. Sprinkle the coarse salt over the pieces of meat. Mix the ground spices and flour together and work the mixture into the beef pieces.
2. Gently heat the oil in a Dutch oven and slowly brown the meat well, in batches. Remove the pieces as they finish browning and set them aside.
3. Add the leeks, garlic, celery, and mushrooms. Sauté them for about 5 minutes, tossing them frequently, until they are limp but not browned.
4. Add the wine and deglaze the bottom of the kettle.

5. Add the browned beef, stock, and the bouquet garni. Cover tightly and simmer over the lowest possible heat for 1¹/₂ hours, or until the beef is fork-tender.
6. Add the bell pepper, olives, peas, tomato sauce, and parsley. Sprinkle the cornmeal over the surface of the stew and whisk it in well to avoid lumps. Cover and simmer for 20 minutes.
7. Discard the bouquet garni. Salt to taste. Serve hot, sprinkled with the grated Fontina.

NOTE: My Frolani friends often serve this stew in a nest of polenta, gnocchi, or plain boiled rice. They then sprinkle on the Fontina and slip the serving dish under the broiler until the cheese melts and begins to take on color.

Florentine Roulade of Beef

SERVES 4 OR 5

*S*tewing or braising stuffed, tightly rolled rump steak to produce both sauce for
pasta and a main dish of sliced, stuffed beef is a very old technique in many
regions of Italy. Unfortunately, it often happens that in an effort to extract the
last drop of nutrition from the sometimes tough, intractable beef, it is cooked far
too long, so that the sauce turns out rich and full-bodied, but the beef is reduced
to tasteless fiber. The trick is to add just enough fat to the stuffing to keep the
rolls succulent and tasty and to cook them only until they are fork-tender. This
Florentine recipe requires a little time and attention, but the attractive result is
worth it.

One 2¹/₂- to 3-pound top rump
   steak, ¹/₄ inch thick
2 cups soft white bread crumbs
¹/₂ cup milk or beef stock
¹/₂ cup grated Parmesan cheese
¹/₄ cup extra virgin olive oil
2 tablespoons finely chopped flat-
   leaf parsley
2 strips breakfast bacon, finely
   chopped
¹/₄ teaspoon *each* ground white
   pepper, dried sage, and ground
   coriander
2 tablespoons anchovy paste
2 plump cloves garlic, crushed to
   a paste with ¹/₂ teaspoon coarse
   salt, using the underside of a
   soup spoon

1 large egg
1 egg white
¹/₈ pound thinly sliced prosciutto
15 blanched toasted almonds
15 cornichons
3 tablespoons flour
5 tablespoons vegetable oil
2 cups Chianti
2 cups unsalted beef stock
One 8-ounce can tomato sauce
1 tablespoon honey
1 small white onion, peeled and
   spiked with 2 cloves
1 bay leaf
1 carrot, halved
3 tablespoons cornstarch dissolved
   in 3 tablespoons cold water
Salt

1. Snip through the integument that surrounds the steak every ¹/₂ inch
   so that it won't curl in braising. Place the steak between two heavy
   sheets of waxed paper on a hard work surface. Pound it all over with
   a mallet or cutlet pounder, taking care not to tear it. Set it aside.
2. Put the bread crumbs, milk, Parmesan, olive oil, parsley, chopped

bacon, white pepper, sage, coriander, anchovy paste, garlic paste, egg, egg white, and 2 tablespoons of water in a food processor and pulse to a thick sticky paste. Add 2 more tablespoons of water if the paste seems too dry to spread.

3. Peel off the top layer of waxed paper and cover the steak with half the prosciutto slices, overlapping them a little so that the steak is entirely insulated. Spread the bread-crumb stuffing evenly over the prosciutto slices to within $1/2$ inch of the edges of the steak. Arrange the almonds and pickles in alternating rows, pressing them into the stuffing. Cover the stuffing with the remaining prosciutto slices, arranging them just as you did before.

4. Starting on a long side, roll up the steak and stuffing like a jelly roll, peeling off the waxed paper as you go. Truss the roll with cotton string and skewer the ends with toothpicks. Dredge the roll in the flour, brushing off the excess.

5. Heat the vegetable oil in a heavy-bottomed braising pan and gently brown the beef well all over. Remove the roll and set it aside.

6. Discard the oil. Add the wine and deglaze the bottom of the pan. Boil the wine over high heat until it has reduced to one third of its volume.

7. Stir in the beef stock, tomato sauce, and honey. Add the meat roll, spiked onion, bay leaf, and carrot. Cover the pan with a double sheet of aluminum foil and press the lid firmly down on top of it. Simmer the roll over the lowest possible heat for 2 hours, or until the roll can be easily pierced with a fork.

8. Remove the roll to a cutting board and allow it to firm up for 10 minutes.

9. Discard the bay leaf, the spiked onion, and the carrot. Stir in the cornstarch mixture. Simmer the sauce for 5 minutes, or until it is thick and smooth. Salt to taste.

10. Remove the trussing strings and the toothpicks. Cut the roll into neat slices, arrange them on a serving platter, and ladle the sauce around them. Serve while the sauce is hot.

NOTE: For an attractive lunch, serve the sauced slices of roulade with a green salad and assorted pickles and relishes. For a hearty dinner dish, arrange the slices on a bed of freshly cooked buttered linguine that has been tossed in the sauce and generously sprinkled with freshly grated Parmesan.

Sweet-and-Sour Cabbage Rolls

Here is my updated version of an old-fashioned recipe for stuffed cabbage. The original recipe came to the States with immigrants from Russia and Central Europe. It is one of those specialties the success of which depended, so old cooks said, on a secret. Not so! The only secret, if secret there be, is taking the time to do it. But it is very easily done, you'll find. Of course, first-rate ingredients, as in every recipe, are of cardinal importance. These rolls will keep in the refrigerator for three or four days; reheat them gently.

One 3-pound head white cabbage

1 small white onion, finely grated

3 tablespoons olive oil

³/₄ pound lean ground beef or veal

¹/₂ cup raw rice

2 tablespoons sugar

2 tablespoons coarse salt

1 large egg, lightly beaten

2 tablespoons fine white bread
    crumbs

¹/₂ teaspoon ground coriander

2 tablespoons vegetable oil

One 8-ounce can tomato sauce

1 cup unsalted beef stock

1 teaspoon finely chopped fresh
    dill

¹/₄ teaspoon sour salt (see Note)
    or 3 tablespoons freshly
    squeezed lemon juice

¹/₂ cup golden raisins

¹/₂ cup halved dried apricots

3 cloves

Salt

1 teaspoon caraway seeds

1. Core the cabbage and blanch the whole head, stem end down, for 10 minutes in a deep kettle holding 6 cups of boiling water. Remove the cabbage and drain it. When it is cool enough to handle, carefully remove the leaves, one by one. With a sharp knife, shave down the thick central rib of each leaf so that it is as thin as the rest of the leaf. The leaves should be whole and limp enough to fold. Cover the leaves with some of the hot blanching water and set them aside.

2. Put the grated onion in a medium-size frying pan with ¹/₄ cup of boiling water and simmer gently until the water disappears. Add the olive oil and fry slowly, scraping the onion back and forth with a wooden spatula until it is a yellowish mass, not browned. Remove the frying pan from the heat and set aside.

3. Knead the ground meat together with the rice, 1 tablespoon of the fried onion, half the sugar, half the coarse salt, the egg, bread crumbs, and coriander.

4. Carefully dry a cabbage leaf with paper towels. Spread the leaf and put 2 heaping tablespoons of the meat mixture in the center. Fold the stem end of the leaf over the stuffing, tuck in the two sides at right angles, and roll toward the thinner end of the leaf. The roll should be about $1^1/_2 \times 3$ inches. Place it, seam side down, on a plate. Repeat, using all the meat mixture. You should have about twelve or thirteen rolls. Set them aside, and chop the remaining cabbage leaves.

5. Pour the vegetable oil into the frying pan holding the remaining fried onion, and add the tomato sauce, stock, dill, the remaining sugar, and the sour salt. Cook gently, stirring continuously with a wooden spatula, and scraping the bottom to prevent scorching.

6. Simmer the cabbage rolls, seam sides down, for 3 minutes in the sauce, then turn them and simmer for 3 minutes on the other side.

7. Transfer the rolls to the bottom of a large heavy-bottomed kettle and pour the sauce over them. Pour in just enough warm water to cover the rolls. Scatter the dried fruit, cloves, and chopped leftover leaves over the rolls. Cover tightly and simmer over the lowest possible heat for $1^1/_4$ hours. Salt to taste.

8. Serve on dinner plates, three rolls to a person. Heap some sauce, stewed fruit, and cabbage over each serving and sprinkle with caraway seeds.

NOTE: Sour salt (citric acid crystals) may be found in the kosher section of large supermarkets.

Short Ribs with Cornmeal Dumplings

G usti Matzner, my Austrian godmother, gave me this recipe, though I have modified her version. Knowing how much my family loved this exquisitely flavored dish, she used to make it for us often during the winter months. I hope it becomes one of your favorites, too.

FOR THE STEW

3 pounds beef short ribs, cut into serving-size pieces

1 teaspoon freshly ground black pepper

1 plump clove garlic, crushed in 1 teaspoon coarse salt, using the underside of a soup spoon

$^1/_4$ cup vegetable oil

1 bay leaf

$^1/_2$ teaspoon caraway seeds

$^1/_2$ teaspoon ground coriander

1 large onion, halved and thinly sliced

3 finely crushed gingersnaps

One 12-ounce bottle ale

1 tablespoon beef concentrate

3 tablespoons cider vinegar

1 teaspoon sugar

FOR THE DUMPLINGS

$^1/_2$ cup yellow cornmeal

$^1/_2$ teaspoon coarse salt

1 large egg, beaten with 2 teaspoons water

$^1/_2$ cup flour

1 teaspoon baking powder

$^1/_4$ teaspoon freshly ground nutmeg

$^1/_2$ teaspoon dried dill

One 8-ounce can whole-kernel corn, drained

Salt

Freshly ground black pepper

Braising the Beef:

1. Wipe the ribs with a damp cloth. With a sharp boning knife, remove and discard as much excess fat from the ribs as you can without separating the meat from the bones.
2. Rub the ribs all over with the black pepper and the garlic paste.
3. Heat the oil in a large heavy-bottomed kettle and brown the ribs in batches until they are very brown. Remove them and set them aside.
4. Discard all but 2 tablespoons of the browning fat. Add the bay leaf,

caraway seeds, coriander, and onion and toss together well over low heat until the onion is translucent.

5. Add the cookie crumbs, ale, 2 cups of warm water, beef concentrate, vinegar, and sugar. Deglaze the kettle. Distribute the browned ribs evenly in the braising liquid, cover the kettle tightly, and simmer over low heat for 2 hours. Skim off and discard all the fat that has risen to the surface.

Making the Dumplings:

6. In a saucepan, mix the cornmeal and salt with 1 cup of water. Stirring constantly, cook the mixture until it is quite thick. Remove from the heat.

7. Beat the egg mixture into the cornmeal mush.

8. Mix the flour, baking powder, nutmeg, and dill together and stir them into the cornmeal mixture. Stir in the corn, mixing it throughout the batter.

9. Bring the thoroughly skimmed braising liquid back to a simmer and drop in the batter by tablespoonfuls. Cover the kettle tightly and steam the dumplings for 15 minutes.

10. Discard the bay leaf, salt to taste, and pepper the dumplings with two or three turns of the peppermill. Place the kettle on the table and serve your guests directly from it.

NOTE: To my mind, all you need to round out a substantial meal are raisin-pumpernickel bread, sweet butter to spread on it, and horseradish and hot mustard for the ribs. Ale or lager are excellent thirst-quenchers for this lively fare.

Flemish Carbonade of Beef

SERVES 6

There is much discussion about the origin of the word carbonade, *which suggests that the beef was grilled before braising, though none of the existing recipes requires grilling. In any case, the stew becomes a marvelous deep brown in braising. There is also disagreement about the word's spelling. There is no disagreement, however, about the excellence of this hearty stew. It is now claimed as an ethnic heritage by Belgium, France, Spain, and Italy. The Flemish insist that they invented the stew and that the occupying troops took it back home with them. I am convinced they are right, so I spell the Flemish version as they do, with one* n. *Here is my version of the Flemish recipe for the stew.*

2 tablespoons light olive oil

Three ¹/₄-inch-thick strips smoked bacon, cut into ¹/₄-inch pieces

1 teaspoon coarse salt

1 tablespoon freshly ground black pepper

2 pounds lean London broil, ³/₄ inch thick, cut into bite-size pieces

2 large yellow onions, cut into ¹/₄-inch slices

2 plump cloves garlic, crushed

2 bay leaves

16 juniper berries, lightly bruised with a mallet

¹/₄ teaspoon dried thyme

¹/₄ teaspoon ground mace

3 tablespoons softened unsalted butter

3 tablespoons flour

1 cup unsalted beef stock

2 cups light beer

1 jigger (1¹/₂ ounces) best-quality gin (optional)

¹/₂ teaspoon sugar

Salt

1. Heat the oil in a large heavy-bottomed kettle and sauté the bacon until it begins to brown along the edges. Remove and set aside.
2. Work the coarse salt and pepper into the pieces of beef. Brown them well all over, in batches. Set them aside with the bacon.
3. Remove all but 2 tablespoons of the browning fat from the kettle. Toss the onions and garlic in the fat and sauté them until wilted but not browned. Add the bay leaves, juniper berries, thyme, and mace and toss well.
4. Preheat the oven to 350°F.
5. Mix the butter with the flour and set aside.

6. Add the stock and beer to the onions and garlic and deglaze the kettle. Drop the butter–and–flour mixture into the kettle, a bit at a time, whisking until it combines completely with the liquids. Add the bacon, beef, and whatever juice has accumulated under the beef.
7. When the kettle boils, remove it from the heat and seal it by placing two thicknesses of aluminum foil over the top and pressing the lid down firmly. Reduce the oven temperature to 300°F and bake the carbonade for 2 hours.
8. Unseal the kettle. Skim off and discard all the fat that has risen to the surface. Discard the bay leaves. Stir in the gin and sugar and light the surface with a match. When the gin stops flaming, salt the stew to taste. If you find the stew is a little bitter from the beer, add a little more sugar. Take the kettle to the table and serve the stew immediately.

NOTE: When I have eaten this dish in Brussels, it has always been accompanied by boiled quartered potatoes tossed in sweet butter and sprinkled liberally with browned scallions and freshly ground pepper. If you are on a fat alert, omit the butter and browned scallions. Glasses of lager and thick slices of buttered dark rye bread are very appropriate offerings to round out this rich dark Flemish fare.

Portuguese *Cosido* with Greens

H ere is a hearty Portuguese stew with a clear, peppery broth and feathery chopped greens that will remind you of certain Thai dishes, or of the country minestre of Italy. This stew, however, is authentically Portuguese; it belongs to an ancient, extensive family of Iberian soups and stews that are familiar fare in villages from Catalonia to the Algarve.

2 pounds beef hocks or lean stewing beef, cut into 2 × 2-inch pieces

¹/₂ teaspoon cracked black pepper

¹/₂ teaspoon ground cumin

3 tablespoons flour

3 tablespoons vegetable oil

2 cups thinly sliced yellow onions

2 plump cloves garlic, finely chopped

1 cup coarsely chopped bell pepper

1 cup coarsely chopped white part of leek (save 2 big green leaves for wrapping the bouquet garni)

¹/₄ teaspoon red pepper flakes (optional)

2 smoked pork hocks (optional)

1 bouquet garni made up of 1 carrot, 4 cloves, and 2 bay leaves, wrapped in 2 leek leaves and tied together with cotton string

2 cups dry white wine

3 cups coarsely chopped cabbage

3 cups coarsely chopped, stemmed kale

2 cups peeled potatoes in 1-inch dice

One 15-ounce can chick-peas, rinsed and drained

Salt

1. Dry the beef with paper towels and sprinkle it with the black pepper and cumin. Dredge the pieces well with the flour, brushing off the excess.

2. Heat the oil in a large heavy-bottomed kettle and brown the beef well. Remove it and set it aside.

3. Add the onions, garlic, bell pepper, leeks, and pepper flakes to the kettle and toss them well in the remaining fat. Reduce the heat and sauté the vegetables until completely wilted but not browned.

4. If you are including the pork hocks, scrub them well with a brush under warm running water.

5. Bury the browned beef, the pork hocks, and the bouquet garni in the sautéed vegetables. Add the wine and 2 cups of water and bring to a rolling boil. Reduce the heat to a simmer, and for the first 15 minutes of simmering, skim off and discard the froth and fat that rise to the surface.

6. Cover the kettle and simmer the stew for 2 hours.

7. Stir in the cabbage, kale, and potatoes, adding more water to cover, if necessary. Cover and simmer for 45 minutes.

8. Add the chick-peas and simmer for 10 minutes.

9. Discard the bouquet garni. Salt to taste. Remove the kettle from the heat and let the stew sit for 5 minutes.

10. Serve hot, in deep soup dishes, straight from the kettle.

NOTE: Other than first-rate crusty bread and, in the States, sweet butter, this very substantial stew requires no accompaniment. It is customary in Portugal to provide a bottle of very hot pepper sauce for those who like their broth fiery.

Quick Chinese Hot Pot

T his is a good, modest, family-size hot pot that is served up individually in the kitchen and brought to each diner. It is much easier to prepare than the gigantic party or celebration hot pot, and you don't need an electric kettle for the table or a plethora of ingredients to make and serve it.

FOR THE BROTH

2 cups unsalted defatted beef stock

2 scallions, trimmed

2 thin slices fresh unpeeled ginger, each 2 inches long

2 tablespoons dry white wine

Soy sauce

FOR THE SOLIDS

1/2 pound lean stewing chuck, sliced very thin

12 canned Chinese straw mushrooms

12 ears canned baby corn

1/4 pound well-cleaned bean sprouts

1 pound freshly cooked rice noodles

24 branches fresh watercress

2 scallions, white parts only, cut lengthwise into very fine julienne

1. Put all of the broth ingredients except the soy sauce into a large stew pot and simmer gently for 15 minutes. Discard the scallions and ginger root and add soy sauce to taste.
2. Bring the broth to a boil, toss in the meat, mushrooms, and corn, and cook for 2 minutes.
3. Serve immediately, layered into individual deep bowls as follows: sprouts in the bottom, then the noodles, mushrooms, and corn, followed by the watercress and the meat. Scatter the julienned scallion on top. Ladle the simmering stock over the solids in each bowl, filling to within 1/2 inch of the top, and serve at once.

NOTE: Provide a Chinese porcelain spoon and chopsticks for each diner, and soy sauce and hot pepper sauce for those who wish to add them.

Saigon Hot Pot

SERVES 4

*V*ietnamese *fellow students taught me to make this dish in Aix-en-Provence in the early fifties. They used to prepare this hot pot in their rooms on a tiny alcohol burner when there was a birthday to celebrate, and they would invite two or three of us to eat it with them. This is a light, somewhat Westernized version of the recipe.*

FOR THE BROTH

1 cup unsalted defatted beef
   stock
1/2 cup dry white wine
2 thin slices fresh unpeeled ginger,
   each 2 inches long
Rind of 1 lemon, peeled in a spiral
1 bag jasmine tea

FOR THE SOLIDS

3 scallions, white parts only, cut
   into paper-thin rounds
8 leaves bok choy or Chinese
   cabbage, cut into bite-size
   pieces
1/2 pound cellophane noodles
   (see Notes), soaked in water
   until soft and cut into 4-inch
   lengths
3/4 pound lean beef chuck, sliced
   paper-thin
Soy sauce
1/4 cup cilantro leaves

1. Simmer the beef stock, 3 cups of boiling water, wine, ginger, and lemon peel for 15 minutes. Put in the tea bag for 2 minutes. Discard it, the ginger, and the lemon peel.
2. Add the scallions, bok choy, and noodles and simmer for 5 minutes. Toss in the beef and simmer for 1 minute. Turn off the heat. Stir in soy sauce to taste.
3. Apportion equally into four deep bowls. Scatter a few cilantro leaves over each and serve immediately.

NOTES: Cellophane noodles can be found in the Oriental foods section of many supermarkets.

Provide a porcelain soup spoon and chopsticks for each diner, and soy sauce and hot pepper sauce for those who wish to add them.

Brittany-Style Veal Stew

SERVES 4 OR 5

Here is a good, simple stew from my friend, Josée Le Bec, who lives near Pouldreuzic on the Brittany coast. It is her mother's recipe; she recommends it as the best home remedy against low spirits on a damp, drafty day. The stew is equally good made with beef or pork.

2 pounds lean stewing veal, cut into bite-size pieces

2 tablespoons vegetable oil

2 tablespoons unsalted butter

1 tablespoon flour

6 plump shallots, thinly sliced

3 bay leaves, stems tied together with cotton string

12 pitted prunes

6 small carrots, peeled and cut into thin rounds

4 medium-size potatoes, peeled and quartered

1 jigger (1½ ounce) Calvados (optional)

Salt and pepper

1. Heat the oil and butter in a large heavy-bottomed kettle, and gently brown the veal all over, turning it often. Sprinkle in the flour and shallots and cook, stirring, for 3 minutes. Add 2 cups of water and deglaze the bottom of the pan over high heat for 5 minutes.

2. Reduce the heat to the lowest possible level. Add the bay leaves, prunes, carrots, and potatoes.

3. Place two sheets of aluminum foil over the kettle and press the lid down firmly to seal it. Simmer the stew gently for 2 hours.

4. Discard the bay leaves, and stir in the Calvados. Season to taste and serve at once.

NOTE: This simple ragoût improves overnight, except for the potatoes. If you make the stew a day ahead, leave out the potatoes. Boil them just before reheating the stew, stir them in hot, and gently reheat the stew.

Ossobuco Milanese

SERVES 4

This luscious braise, simmered in a rich sauce until the meat is almost melting, then sprinkled just before serving with a nippy topping called gremolata, is one of the great accomplishments of northern Italian regional cooking. Veal shins are not a bargain these days. Since you will be paying dearly for them, make sure you get what you need: They must be meaty, at least 2 inches thick, the central bone sawed neatly through so that it will stand up. That bone should be full of marrow. Ossobuco means "hollow bone"; you'll know why when you see what your guests have left on their plates when they've finished.

3 tablespoons unsalted butter

1 medium-size carrot, peeled and finely chopped

1 medium-size yellow onion, finely chopped

1 plump clove garlic, finely chopped

1 rib celery, finely chopped

1 tablespoon finely chopped flat-leaf parsley

4 slices veal shin, each 2 inches thick, marrow bones neatly sawed through

1 teaspoon coarse salt

1/2 teaspoon freshly ground black pepper

1/4 teaspoon ground sage

2 tablespoons flour

3 tablespoons light olive oil

1/2 cup dry white wine

One 16-ounce can stewed tomatoes, drained and coarsely chopped

3/4 cup unsalted beef stock

FOR THE GREMOLATA

1 tablespoon finely grated lemon peel

1 small clove garlic, finely chopped

3 tablespoons finely chopped flat-leaf parsley

2 flat anchovy fillets, finely crushed

1. Choose a medium-size heavy-bottomed kettle or braising pan that will accommodate the veal neatly, with the bones erect. Heat the butter in it and gently sauté the carrot, onion, garlic, celery, and parsley for 15 minutes, or just until they begin to take on color. Scrape them back and forth with a wooden spatula to prevent sticking. Remove the kettle from the heat. Blot the sautéed vegetables with a wad of paper towels and set the kettle aside.

2. Sprinkle the veal with the salt, pepper, and sage, then dredge it lightly in the flour, brushing off the excess. Heat the oil in a large frying pan and brown the veal on both sides. Remove the browned veal slices and place them snugly in the kettle on top of the sautéed vegetables.

3. Discard the oil from the frying pan and deglaze the bottom with the wine over high heat. Pour the boiling wine over the veal and simmer over low heat until the foaming stops. Add the tomatoes and the stock.

4. Seal the kettle by placing two sheets of aluminum foil over it and pressing the top down firmly. Simmer at the lowest possible heat for 2 hours, shaking the kettle gently from time to time to prevent sticking.

5. Meanwhile, mix the *gremolata* ingredients together.

6. After 2 hours of braising, unseal the kettle and sprinkle the *gremolata* over the meat. Spoon a little of the sauce over the meat and carefully remove the slices to a serving platter or to individual plates. Serve at once.

NOTE: The usual accompaniment is *risotto alla milanese*, but plain boiled rice or an assortment of freshly blanched buttered vegetables may suit you better if you want to keep the calories in check. Lacking proper marrow spoons, provide your guests with little knives so they can dig out the treasured marrow and spread it on their bread.

Veal with Onions and Mushrooms

SERVES 4 OR 5

This succulent veal stew is the all-time favorite in France, whether home-made or bistro-made. My late friend, Marguerite Béchet, taught me how to make this blanquette (as well as almost every other Burgundian dish I know) in her sunny kitchen in Mâcon. Formerly, it was customary to whisk in as many as four eggs and a cup of heavy cream before serving it. This version is much lighter than Marguerite's original, but I don't think she'd mind.

2 pounds stewing veal, cut into bite-size pieces

$^1/_2$ teaspoon freshly ground white pepper

1 medium-size white onion, coarsely chopped

1 medium-size carrot, peeled and sliced into $^1/_8$-inch rounds

$^1/_2$ cup dry white wine

1 bouquet garni made up of 1 bay leaf, 1 rib celery, and 1 sprig fresh thyme, all bound together with cotton string

16 to 20 small white mushrooms, wiped clean, stem ends trimmed

3 tablespoons unsalted butter

3 tablespoons flour

1 tablespoon freshly squeezed lemon juice

1 egg yolk

Salt

1 tablespoon finely chopped flat-leaf parsley

1. Wash the meat under cold running water and blot it dry with paper towels. Work the pepper into the pieces.
2. Put the veal, onion, carrot, wine, and bouquet garni in a medium-size heavy-bottomed kettle and pour in 6 cups of cold water.
3. Slowly heat the water to a rolling boil and maintain it there for 3 minutes. Reduce the heat immediately to the lowest possible level, cover, and simmer gently for 1 hour. Skim off and discard the coagulated froth that rises during the first 15 minutes of simmering.
4. Add the mushrooms and simmer for 15 minutes. Remove the solids with a slotted spoon and set them aside. Pass the stock through a fine sieve into a bowl and set aside. Discard the bouquet garni.
5. Clean the kettle, dry it, and heat it again slowly. Melt the butter. When it is bubbling, stir in the flour with a wooden spatula. Fry this

white roux for just 1 minute. Stir in the reserved stock, whisking until the roux disappears and the stock thickens uniformly.

6. Add the meat and vegetables. Cover and simmer for 20 minutes.

7. Whisk the lemon juice, egg yolk, and 2 tablespoons of water together in a bowl. Add about 3 tablespoons of the hot thickened stock, stirring it all together well. Remove the kettle from the fire and whisk in the egg mixture for 15 seconds. Salt to taste.

8. Serve hot, sprinkled with the chopped parsley.

NOTE: Plain boiled rice or potatoes are the usual accompaniment. Buttered noodles, though untypical, are a dream with this dish. Have plenty of thick slices of crusty French bread on hand to mop up the delicious white sauce.

Veal Submarines with Peppers and Onions

SERVES 4

This is the stew that made the first New York submarine sandwiches stellar in quality. Unfortunately, those gourmet submarines have gone the way of all high-quality submarines, blown out of the water by the more plebeian meatball or chile subs. Well, here's good news for those who loved the gourmet type: You can still have them if you make them yourself. Here's how.

2 pounds lean stewing veal, cut into bite-size pieces

1 teaspoon freshly ground black pepper

1 plump clove garlic, crushed to paste with ¹/₂ teaspoon coarse salt, using the underside of a soup spoon

3 tablespoons flour

3 tablespoons light olive oil

1 cup dry white wine

1 cup unsalted beef stock

3 bay leaves

¹/₄ teaspoon finely crumbled dried oregano

4 medium-size white onions, peeled and quartered

3 large green bell peppers, cut into ¹/₂-inch strips

Salt

4 fresh submarine rolls

1. Wash the veal under cold running water and blot it dry with paper towels. Work the pepper and garlic paste into the pieces with your fingers. Dredge lightly with the flour.

2. Heat the oil gently in a large heavy-bottomed kettle or braising pan and blanch (don't brown!) the veal in batches. Remove the veal and set it aside.

3. Deglaze the bottom of the kettle with the wine and stock over high heat. Reduce the heat to the lowest possible level and add the veal, bay leaves, oregano, onions, and peppers. Toss the ingredients together to mix them. Cover tightly and simmer for 1¹/₄ hours, or until the meat is fork-tender but not falling apart.

4. Discard the bay leaves. Continue simmering, uncovered, for 20 minutes. The sauce should reduce to one third of the original volume. Salt to taste.

5. Split the rolls, stuff them with the stew, and serve.

NOTE: This excellent *stufato* can be made into a main course by adding four ribs of trimmed celery cut into 1-inch pieces and several halved artichoke hearts in Step 4, in which case, simmer, *covered*, for 20 minutes. Serve with rice boiled in stock. Provide plenty of freshly grated Parmesan and finely chopped parsley to accent the tastes and textures.

Swedish Meatballs with Turnips and Cabbage

SERVES 4 OR 5

This is a wonderfully light stew that is fragrant and filling. It is very adaptable to individual tastes and needs; once you know it, you may decide to add carrots, potatoes, apples, or other ingredients.

2 large slices rye bread, crusts
  removed

$^1/_2$ cup milk

1 medium-size onion, finely
  grated

$^3/_4$ pound ground veal

$^1/_2$ teaspoon coarse salt

$^1/_4$ teaspoon freshly ground black
  pepper

$^1/_2$ teaspoon ground cardamom

$^1/_4$ teaspoon freshly grated nutmeg

2 egg yolks, lightly beaten with
  1 tablespoon light olive oil

$^1/_2$ cup flour

$^1/_4$ cup vegetable oil

2 cups unsalted beef stock

4 medium-size turnips, peeled,
  halved, and cut into $^1/_8$-inch
  slices

4 cups coarsely shredded white
  cabbage

4 tablespoons freshly squeezed
  lemon juice

1 tablespoon sugar

$^1/_2$ tablespoon caraway seeds

$^1/_2$ tablespoon finely crumbled
  dried dill

Salt

1. Soak the bread in the milk. When soft, stir together with the grated onion in a large bowl.
2. Knead the bread and onion, veal, salt, pepper, cardamom, nutmeg, egg yolks, and oil together until completely mixed. Roll into walnut-size balls and dredge lightly in the flour. Place the meatballs on an oiled plate to dry for 10 minutes.
3. Heat the vegetable oil in a large, deep frying pan and fry the meatballs slowly, browning them evenly on all sides.
4. Discard the frying oil. Pour the stock over the meatballs. Cover tightly, and simmer gently for 1 hour.

5. Toss the turnips, cabbage, lemon juice, sugar, caraway seeds, and dill together well. Place them in the kettle on top of the meatballs. Cover the kettle and simmer for $^1/_2$ hour, or until the vegetables are tender. Salt to taste.

6. Toss the meatballs, vegetables, and sauce together and serve hot.

NOTE: This dish is often served with heavy cream. I find it very satisfying without the cream, however, and it's so much better for the waistline.

North African Meatballs and Couscous

SERVES 6

V ersions of this dish can be found all over North Africa and the Middle East. Friends in Algiers assure me that the original was brought to North Africa by those masters of the koufta (or kefta), the Turks, who maintained close trading liens with North Africa for centuries. This version makes a substantial one-dish meal.

1¹/₂ cups rice

1 cup dry white wine

1 pound ground veal

1 plump cloves garlic, finely
crushed to paste with
¹/₂ teaspoon coarse salt, using
the underside of a soup spoon

1 small white onion, finely grated

¹/₂ teaspoon cracked black pepper

¹/₂ teaspoon ground coriander

¹/₂ teaspoon ground cinnamon

¹/₂ teaspoon fennel seeds

1 large egg, lightly beaten with
2 tablespoons olive oil

2 tablespoons fine white bread
crumbs

³/₄ cup flour

¹/₄ cup vegetable oil

One 15-ounce can peeled
tomatoes, with their juice

3 cups unsalted beef stock

1 large yellow onion, peeled and
cut into six wedges

3 medium-size carrots, peeled
and sliced into thin rounds

3 medium-size turnips, peeled
and quartered

4 ribs celery, trimmed and cut
into 1-inch pieces

¹/₄ cup golden raisins

¹/₄ cup currants

¹/₂ teaspoon red pepper flakes

3 tablespoons brown sugar

2 cups instant couscous
(see Notes)

3 tablespoons freshly squeezed
lemon juice

¹/₄ teaspoon orange extract
(optional)

Salt

1. Soak the rice in the wine for 15 minutes. Set aside.
2. Using your hands, knead the veal with the soaked rice, garlic paste, grated onion, pepper, coriander, cinnamon, fennel seeds, egg and olive oil, and the bread crumbs. Wet your fingers and palms and roll the mixture into walnut-size balls. Dredge them lightly in the flour and set them on waxed paper for 15 minutes to dry.
3. Heat the vegetable oil gently in a large heavy-bottomed kettle. Brown

the meatballs all over in batches. Remove them as they finish browning and set them aside.

4. Remove the frying oil and set it aside. Wipe out the kettle with a paper towel, then deglaze it with the tomatoes, torn into small pieces, and their juice, 2 cups of beef stock, and 2 cups of warm water.

5. Add the meatballs, yellow onions, carrots, turnips, celery, raisins, currants, pepper flakes, and brown sugar. Bring to a rolling boil, then reduce the heat to the lowest possible level. Cover the kettle and simmer for 1 hour.

6. Mix the reserved frying oil and 3 tablespoons of cold water well through the couscous by pinching and rolling the grains between your thumbs and forefingers. Break up all the clumps.

7. Stir the lemon juice and orange extract into the stew. Salt to taste.

8. Sprinkle the couscous evenly over the stew. Cover and simmer for 5 minutes.

9. Heat the remaining 1 cup of stock.

10. Heap the stew and couscous into six deep soup plates. Ladle a little of the hot stock over each and serve at once.

NOTES: Near East or other brands of instant couscous can be found in the pasta-and-rice section of supermarkets.

If you wish, you may extend the stew by adding one 10-ounce can of well-rinsed chick-peas in Step 4. Other than pepper sauce, pepper relish, and wedges of warmed pita bread, nothing else is needed.

Pork Stews

Introduction to Pork Stews

In the States we are familiar with the sauerkraut-and-smoked pork stews of Central Europe and the sweet-and-sour pork stews of Chinese cooking, yet we are almost totally ignorant of the hundreds of delicious stews made with fresh pork. We grill pork chops and barbecue spareribs, but we rarely think of those cuts as destined for the stewpot. I haven't discovered why. Pork is, after all, the most popular, most consumed meat in the world. Despite the millions of people who, because of religious interdiction, eat no pork at all, the pig population of the world is estimated at 1 pig per 10 persons, an astonishing 500 million porkers.

It is easy to guess why pork is so popular. The pig furnishes more edible flesh in proportion to its feeding costs than any other animal raised for human consumption. Pork is only slightly more expensive than most commercial chicken. When you compare the loss in discarded skin and fat in defatting a chicken, pork, with less waste in fat and fewer bones, comes to about the same price. To my mind, pork is much pleasanter to defat; the fat is usually smoothly striated, firmer, and far easier to excise neatly. Pork fat becomes white and brittle on cooling, so that every speck of it is visible and can be removed from the finished stew, if you can allow the stew to chill before reheating it for serving. Pork makes the most succulent of stews; the flesh is firm but short-fibered, and if overcooked, it disintegrates instead of becoming tough and stringy.

I have confined my choice of stews in this chapter to twenty, all made principally with cuts from the neck, shoulder, spine, and ribs of the pig, because those cuts are familiar and readily available in most butcher shops and supermarkets.

It is worth recalling that we once kept leftover dripping for sautéing and frying. With the arrival of the rather fanatical lipophobia that has fastened like a limpet on our dietary and cooking habits of late, dripping has disappeared from most kitchens and most recipes. Let me say in its defense that with a little purifying, dripping is probably better for us, in some instances, than butter. Since the burning point of pork fat is 400°F and that of butter 250°F, pork dripping is often easier and safer for sautéing. Stow those practical considerations away for your own use. It is, of course, very important to know which kinds of fat are permitted to you and your guests, but remember that good nutrition for those who are normally healthy means that up to 30 percent of our caloric intake can come from fat. That means low fat, not no fat.

When choosing fresh pork for stewing, the old saw about "light pink only" may not apply in the way that it does for loin chops and other expensive cuts of pork. The natural color of the flesh from the shoulder, which many of these recipes require, is brick red. In judging the freshness of all cuts, however, steer clear of any variation in color, especially around the edges of packaged cuts. Other than a very faint, sweet, fresh aroma, fresh pork has no appreciable odor, and the fat should be pure white and firm. A greasy surface and flaccid, off-white fat are usually signs that the cut is nearing or past its limit of freshness. Always read the date on the label when buying packaged meat. On principle, always wash stewing pork under lukewarm running water to remove the surface bacteria and any bone dust left there by the power saws used to cut it. If the next step in the recipe is browning the pork, dry the pieces well with paper towels to prevent excessive spattering.

I envy you your first encounter with these delicious pork stews. I hope that many of them will become part of your regular cooking repertoire.

Pork and Puffed Dumplings

When I was a small child, this simple but rich stew was served for supper to all hands on my great-grandmother's farm after a long day of pork salting, ham curing, and sausage making. In those days the stew was made with large chunks of stripped chine (backbone) from the pigs that had been slaughtered that day.

Nowadays, pork chine is not easy to come by; however, fresh pork neck bones are available in most markets, and they are a good substitute. You may also substitute lean pork stew meat or spareribs. The trick in making this stew is to defat it as completely as you can, since the quenellelike dumplings, for all their velvety lightness, are rather substantial.

FOR THE STEW

2 pounds fresh pork neck bones, cut into manageable pieces

1 pound lean stewing pork, cut into bite-size pieces

2 tablespoons coarse salt

$^1/_2$ teaspoon finely crumbled dried marjoram

1 teaspoon finely crumbled dried sage

$^1/_2$ teaspoon freshly grated nutmeg

$^1/_2$ teaspoon cracked black pepper

2 bay leaves

1 plump clove garlic, crushed

1 medium-size onion, peeled and spiked with 3 cloves

3 tablespoons cider vinegar

$^1/_4$ cup Wondra flour

Salt and black pepper

FOR THE DUMPLINGS

1 cup pork broth (from the stew)

$^3/_4$ stick (6 tablespoons) unsalted butter or margarine

1 cup sifted all-purpose flour

2 large eggs

1. Wash the pork well. Sprinkle the pieces with $1^1/_2$ tablespoons of the salt, the marjoram, sage, nutmeg, and cracked pepper. Place in a large heavy-bottomed kettle with the bay leaves, garlic, spiked onion, vinegar, and 2 quarts of cold water. Bring to a rolling boil, then reduce to a low simmer. Cover the kettle and simmer for 2 hours.

2. Half an hour before the stew finishes simmering, make the dumplings: Place 1 cup of broth from the stew in a medium-size stewpan with a long single handle and bring it to a boil. Add the butter. When it has

melted completely, grasp the handle firmly with one hand and stir in the all-purpose flour and the remaining $1/2$ tablespoon coarse salt to make a smooth paste. Hold the pan over the heat as you stir and continue to dry out the mixture until it leaves the sides of the pan. Turn off the heat. Cool the dough for 5 minutes. One by one, incorporate the eggs, stirring them in vigorously and thoroughly.

3. Remove the stew from the heat and skim off and discard all the fat that has risen to the surface. Mix the Wondra flour with $1/2$ cup of cold water and stir it into the stew. Resume the simmering for 3 minutes, then salt and pepper to taste. Discard the bay leaves and the spiked onion.

4. With two soup spoons dipped in cold water, make egg-shaped dumplings of the dough, dropping them one at a time into the simmering stew. Poach the dumplings, covered, for 10 minutes. Turn off the heat and allow them to puff for 5 minutes.

5. Serve the stew in large individual soup bowls, divvying up the neck bones and meat, the thickened broth, and the dumplings among the diners.

NOTE: Serve this old-fashioned, bone-sucking stew with thickly sliced fresh country bread. You won't need much else except a nap.

Barrio Pork Stew

SERVES 6

This is my version of a very savory Latino pork stew that both Puerto Ricans and Dominicans will recognize, despite a few minor changes.

2 pounds lean boneless pork shoulder, cut into 1-inch cubes

3 plump cloves garlic, peeled

1 tablespoon coarse salt

1 teaspoon freshly ground black pepper

2 tablespoons distilled vinegar

2 tablespoons Worcestershire sauce

3 tablespoons light brown sugar

$1/4$ cup flour

$1/4$ cup vegetable oil

1 tablespoon *achiotina* (see Note)

2 medium-size yellow onions, thinly sliced

2 medium-size carrots, peeled and cut into 1-inch rounds

1 large parsnip, peeled and cut into $1/4$-inch rounds

2 cups unsalted chicken stock

1 package coriander-and-annatto seasoning (see Note)

2 bay leaves

10 black peppercorns, cracked

2 medium-size white potatoes, peeled and cut into 1-inch-thick chunks

2 medium-size sweet potatoes, peeled and cut into 1-inch-thick chunks

2 medium-size zucchini, cut into 1-inch pieces

2 medium-size ripe red tomatoes, peeled, seeded, and coarsely chopped

1 cup shelled green peas (thawed frozen ones may be substituted)

Salt

2 tablespoons finely chopped cilantro

1. Wash the pork well and pat it dry.
2. Make an *adobo* by crushing the garlic with the salt against a flat, hard surface with the underside of a soup spoon and mixing this paste with the black pepper, vinegar, Worcestershire sauce, and brown sugar. With your fingers, work the *adobo* into all the pieces of pork, then set them aside in a bowl at room temperature for at least 1 hour.
3. Wipe the *adobo* off the pork cubes with paper towels. Dredge the cubes lightly in the flour, shaking off the excess.

4. In a large heavy-bottomed kettle, heat the oil and *achiotina* together and gently brown the pork cubes in batches, removing them and setting them aside as they finish browning.
5. Discard all but 2 tablespoons of the oil. Add the onions and toss them thoroughly in the oil. Sauté them until wilted. Add the carrots, parsnip, chicken stock, 1 cup of cold water, the coriander-and-annatto seasoning, the bay leaves, and the peppercorns. Simmer gently, covered, for 1½ hours.
6. Add the potatoes, sweet potatoes, zucchini, tomatoes, and peas, and simmer for 30 minutes, or until the potatoes are fork-tender. Discard the bay leaves and salt to taste.
7. Serve the stew in a large, deep bowl, sprinkling the surface with the chopped cilantro.

NOTE: Coriander-and-annatto flavoring is marketed by Goya brand as one of its many varieties of Sazón. The same company produces *achiotina*, annatto-flavored lard, in small jars. Look for these products in the Latino section of your supermarket.

Pork and Green-Chili Stew

SERVES 4

Here is a zesty pork stew invented by chili-pepper fanciers in northern California. I stipulate canned green chilies here because they are available almost everywhere in the Latino food section of markets. If you have fresh green chilies on hand, then by all means use them instead. This stew pairs well with pinto beans and Mexican-style rice. It also makes excellent tacos.

One 4-ounce can peeled mild green chilies, drained

1 jalapeño pepper, stemmed and seeded (wash your hands at once, if you handle the seeds)

4 dried *pequin* chilies (more, if you like), crumbled (see Notes)

1 teaspoon crumbled dried oregano

1 medium-size onion, finely chopped

1 plump clove garlic, coarsely chopped

2 pounds tomatillos (see Notes), hulled and halved

1 1/2 pound lean stewing pork, cut into 1/2-inch cubes

1 teaspoon coarse salt

3 tablespoons *masa harina* (tortilla flour)

3 tablespoons vegetable oil

1 cup unsalted chicken stock

Salt

2 tablespoons coarsely chopped cilantro

1. Put the green chilies, jalapeño, pequin chilies, oregano, onion, and garlic in a food processor and pulse them to a loose paste. Add the tomatillos and process to a smooth paste. Reserve.
2. Wash the pork cubes and pat them dry. Salt them all over and dredge them lightly with the tortilla flour, brushing off the excess. Set them aside.
3. In a medium-size heavy-bottomed kettle, heat the oil and gently brown the pork cubes in batches, removing them to a plate once they have finished browning.
4. Empty the raw purée into the kettle and fry it for 5 minutes, raking it back and forth continuously. Add the pork cubes and toss them well in the sauce. Add the stock, cover tightly, and simmer gently for 50 minutes, or until the pork is tender.
5. Salt to taste and serve hot, sprinkled with the chopped cilantro.

NOTES: The *pequin* is a tiny, very hot chili, usually sold in cellophane envelopes in the spice section of Latino groceries.

Tomatillos, frequently used in raw salsas, belong to the gooseberry family. They can be found in most Latino markets and, sometimes, in the produce section of large supermarkets.

Mexicali Hot Pot

SERVES 4

This lively pork-and-vegetable stew is peppery and fragrant. Serve it in big, deep, individual bowls, topped with a generous ladle of steamed brown rice.

1¹/₂ pounds lean pork shoulder, cut into bite-size pieces

¹/₂ teaspoon cracked black pepper

¹/₂ teaspoon coarse salt

3 tablespoons vegetable oil

2 bay leaves

2 plump cloves garlic, coarsely sliced

One 8-ounce can tomato sauce

1 vegetarian bouillon cube, crumbled

2 tablespoons red wine vinegar

1 teaspoon sugar

2 cups coarsely chopped white cabbage

2 medium-size yellow potatoes, peeled and cut into ¹/₂-inch cubes

12 to 16 pearl onions, peeled

4 to 6 *chiles petines*, crumbled (see Note)

¹/₂ tablespoon crumbled dried sage

¹/₂ teaspoon crumbled dried epazote (see Note)

Salt

1. Wash the pork and pat it dry. Sprinkle it with the cracked pepper and salt and set it aside.
2. Heat the oil in a large heavy-bottomed kettle and gently brown the pork well, turning it occasionally so that all sides brown evenly and well.
3. Toss in the bay leaves and garlic and stir them about briefly.
4. Add the tomato sauce, the crumbled bouillon cube, 3 cups of warm water, the vinegar, and sugar, and deglaze well.
5. Stir in the cabbage. Cover tightly and simmer for 1¹/₂ hours.
6. Add the potatoes, onions, chili peppers, sage, and epazote. Stir together thoroughly. Simmer, covered, for 30 minutes.
7. Salt to taste. Discard the bay leaves and serve.

NOTE: The tiny hot *petines* and dried epazote can usually be found in small cellophane bags in Latino markets. Ground cayenne is a possible substitute for the *petines*. However, epazote (*Chenopodium ambrosioides*) is unique in taste and is worth making a real effort to find.

Pozolli, Pozole, or Posole?

Posole (poh–SOH–lay), the humble stew that many Anglos of northern New Mexico refer to disparagingly as "hog 'n' hominy," has an impressive pedigree. Consequently, the stew deserves a somewhat longer introduction than the other stews in this collection. It is the direct descendant of pre-Columbian *pozolli*, the oldest stew in the Western Hemisphere. It takes it name from the Nahuatl word for the lime-leached, kiln-dried white maize that was—and still is—the stew's main ingredient. The Aztecs revered *pozolli* as a sacrament, associating deeply with their mythic origins. In preparing and consuming the stew, they also celebrated their dependence on maize, the staff of life given to them by their gods. On solemn occasions their priests prepared a ceremonial *pozolli* by braising with the leached corn and chilies the choicest muscles of the arms and thighs of their handsomest sacrificial victims. According to the sixteenth-century chronicler, Fray Bernardino de Sahagún, the Aztecs believed that the moral and physical strengths of their victims would literally be transferred to them in partaking of the stew. A completely secularized version of that holy *pozolli* still exists as *pozole* in the region of Jalisco; it is a leached corn-and-chili stew in which a pig's feet and head have been ironically substituted for the warriors' flesh.

Priscilla Vigil of Tesuque Pueblo in northern New Mexico, my Tewa adviser on posole, told me that her people completely ignored the history of *pozolli* among the Aztecs but that they did indeed know that posole was the oldest corn stew. She said that the festive posole her mother used to make was always full of the fattest parts of a freshly slaughtered pig, and, according to custom, was always swimming in liquid lard. It was thought that the fatter the posole the better. Today, Mrs. Vigil prepares a completely defatted version. She explained to me in detail how in the old days she and her mother prepared the posole from scratch: burning the juniper needles for ash with which to make the lye to leach the corn; soaking the corn for a day or two; removing its husks; drying it in an outdoor oven—like the one she has just outside her back door—boiling the corn for hours; preparing the chilies; and simmering the stew with the fat-pork parts for at least six hours. "Now," she said with a smile, "we buy the posole corn frozen, and it's no trouble at all." When I asked if the Tewas still felt reverence toward the stew, she said that she could not answer for others, but that to this day, she always begins her cooking with a prayer.

Red-Chili Posole

I arrived at this version of New Mexican red-chili posole after tasting half a dozen variations in as many places. This recipe is slimmed to the limit. I discovered in experimenting with it that as I defatted the stew, the incomparable perfumes of the leached corn (hominy) and the chili peppers became more pronounced, more refined, and the lean pork more savory. You can make this recipe with yellow hominy and other chilies if you wish—I have when necessary. That posole will be good, but it won't be half as exquisite.

Two 15 1/2-ounce cans white hominy (see page 148), rinsed and drained

8 dried New Mexican *ristra* peppers (see Note), stemmed, loose seeds discarded (many will remain attached inside)

1 1/2 to 2 pounds lean pork shoulder, cut into 1 × 2-inch chunks

1 pound lean pork neck bones, cut into manageable pieces

1/2 teaspoon *each* cracked black pepper, ground cumin, ground cloves, and ground cayenne

1/2 teaspoon finely crumbled dried oregano

1 bay leaf

1 large yellow onion, finely chopped

2 plump cloves garlic, crushed and finely chopped

Salt

2 pickled Tabasco peppers, finely chopped

2 tablespoons finely chopped flat-leaf parsley

2 large scallions, white and green parts, trimmed and coarsely chopped

12 to 18 cilantro leaves

1. Put the hominy in a large heavy-bottomed kettle with 6 cups of water and simmer gently, covered, for 1 1/2 hours, or until the kernels split and open like flowers. Don't worry about overcooking the hominy. I have sometimes simmered it in a crockpot for 6 hours.

2. This step sets forth the old-fashioned way to make chili paste. Today many cooks simply let the food processor do it, without bothering to remove the skins. The skins on almost all capsicums trouble the digestion of many diners, myself included, so I prefer removing them. Here is the rather universal method for dealing with chilies:

Put the chilies on a clean hot griddle and keep turning them so that they discolor on all sides. (This operation should take no more than 5 minutes.) Take care not to burn them. Put them in a pan, add cold water to cover, and simmer them for 30 minutes. Let them cool in the water. When they are cool enough to handle, split them open down one side, spread them flat, and, using a metal spatula or a dull knife, scrape the flesh and seeds off the cellophanelike skins. Discard the skins. Put the flesh and seeds into a sieve and press the flesh through it. This should remove all the seeds and threadlike filaments and produce about $1/3$ cup bright red chili paste. (I find it difficult to discard the beautiful cochineal-hued, fragrant water in which the chilies simmered, so I add as much as a cup of it to the simmering hominy.) Wash your hands thoroughly with soap and water to remove the capsaicin. *Ristra* chilies are not very hot, but their capsaicin content can still irritate your eyes, nose, and lips if you touch them.

3. Add the chili paste to the simmering hominy.

4. Wash and dry the pork. Add it to the hominy along with the black pepper, cumin, cloves, cayenne, oregano, bay leaf, onion, and garlic. Simmer, covered, for $1^1/2$ hours, or until the meat is falling off the bones. At this point you may remove and discard the bones before serving the posole. Like many posole lovers, I love gnawing on the bones, so I leave them in.

5. Discard the bay leaf. Salt the posole to taste. Serve the stew hot in large, deep bowls sprinkled with a little chopped Tabasco pepper, parsley, scallions, and a few cilantro leaves.

NOTE: *Ristra* is the name for both a string of dried chilies and the chilies themselves. A New Mexican *ristra* contains about seventy 7-inch-long dried pasado-type peppers. When seeded, soaked, and scraped away from their cellophane-like skins, the peppers yield a bright vermillion paste that has a unique, slightly smoky, mildly piquant flavor. There really is no substitute. If you can't find a supplier for New Mexican *ristras* in your area, I suggest you get in touch with Susan Curtis or one of the members of her fine staff at the Santa Fe School of Cooking, (505) 983-4511. I have always found them most cordial and helpful.

Caribbean Pork Stew

SERVES 8

Sancocho *is a festive stew found mainly in Caribbean and Central Ameri-can cooking. It consists of an abundance of almost any kind of meat—fresh or smoked—or seafood, and tropical fruits and vegetables. A true* sancocho *usu-ally contains some ingredients that are simmered for a long time and others that are simply poached. There are so many versions of the stew that one could easily write a cookbook on sancochos alone. Here is a version of the stew that I make when I have more than half a dozen hungry guests to feed. It requires many in-gredients, but it is easy to make, delicious, satisfying, and impressive. I usually cook the smoked hocks the night before.*

4 to 6 smoked pork hocks

3 pounds lean stewing pork, cut into 1 × 2-inch pieces

1½ teaspoons coarse salt

1 tablespoon Five Pepper Blend (see Notes)

3 medium-size yellow onions, coarsely chopped

3 medium-size leeks, white parts only, split, well washed, and coarsely chopped

1 whole head garlic, unpeeled, halved across the cloves

2 large bay leaves

1 tablespoon finely chopped flat-leaf parsley

1 tablespoon finely chopped cilantro

1 teaspoon red pepper flakes

3 tablespoons freshly squeezed grapefruit juice

1 teaspoon finely grated grapefruit peel

3 tablespoons freshly squeezed orange juice

1 tablespoon distilled vinegar

2 tablespoons brown sugar

1 pound fresh hot Italian sausage

3 tablespoons vegetable oil

4 green plantains

3 tablespoons freshly squeezed lime juice

3 medium-size sweet potatoes, peeled and cut into 1-inch-thick chunks

2 medium-size potatoes, peeled and cut into 1-inch-thick chunks

4 medium-size yellow squash, thinly sliced

4 ears sweet corn, cut through the cob into 2-inch pieces

1 package cilantro-and-annatto seasoning (see Notes)

One 16-ounce can chick-peas, washed and drained

Salt

1. Scrub the hocks well with a vegetable brush under warm running water. Put them in a large heavy-bottomed kettle with 6 cups of cold water and simmer them, covered, for 2 hours. Let the hocks cool in the stock. Remove the hocks and set them aside. Defat and strain the stock. Set the stock aside. Wash and dry the kettle. These steps may be done a day ahead, provided that both the stock and hocks are refrigerated.

2. Wash and dry the pieces of stewing pork. Sprinkle them all over with the salt and Five Pepper Blend. Return the stock to the cleaned kettle with the pork pieces, onions, leeks, garlic, bay leaves, parsley, cilantro, red pepper flakes, grapefruit juice and peel, orange juice, vinegar, and brown sugar. Simmer gently, covered, for 1 hour.

3. Meanwhile, prick the Italian sausage all over with a darning needle or toothpick. Heat the vegetable oil in a frying pan and gently brown the sausage. Remove the sausage, allow it to cool, cut it into 1-inch pieces, and set aside. Discard the browning fat or reserve it for another purpose.

4. Peel the plantains, cut them into 1-inch pieces, and marinate them in the lime juice for at least 15 minutes.

5. Add the sausage, plantains, sweet potatoes, potatoes, yellow squash, corn, and cilantro-and-annatto seasoning to the stew and continue simmering over low heat, covered, for 30 minutes.

6. Bone the hocks, keeping only the lean parts. (The skin and fat are greatly prized by many *sancocho* lovers, but they are not recommended for those on low-fat diets.) Add the lean parts of the hocks and the chick-peas to the stew and let them heat through thoroughly. Discard the bay leaves. (The garlic is usually served, if it is still intact.) Salt the stew to taste.

7. Arrange the meats and vegetables attractively on a large, deep serving platter. Moisten them with a ladle or two of the broth. Serve hot.

NOTES: This stew is often dressed up at serving time with quartered hard-boiled eggs, bottled pimientos, capers, and sliced radishes. It is customary to provide Tabasco sauce for those who like the stew spicy.

Williams-Sonoma sells the blend of five peppers in 2-ounce bottles. Look for cilantro-and-annatto seasoning in the Latino grocery section of your supermarket.

Pork Stewed with Broccoli Raab

SERVES 4 OR 5

This is a zesty, brothy stew for those who love boiled field greens. It produces a fair amount of that delectable, iron-laden broth that Southerners
call "pot liquor," in which they like to crumble freshly baked corn bread—a custom not to be knocked if you haven't tried it. Other greens, such as fresh
spinach, may be substituted for broccoli raab—even mustard or turnip greens,
provided they are tender. If kale is used, it should be stripped of its toughest
stems, parboiled separately for at least an hour, squeezed out, and coarsely
chopped before adding it to the stew.

2 pounds lean stewing pork, cut
   into 1-inch cubes

1 1/2 teaspoons coarse salt

1/2 teaspoon freshly ground black
   pepper

1/4 teaspoon ground allspice

3 tablespoons vegetable oil

One 1/4-inch-thick slice smoked
   bacon, cut into 1/4-inch pieces

6 large scallions, white parts only,
   coarsely chopped

3 plump cloves garlic, finely
   chopped

2 cups unsalted chicken stock

One 2-inch piece fresh unpeeled
   ginger, split lengthwise

2 medium-size waxy potatoes,
   peeled and cut into 1/2-inch
   cubes

3 medium-size turnips, peeled,
   halved, and cut into 1/4-inch
   slices

Salt

1 1/2 pounds fresh young broccoli
   raab, well washed, thick stems
   discarded, cut into 3-inch
   sections

1. Wash the pork cubes and pat them dry. Sprinkle them with the salt,
   pepper, and allspice and set aside.
2. In a large heavy-bottomed kettle, heat the oil and slowly sauté the
   bacon until it begins to take on color. Add the chopped scallions and
   garlic, tossing them thoroughly with the oil and bacon. Sauté for 7
   minutes, tossing from time to time to prevent scorching.
3. Add the pork cubes, stock, 2 cups of cold water, and the ginger.
   Simmer, covered, for 1 1/4 hours.

4. Add the potatoes and turnips and simmer for 30 minutes. Salt to taste.
5. Discard the ginger. Add the broccoli raab, cover tightly, and simmer for 2 to 6 minutes, depending on whether you prefer the greens crisp or well done. Broccoli raab will simply collapse after 7 minutes, so beware.
6. Serve the stew in deep bowls, allotting each guest equal amounts of pork, vegetables, greens, and broth.

NOTE: Provide a cruet of distilled vinegar and a bottle of Tabasco for those who like their greens piquant.

Aunt Harriet's Southern Ham Stew

*A*unt Harriet was an ex-slave, midwife, conjuring woman, and cook whom I got to know when I was 14. I spent the summer with a family of friends who lived in the then piney woods north of Evans, Georgia. Aunt Harriet had brought them all into the world, and they were attached to her. Several times that summer she made this stew for us of leftover ham and what she called "havin's"—in other words, whatever she had at hand. I found the stew as colorful, consoling, and quintessentially Southern as she was. You don't have to be Southern to relish its typical savors, textures, and pot liquor, but if hot corn bread is served up with it and you're a Southerner, you may just die from excess of pleasure. This version of Aunt Harriet's stew is all the more attractive; I have slimmed it down and reduced the salt without sacrificing a tad of its taste.

1¹/₂ cups lean, defatted, leftover ham, cut into ¹/₂-inch cubes (include the ham bone, if it's available)

1 plump clove garlic, thinly sliced

4 medium-size garden onions, bulbs only, trimmed and halved (see Notes)

1 tablespoon vegetable oil

¹/₂ teaspoon cracked black pepper

One 1-pound bunch tender young collard greens, stemmed and well washed

One 14¹/₂-ounce can unsalted stewed tomatoes, with their juice

One 15¹/₂-ounce can white hominy (see Notes), well rinsed and drained

One 16-ounce can black-eyed peas (see Notes), well rinsed and drained

1 cup fresh young okra pods, stemmed (10 ounces thawed frozen okra pods may be substituted)

Salt

1. In a large heavy-bottomed kettle, place the cubed ham, the ham bone (if you have it), the garlic, onions, and oil. Sprinkle in the cracked pepper and toss the ingredients until lightly coated in the oil. Layer the wet greens on top, cover, and sweat the ingredients over very low heat for 15 minutes.
2. Add the tomatoes and their juice, 3 cups of warm water, the

hominy, and the black-eyed peas. Toss the ingredients thoroughly again and simmer, covered, for 1 hour.

3. Mix in the okra pods and simmer the stew, covered, for 15 minutes, or until the okra is just done but not entirely soft. Salt to taste and serve the stew hot in large, deep soup plates, ladling in plenty of the pot liquor. Hot cornbread, lightly salted butter, and a bottle of pickled Tabasco peppers are de rigueur as accompaniments.

NOTES: If you don't find hominy among the canned goods in your supermarket, ask the manager to order it from Bush Brothers and Company, Dandridge, Tennessee.

I recommend Goya Brand canned black-eyed peas for this stew. They are perfectly cooked and, unlike many others, don't disintegrate with long simmering.

Garden onions are not scallions but spring onions halfway to full maturity. They have a bulb that is about $1\frac{1}{4}$-inch thick. Pearl onions may be substituted, but the taste will be much sweeter. Small dried yellow onions may also be substituted. They will be delicious, but the stew will lack the lively, exciting taste of the young garden onions.

Pork Jambalaya

SERVES 6

There are many alleged etymologies for the word jambalaya, each with its fervent adherents. I have no intention of opening that Pandora's box, but I can safely say that jambalaya is a Spanish-Creole-African-American elaboration of the colonial sopa seca. A good jambalaya ranks in excellence with a good risotto milanese, paella valenciana, or Levantine pilaf. An old hand at making jambalaya once told me that there are more varieties of jambalaya than you can shake a stick at. The main thing, she insisted, was the rice. To put a fine point on it, the finished rice should be soft but loose, fragrant and savory, yet as free of fat as you can make it. This version of jambalaya is updated from an old New Orleans recipe. It makes a substantial main course that needs only a salad of mixed greens to turn it into a meal of unusual distinction. After you have made this version, you should feel free to improvise with other ingredients. Just remember that the main thing is the rice.

¹/₂ pound lean, boneless pork shoulder, cut into ¹/₂-inch cubes

3 tablespoons vegetable oil

6 links dinner-size country sausage, cut into ¹/₂-inch rounds

1 cup cooked ham, cut into ¹/₂-inch cubes

2 medium-size green bell peppers cut into ¹/₂-inch squares

2 medium-size onions, finely chopped

3 plump cloves garlic, finely chopped

4 ribs celery, coarsely chopped

3 tablespoons finely chopped flat-leaf parsley

1 tablespoon finely chopped cilantro

2 large scallions, green and white parts, trimmed and coarsely chopped

1 bay leaf

¹/₄ teaspoon *each* ground cloves, ground allspice, grated nutmeg, cracked black pepper, and dried thyme

¹/₂ teaspoon red pepper flakes

2 cups unsalted chicken stock

1 tablespoon molasses

2 cups medium-grain rice

Salt

1. Wash and dry the pork cubes. Heat the oil in a large heavy-bottomed Dutch oven and gently brown the pork cubes, sausage, and ham in batches, removing them as they finish browning. Take care to rake

the meat about often and see that the precious crust forming on the bottom does not burn; it is the source of much of the dish's incomparable taste. Set the meat aside. Discard the browning fat and quickly wipe out the Dutch oven with a paper towel. Pour in $1/2$ cup of warm water and deglaze the pan completely over high heat.

2. When the deglazing liquid has reduced to one third of its original volume, reduce the heat to very low and return the meats to the pan. Add the bell peppers, onions, garlic, celery, parsley, cilantro, scallions, the bay leaf, the spices and thyme, and the pepper flakes. Toss all of these ingredients together thoroughly with a wooden spatula. (Use the wooden implement from this point on in the preparation of this dish.) Cover and sweat the ingredients for 7 minutes, tossing them from time to time to ensure that they intermingle.

3. Mix the stock with the molasses and 2 cups of warm water. Stir this mixture into the ingredients in the pot and bring the stew to a rolling boil. Reduce the heat to medium, and allow the stew to bubble, uncovered, for 15 minutes. Carefully skim off and discard all the fat that has risen around the rim of the pot.

4. Meanwhile, put the rice in a sieve and, using your fingers, rinse the grains thoroughly with cold running water. Stir the rinsed rice into the stew. When the stew is boiling again, stir the ingredients together thoroughly once more, and salt to taste. Discard the bay leaf.

5. Reduce the heat and let the liquid boil away gently without stirring the stew. When the liquid has disappeared, stir the stew briefly one last time, cover, and cook over the lowest possible heat for 10 minutes.

6. Turn off the heat. Allow the jambalaya to sit, covered, for 30 minutes before serving.

NOTE: To savor fully the complex bouquet of a good jambalaya, you should eat it warm. If you have any left over, don't add a drop of liquid to the delicately steamed rice. Reheat the dish just as it is in a microwave or at 250°F in the oven.

Pork with Red Cabbage

*L*ike so many others, I find braised red cabbage irresistible; I also very often find it difficult to digest. Besides being the most hard-headed of all the members of the cabbage family, red cabbage possesses a few other unpleasant idiosyncracies, and even the techniques of old Austrian and Alsatian friends who have been preparing red cabbage for several lifetimes don't always work. Nevertheless, here is a Belgian method of braising red cabbage and fresh pork that seems to work well-nigh perfectly every time. Don't be appalled at the prospect of braising the dish for 3 hours. Once the kettle is sealed and the stew is braising, you have to interrupt what you are doing only once in the 3 hours to give it a quick stir. The long braising is needed to work the hermetic alchemy that transforms the intractable red cabbage to velvety lusciousness and easy digestibility.

1 tablespoon unsalted butter

1 tablespoon vegetable oil

2 strips very streaky breakfast bacon, cut into $^1/_8$-inch pieces

1 large sweet onion, halved and thinly sliced

1 bay leaf

$^1/_2$ teaspoon caraway seeds

4 cloves

$^1/_4$ cup dry white wine

1 firm 2-pound head red cabbage

3 tablespoons red wine vinegar

3 tablespoons light brown sugar

$1^1/_2$ pounds lean pork shoulder, cut into 2 × 2-inch chunks

1 large Granny Smith apple, peeled, quartered, cored, and thinly sliced

1 tablespoon ground cinnamon

1 teaspoon coarse salt

Salt

3 tablespoons cornstarch

1. In a large, nonaluminum, heavy-bottomed kettle, heat the butter and oil. When the butter sizzles, add the bacon, onion, bay leaf, caraway seeds, and cloves and toss them well in the hot fat. Add the white wine, and braise very gently, covered, for about 20 minutes, until the onion has almost melted.

2. Meanwhile, prepare the cabbage. Pull off and discard any damaged outer leaves. Quarter the head, cut out and discard the core, and julienne each quarter. Rinse the cabbage quickly in cold water, shake out the shreds by the double handfuls, and work the vinegar

and sugar through them. (The sink is the best place to do this.) Pile the cabbage in a large colander. Set aside.

3. Wash the pork, and set it aside to drain.

4. Place half the cabbage in the kettle on top of the bacon and onion. Make a nest in the center and place the pork and apple slices in it. Sprinkle cinnamon and salt over them, and cover them up with the rest of the cabbage. Seal the kettle with a sheet of aluminum foil and press the lid down securely over it. Braise for 2 hours over the lowest possible heat.

5. At the end of 2 hours, break the seal. Salt to taste, and gently fold the braise together. The pork will be very tender, and you don't want to break it up too much. Replace the lid but not the foil and braise, covered, for another 30 minutes. Uncover the kettle and allow the liquids to reduce a little for 30 minutes.

6. Mix the cornstarch with 3 tablespoons of cold water. Stir this mixture into the braise and allow a little time for it to thicken. Adjust the flavoring for salt, sugar, and vinegar. Serve hot.

NOTE: Coarsely torn romaine, finely chopped fresh dill, and a generous dollop of sour cream or plain yogurt are good accents for this dish; mashed potatoes, made from scratch, are a natural accompaniment.

Pacific Rim Pork Stew

SERVES 4

Did you ever wonder how you might prepare one of those family packs of thinly sliced pork chops offered so often at such attractive prices in the supermarket? Here is a very good solution that may become a family favorite. You will need at least two very thin chops per person.

$^1/_4$ cup light soy sauce

3 tablespoons honey

2 plump cloves garlic, peeled

4 cloves

1 envelope ham concentrate (see Note)

1 tablespoon Dijon mustard

2 tablespoons cider vinegar

$^1/_4$ teaspoon freshly ground black pepper

8 thinly sliced pork chops, with bone

$^1/_4$ cup cornstarch

3 tablespoons vegetable oil

3 ribs celery, cut diagonally into $^1/_8$-inch slices

3 large scallions, white and green parts, coarsely chopped

1 cup pineapple juice

1 cup unsalted chicken stock

3 tablespoons smooth peanut butter

$^1/_8$ teaspoon red pepper flakes

Salt

2 slices canned pineapple, quartered

$^1/_4$ cup dry-roasted unsalted peanuts, coarsely crushed

1. In a food processor or blender, pulse the soy sauce, honey, garlic, cloves, ham concentrate, mustard, vinegar, and black pepper to a fine paste.
2. Wash and dry the chops. Brush them all over with the paste. Place them in a nonreactive dish to marinate for at least 1 hour at room temperature.
3. With a dampened paper towel, wipe off the paste. Dredge the chops lightly in the cornstarch, shaking off the excess.
4. In a large heavy-bottomed kettle, heat the oil and gently brown the chops, making sure they do not stick. Remove them as they finish browning. Set them aside.
5. Discard all but 1 tablespoon of the browning oil. Add the celery and scallions and toss them thoroughly in the remaining oil. Sauté them for 5 minutes, tossing them frequently.

6. Place the chops over this sauté and add the pineapple juice and the stock. Cover tightly and simmer very gently for 1¹/₂ hours, or until the meat is about to fall off the bone.
7. Mix the peanut butter and pepper flakes with a little of the simmering sauce and stir the mixture into the stew. Simmer, uncovered, for 5 minutes. Salt to taste.
8. Serve the hot stew on a bed of plain boiled rice. Garnish with the pineapple and crushed peanuts.

NOTE: Ham concentrate is sold in eight-envelope packages by Goya Food, Inc. If you can't obtain it, make the substitute on page 35.

Hot-and-Sour Pork Stew

Here is my favorite of all the hot-and-sour stews, a spicy vindaloo from Goa. It is one of the few East Indian dishes made with pork, and it has quite a different flavor from the others in this collection. Like many Far Eastern recipes, vindaloo is prepared in individual steps that seem quite unrelated to each other until the components are combined at the end to produce a dish that is marvelously complex in taste and texture. Just follow the instructions step by step, without hurrying, then relax and enjoy the wonderful dish you have created. Serve the vindaloo with a fluffy steamed long-grain rice such as basmati, sprinkled with a few golden raisins, shredded coconut, and slivered almonds. The stew is highly flavored, and it already contains substantial amounts of stewed potatoes and tomatoes, so the best choice of accompaniments is a simple steamed or poached green vegetable such as broccoli or chard. The fresh cilantro leaves and the chopped scallions should be placed in little bowls on the table, along with your favorite hot pepper sauce; each diner may then compose and accentuate his or her meal ad libitum.

1¹/₂ teaspoons black mustard seeds (see Note)

1 teaspoon black peppercorns

4 cloves

One 2-inch cinnamon stick

1 teaspoon cumin seeds

1 teaspoon red pepper flakes

1 teaspoon fenugreek seeds

¹/₄ cup distilled vinegar

1 teaspoon coarse salt

1 tablespoon light brown sugar

6 tablespoons vegetable oil

1 large yellow onion, halved and finely sliced

6 plump cloves garlic, peeled

One 2-inch piece fresh ginger, peeled and coarsely chopped

3 pounds lean pork shoulder cut into 1 × 2-inch pieces

1 tablespoon ground coriander

¹/₂ teaspoon ground turmeric

3 medium-size potatoes, peeled, halved and cut into 1-inch chunks

2 medium-size firm red tomatoes, quartered

18 to 24 cilantro leaves

2 large scallions, green and white parts, coarsely chopped

1. Put the mustard seeds, peppercorns, cloves, cinnamon stick, cumin seeds, red pepper flakes, and fenugreek seeds in a small, clean frying pan and dry toast them by shaking the pan continuously over medium heat for about 1 minute, or until you can smell the aromatic oils. Before the spices have a chance to burn, turn them out on a paper towel. Transfer them to a food processor or blender and pulse them to a coarse powder. Add the vinegar, salt, and sugar and pulse to a smooth paste. Leave the paste in the machine.

2. In a large heavy-bottomed kettle, heat 3 tablespoons of the oil. Add the onion and toss the slices thoroughly in the oil. Continue to toss from time to time as the onion sautés. When the slices are just beginning to crisp along the edges, remove them to a bowl and set them aside. Turn off the heat.

3. Add the browned onion to the paste in the machine and pulse until the onion is smoothly combined with the spice paste. This is the famous vindaloo paste. It can be made well in advance—even frozen for future use—if you wish. Remove the paste to a bowl and set it aside. Clean the machine.

4. Put the garlic, ginger, and 3 tablespoons of water into the machine and pulse to a smooth paste. Remove this paste to a bowl and set it aside. You won't need the machine again for this recipe.

5. Wash and dry the pieces of pork. Heat the remaining 3 tablespoons of oil in the kettle and gently brown the pork pieces in batches, removing them to a plate as they finish browning.

6. Add the garlic-and-ginger paste to the kettle and fry it for 15 seconds, stirring continuously. Add the coriander and turmeric and continue to fry, stirring for another 15 seconds. Add the pork and whatever juice has accumulated in the plate, the vindaloo paste, and $1^1/2$ cups of warm water. Stir thoroughly and simmer gently, covered, for 1 hour, stirring from time to time.

7. Stir in the potatoes and simmer again, covered, for 20 minutes, then stir in the tomatoes and simmer, covered, for 10 minutes.

8. Serve hot, following the suggestions in the headnote.

NOTE: Black mustard seeds, fenugreek seeds, and the other spices in this recipe are usually available in Oriental food speciality shops. If you have the good fortune to live in or near an Oriental neighborhood, you may be able to buy your spices in just the amounts the recipe requires, if you can figure the amounts in grams or ounces. In any case, if you have the chance to familiarize yourself with an Oriental spice market, by all means, do so. Ask questions! I couldn't tell you how many precious bits of information I have learned about spices and their uses from spice sellers simply because I asked.

Pork Stewed in Milk

SERVES 4 OR 5

Through the ancient Iberian recipe for lomo en leche, I have known for years about the alchemy of pork cooked gently in milk. While reading about pish-pash of chicken in Norman Douglas's Venus in the Kitchen, it occurred to me that a pish-pash of pork might be magic. It is. The combination of pork and milk produces a light, risottolike dish full of succulent, exquisitely flavored chunks of pork.

1¼ pounds lean shoulder of pork, cut into 1-inch cubes
½ teaspoon ground cardamom
½ teaspoon freshly ground Five Pepper Blend (see Notes)
4 cups milk
1 bay leaf
1 sprig fresh thyme

1 small white onion, peeled, spiked with 4 cloves
3 plump shallots, thinly sliced
⅔ cup medium-grain rice (see Notes)
Salt
2 tablespoons finely chopped flat-leaf parsley

1. Wash and dry the pork cubes. Sprinkle them with the cardamom and Five Pepper Blend.
2. Put the pork in a large heavy-bottomed kettle with the milk, bay leaf, thyme, spiked onion, and shallots. Heat very slowly and simmer over the lowest possible heat, uncovered, for 1 hour. The milk solids will stick to the kettle, so scrape and stir the bottom and sides of the kettle from time to time with a wooden spatula to prevent scorching.
3. Remove the pork cubes with a slotted spoon and set them aside. Strain the reduced milk through a coarse sieve, discarding everything the sieve catches. Scrub out the kettle and rinse it well.
4. Return the pork cubes and the reduced milk to the kettle, stir in the rice, and simmer for 14 minutes, or until the rice is al dente. Add salt to taste.
5. Serve hot, sprinkled with the chopped parsley.

NOTES: Five Pepper Blend is bottled and marketed by Williams-Sonoma. Look for it in gourmet food shops.

Medium-grain rice can still be found in most Latino groceries. Long-grain rice won't produce the velvety, sticky texture the dish requires.

Cantonese Dry-Braised Spareribs

SERVES 4

*D*ry-braising spareribs, originally a Cantonese cooking technique, it seems, is the easiest way I know to prepare barbecued ribs in an apartment. The ribs braise in just their own juices, a few tablespoons of marinade, and another few tablespoons of glazing sauce. They are delicious, easy to prepare, require neither a secret barbecue sauce nor a charcoal grill—and, if you follow instructions, they won't set off the smoke alarm.

2 pounds lean baby back spareribs
1 tablespoon whiskey
2 tablespoons sugar
3 tablespoons distilled vinegar
¼ cup light soy sauce
2 plump cloves garlic, crushed and finely chopped

1 tablespoon finely grated fresh ginger
1 tablespoon Worcestershire sauce
2 tablespoons catsup
2 slices canned pineapple, quartered
1 large scallion, finely chopped

1. Remove and discard all visible fat from the ribs. Wash and dry them and cut them into manageable pieces.
2. Mix the whiskey, sugar, vinegar, and soy sauce and coat the ribs all over with the mixture. Put the ribs in a large heavy-bottomed braising pan or kettle. (The pan should be large enough to accommodate most of the ribs in a single layer, and it must have a tight-fitting lid.) Seal the top of the pan with two sheets of aluminum foil, pressing the lid down firmly over them. Braise the ribs over the lowest possible heat for 45 minutes, shaking the kettle from time to time to turn the ribs.
3. In a blender, make a paste of the garlic, ginger, Worcestershire sauce, and catsup. Coat the ribs with the paste, first on one side, then on the other. Seal the kettle again and steam the ribs very gently for 20 minutes.
4. Pile the ribs attractively on a serving platter. Scatter the chunks of pineapple and the finely chopped scallion over them, and serve them while still warm.

NOTE: In this fat-fearing era, it was exciting for me to discover that these ribs rendered just enough fat and sweated just enough juice to braise themselves beautifully. What's more, they left most of that fat on the bottom of the pan.

Provençal Summer Stew

SERVES 4 OR 5

This fragrant, brothy stew will remind you of soupe au pistou and other dishes made in Provence in summer from the superabundance of locally grown fresh vegetables. For anyone who has lived in Provence, getting a whiff of the distinctive fragrance of this stew is like meeting a beloved old friend again. In the States we don't think of hot stews and soups as summer fare. Yet, in the warmest days of the scorching Provençal summer, these stews remain popular favorites, as their tantalizing aroma at noon in every Provençal village will attest.

1 pound lean stewing pork, cut into ¹/₂-inch cubes

3 tablespoons light olive oil

One ¹/₄-inch-thick slice smoked bacon, cut into ¹/₄-inch pieces

1 small onion, finely chopped

6 plump cloves garlic, peeled

3 flat anchovy fillets

2 tablespoons finely chopped flat-leaf parsley

3 ripe red tomatoes, skinned, seeded, and coarsely chopped

¹/₄ teaspoon *herbes de Provence*

1 jigger (1¹/₂ ounces) brandy (optional)

¹/₂ teaspoon sugar

3 cups unsalted chicken stock

3 medium-size potatoes, peeled and cut into ¹/₂-inch cubes

1 cup green beans, stemmed and tailed and cut into 1-inch pieces

12 saffron threads, dry-toasted and crumbled (see Note)

2 medium-size zucchini, cut into ¹/₂-inch cubes

¹/₂ cup ditalini or other tiny pasta

12 black Provençal olives, pitted

Salt

¹/₂ cup extra-virgin olive oil

12 fresh basil leaves, stemmed and torn into bits

1 cup grated Gruyère cheese

1. Wash and dry the pork.
2. Heat the oil gently in a large heavy-bottomed kettle and sauté the pork and the bacon until they begin to take on color around the edges. Remove them immediately with a slotted spoon and set them aside.
3. Discard all but 1 tablespoon of the oil. Make a *soffritto* by slowly sautéing the onion until it is transparent, then adding the garlic, anchovy fillets, parsley, tomatoes, and *herbes de Provence*, scraping them

back and forth with a wooden spatula until they have become a soft mass. (Old Provençal cooks say that a proper *soffritto* requires a good 7 minutes to prepare.)

4. Add the pork and the bacon. Toss them together thoroughly with the *soffritto*. Throw in the brandy and light it, stirring the ingredients until the flames go out. Sprinkle in the sugar.

5. Add the stock, 2 cups of water, the potatoes, green beans, and the crumbled toasted saffron. Cover tightly and simmer gently for $1^1/_4$ hours.

6. Add the zucchini and the pasta and simmer for 7 minutes.

7. Stir in the olives, and salt the stew to taste.

8. Mix the oil and the torn basil leaves together.

9. Serve the stew boiling hot in large soup plates. Drizzle each serving with a little of the oil and basil leaves. Pass the grated cheese at the table for those who wish it.

NOTE: Authentic saffron is expensive, so wise cooks use it judiciously. Toasting the stamens intensifies their flavor (so you need less), and it makes the tough little stamens friable. Here's the method: Shake the saffron threads very briefly (they are very susceptible to heat) in a dry frying pan that has been heated and removed from the stove. Turn them out at once on a piece of waxed paper. Crumble the saffron to a powder with the back of a spoon, and use it immediately.

Country Spareribs with Ratatouille

F or those who love pork chops and spareribs, country spareribs are the best of all possible worlds, since they combine both cuts. Here the chops are braised in a fragrant, chunky Provençal ratatouille. Make the dish for a festive occasion in high summer when vegetables are plentiful, field-fresh, and inexpensive. Preparing the ratatouille step by step takes a little time and patience, but the results warrant all the love and attention you can lavish on them. The dish is equally delectable served warm or cold. Served too hot, many of the subtler tastes you labored to incorporate will be obscured—love's labor's lost.

6 large, lean country pork chops, cut apart from one another

$^1/_2$ teaspoon cracked black pepper

$^1/_2$ teaspoon ground sage

1 large eggplant (about 1 pound), cut into 1-inch-thick chunks

1 tablespoon coarse salt

$^1/_4$ cup vegetable oil

3 tablespoons flour

1 cup dry red wine

1 teaspoon sugar

2 large bell peppers, flame-roasted (see Notes), cut lengthwise into 1-inch wide strips

3 plump cloves garlic, peeled and halved lengthwise

4 scallions (1 to 1$^1/_4$ inches in diameter), halved

4 medium-size ripe red tomatoes, skinned, halved and seeded

2 medium-size zucchini, cut into 1-inch pieces

1 bouquet garni made up of 1 bay leaf, one 1 × 2-inch piece orange peel, 3 sprigs fresh thyme, and 1 sprig fresh rosemary, tied together with cotton string

$^1/_2$ teaspoon fennel seeds

12 black oil-cured olives, pitted

$^1/_4$ cup capers, rinsed and drained

Salt

3 tablespoons finely chopped flat-leaf parsley

12 fresh basil leaves

1. Wash and dry the pork chops and pat the cracked pepper and sage into them. Set them aside.
2. Put the eggplant in a colander in the sink. Sprinkle all the chunks well with the coarse salt and allow them to leach for 20 minutes.
3. Heat the oil in a large heavy-bottomed (preferably enameled) kettle

and gently brown the chops well all over. Remove them as they finish browning and set them aside.

4. Rinse the eggplant chunks well under cold running water. Squeeze them out and pat them dry with paper towels. Dredge them with the flour and brown them, in batches, on all the cut sides. Remove the chunks as they finish browning and set them aside.

5. Discard all the oil in the kettle. Add the red wine and sugar, and, using a wooden spatula, thoroughly deglaze the bottom.

6. Return the ribs and eggplant chunks to the kettle. Add the green peppers, garlic, scallions, tomatoes, zucchini, bouquet garni, and fennel seeds, and toss the ingredients together briefly but thoroughly. Cover the kettle tightly and simmer gently for 45 minutes. Scrape the bottom of the kettle with a wooden spatula from time to time to prevent scorching.

7. Stir in the olives and capers and simmer, uncovered, for 5 minutes. Salt to taste. If the stew seems "brothy," increase the heat and reduce it. Take care, it scorches easily. Discard the bouquet garni.

8. Arrange the stew on a large, deep serving platter and sprinkle well with the chopped parsley. Just before serving the stew, stem the basil leaves, tear them into bits, and scatter them over the parsley. Serve at once.

NOTES: When Nicole Roman taught me to make ratatouille in Aix-en-Provence more than forty years ago, it was traditional to fry the eggplant and zucchini until they were almost burned and, once the vegetables were combined, to stir the ratatouille a great deal while cooking until it was a dark purée. The result was not very pleasing to the eye, but it was delicious and compelling to the tongue. Chilled and spread on a canapé of toasted bread, it was a knockout, the perfect accompaniment to a glass of good red wine. You might want to try it that old-fashioned method sometime. Today, however, most of us prefer to keep the vegetables somewhat underdone, chunky, and recognizable, as they are in this dish.

Roast bell peppers by holding them on a long fork over an open flame and turning them until they are evenly blackened. Place them in a paper bag until they cool, then wash off the blackened skin under cold running water. Remove any stubborn bits of skin with a paring knife. Stem the peppers, seed them, and tear them lengthwise into large pieces.

The peppers are now ready to eat with salt, lemon juice, oil, and thinly sliced garlic as an hors d'oeuvre, or to use as directed in a recipe. If you don't have a gas stove, put the peppers in a foil-lined roasting pan and grill them in the oven.

Pork with Spring Vegetables

SERVES 6

When I went to live in the south of France more than forty years ago, Nice was the first city to enchant me. She had a culture all her own and an old elegance, neither French nor Italian, and I adored her food. At that time Old Nice was full of small, good, family-run restaurants where local specialties were always the order of the day, and everyone could afford them. There, in the last days of spring, we often enjoyed a ragout made from the first tiny vegetables of the season called lou poutité dè prima à la Nissarda. Each cook made a slightly different version, but, in the main, this is how they all made the stew. To create the true Nissarda taste, you'll need the freshest, tiniest spring vegetables you can get your hands on. If they come from your garden, all the better. They ought to be gathered while the dew is still on them.

2 pounds lean pork shoulder, cut into 1 × 2-inch chunks

1 pound pork neck bones, cut into manageable pieces

2 tablespoons vegetable oil

One 1/4-inch-thick strip smoked bacon, cut into 1/4-inch pieces

3 tablespoons flour

4 walnut-size garden onions, trimmed and quartered (page 148)

3 plump cloves garlic, crushed and finely chopped

3 baby carrots, thinly sliced

2 cups unsalted defatted chicken stock

2 tablespoons red wine vinegar

1/2 cup dry white wine

3 medium-size ripe red tomatoes, skinned, seeded, and coarsely chopped

1 bouquet garni made up of 2 bay leaves, 3 sprigs fresh thyme, 1 sprig fresh rosemary, and 4 sprigs fresh parsley, bound with cotton string

6 to 8 stalks Swiss chard, ribs only, cut into 1/4 × 2-inch pieces

1 cup tiny sugar snap peas, stemmed and tailed but left whole

3 tablespoons freshly squeezed lemon juice

2 medium-size potatoes, peeled and cut into 1/2-inch cubes

1/2 pound tiny elbow macaroni

3 tablespoons fruity olive oil

12 fresh basil leaves, stemmed and torn to bits

Salt and black pepper

Freshly grated Parmesan cheese

1. Wash the pork chunks and neck bones under warm running water and dry them well with paper towels.
2. Heat the vegetable oil in a large heavy-bottomed kettle and brown the pork chunks, neck bones, and bacon, tossing them frequently with a wooden spatula so that they brown evenly but do not burn.
3. Tip the kettle and spoon out and discard as much fat as you can. With a wad of paper towels, blot the rest of the fat. Sprinkle the flour over the meat and toss until the flour clings to the meat and loses its white color.
4. Put the onions, garlic, and carrots in the kettle and toss together thoroughly. Cook, tossing from time to time, until the onions have wilted (about 5 minutes). Add the stock, vinegar, wine, and 1 cup of warm water. Bring the liquid to a rolling boil to deglaze the bottom of the kettle, then reduce the heat to a faint simmer. (In Nice one cook used to say that the surface of the stew should smile and murmur without bubbling.) Add the tomatoes and the bouquet garni. Cover and simmer gently for 1½ hours.
5. Meanwhile, blanch the chard for 10 minutes, the peas for 5, in 3 cups of water to which the lemon juice has been added. Drain them and set them aside.
6. Stir the potatoes into the stew, and simmer gently for 30 minutes.
7. Boil the macaroni until it is al dente, drain it, and toss it with the olive oil and the basil leaves in the hot pan in which it was cooked.
8. Salt and pepper the stew to taste. Skim off and discard any fat that may have risen to the surface. Discard the bouquet garni. Combine the chard, peas, and macaroni with the stew, tossing all the ingredients together well.
9. Serve the stew hot in large, deep soup plates. Pass freshly grated Parmesan for those who wish it.

NOTE: Start the meal with tiny radishes and curls of sweet butter, a fresh loaf of crusty bread, and a carafe of cold white wine. Then serve your stew. Follow it with a salad of mesclun, a very fresh young goat cheese, some fruit of the season, and, for a full stop, a thimbleful of excellent black coffee with a dot-sized piece of lemon peel. You will have had the ideal spring lunch à la Nissarda.

Spanish-Style Pork and Summer Vegetables

SERVES 6

This perfectly delicious hodgepodge of pork, ham, and summer vegetables lightly bound together with beaten eggs is a Spanish specialty from the region of Don Quixote. Pisto, as it is known, is real peasant fare, consistent and tasty, if somewhat lacking in elegance. Nevertheless, it is one of the most popular dishes of the Spanish repertoire, one you will often find on the menus of good restaurants in Spain. Make the dish in early summer when tiny zucchini, baby asparagus, and tender sugar snap peas are available. The dish is sometimes made without meat or with only a few bits of mountain ham to give it a distinctive flavor. This version is a little posh, but it is substantial enough to serve as a good main course. Is pisto really a stew? Yes, a very thick one. As for stirring in a few eggs, precedents abound in the cooking of rural Spain, France, and Italy. The classic Castilian recipe for pisto manchego calls for ten to twelve eggs. Here I have cut the quantity by about half.

2 large red bell peppers, flame-roasted (see page 163) and cut into ¹/₄-inch strips

1 pound lean pork shoulder, cut into ¹/₂-inch cubes

2 tablespoons olive oil

3 tablespoons unsalted butter

¹/₂ cup lean cooked ham, cut into ¹/₂-inch cubes

2 medium-size onions, thinly sliced

2 medium-size zucchini, halved and cut into 1-inch pieces

¹/₂ teaspoon baking soda

2 medium-size ripe red tomatoes, skinned, halved, seeded, and coarsely chopped

1 medium-size potato, peeled, quartered, and sliced thin

1 medium-size yellow squash, halved, and cut into ¹/₄-inch slices

1 cup shelled green baby lima beans (thawed frozen ones may be substituted)

1 cup unsalted chicken stock

¹/₂ cup shelled baby sugar snap peas (thawed frozen snowpea pods may be substituted)

3 or 4 tiny fresh asparagus spears, cut into ¹/₂-inch pieces

6 eggs

¹/₂ teaspoon coarse salt

¹/₄ teaspoon freshly ground black pepper

3 tablespoons finely chopped flat-leaf parsley

1. Prepare the bell peppers well in advance.

2. Wash and dry the pork cubes. Heat the oil and butter in a large heavy-bottomed braising pan or kettle. When the butter is sizzling, brown the pork cubes in batches, removing them as they finish browning. Set them aside.

3. Taking care that the fat does not burn, gently brown the ham cubes. Add the onions and toss together thoroughly until the onions have wilted. Add the zucchini and toss with the ham and onions. Sauté for 3 or 4 minutes.

4. Mix the baking soda thoroughly with the tomatoes and set the mixture aside.

5. Layer in the pork cubes, bell peppers, potato, yellow squash, and lima beans. Add the stock, and cover the pan with two sheets of aluminum foil, pressing the lid down firmly to seal up the stew. Reduce the heat to the lowest possible level and simmer gently for 30 minutes. Unseal the pan and add the peas and asparagus, tossing them in with a wooden spatula. Replace the lid but not the foil and continue to simmer gently for 10 minutes. Add a little water if necessary, but don't stir, or the vegetables will lose their identities.

6. Beat the eggs lightly with 6 tablespoons of cold water, the salt, black pepper, parsley, and the neutralized tomatoes. Fold this mixture quickly into the already thick stew and serve before the eggs have time to set.

NOTES: The authentic consistency of this dish is drooly, like a genuine French *omelette baveuse*. That is how *pisto* lovers like it. If you insist on cooking it longer, it will cease to be a *pisto* and become a *tortilla de legumbres*.

Have plenty of fresh, crusty, thickly sliced bread on hand. With a salad of mesclun (in a light dressing of rice vinegar, Dijon mustard, salt, and a pinch of sugar), this *pisto* provides you with a completely delicious and well-balanced rustic lunch.

Balkan Pork and Vegetables

*T*here are many dishes from the Balkans and the Middle East in which the vegetables and meat are softened by gentle braising in a great deal of oil or pork dripping. They are distinctive and delicious, but their fat content makes them taboo for most of us. Here is my version of an old Balkan favorite in which I have carefully reduced the fat content without destroying its rich taste and texture. Serve it on a bed of steamed groats such as kasha (buckwheat) or bulgur. Top each serving with a dollop of yogurt sprinkled with a few toasted caraway seeds or a little finely chopped fresh dill. Thick slices of soft-crumbed bread are a good choice to balance the buttery richness of the peppers and pimientos.

1 1/2 pounds lean stewing pork, cut into bite-size pieces

2 teaspoons coarse salt

1/2 teaspoon cracked black pepper

1/4 cup vegetable oil

3 medium-size onions, very finely chopped (use a food processor if possible)

1 teaspoon paprika

3 medium-size green bell peppers, cut lengthwise into 1/2-inch strips

1 medium-size eggplant, peeled and cut across the width into 1/2-inch slices

One 14 1/4-ounce can peeled tomatoes, drained and coarsely chopped

2 cups unsalted chicken stock

3 tablespoons cider vinegar

1 tablespoon sugar

One 11 1/2-ounce jar fancy pimientos, drained and cut lengthwise into 1/2-inch strips

2 cups yellow squash, halved and cut into 1/4-inch slices

1 tablespoon finely chopped flat-leaf parsley

1 tablespoon finely chopped fresh dill

Salt

1. Wash the pork and blot it dry with paper towels. Sprinkle the pieces all over with 1 teaspoon of the salt and all the black pepper. Set aside.

2. Heat the oil in a large heavy-bottomed kettle and gently brown the pork in batches, removing the pieces to a plate as they finish browning.

3. Add the onions, paprika, and bell peppers to the kettle, tossing them thoroughly to coat them well with the fat and paprika. Cover tightly and sweat the vegetables over very low heat for 20 minutes, shaking

the pan and tossing the vegetables from time to time to prevent scorching.

4. Salt the eggplant slices with the remaining 1 teaspoon of salt and poach them in 2 cups of boiling water for 10 minutes. Drain them and rinse them under cold running water. Squeeze them out and pat them dry with paper towels. Set them aside.

5. Add the meat, tomatoes, stock, vinegar, and sugar to the kettle and mix everything together thoroughly. Simmer gently, covered, for $1^{1}/_{4}$ hours, or until the meat is fork-tender. Remove the lid, stir in the eggplant, pimientos, squash, parsley, and dill, and simmer, uncovered, for 30 minutes, letting the liquids reduce. The braise should be very thick but unscorched.

6. Salt to taste and serve as suggested in the headnote.

NOTE: Like many such braises, this one is delicious chilled. It can be served cold as a first course, sprinkled with more finely chopped parsley and a few rinsed capers, or as a main course, accompanied by a rice salad.

Danubian Pork and Sauerkraut Stew

SERVES 4 TO 5

*T*his is another Middle European stew I learned through my Austrian god-mother. I have known this luscious, peppery dish for half a century, so my appreciation of it is completely biased. Just smelling it simmer gives me a Pavlov-ian seizure. It is a pleasure for me to introduce you to my updated version of this wonderful Old World dish.

³/₄ pound lean pork spareribs, cut apart

¹/₂ teaspoon freshly ground Five Pepper Blend (see Note)

3 tablespoons vegetable oil

1¹/₂ cups lean cooked ham, cut into 1-inch cubes

3 small bay leaves

6 juniper berries, bruised

¹/₂ teaspoon dried thyme

¹/₂ teaspoon caraway seeds

1 tablespoon sweet Hungarian paprika (see page 45)

2 medium-size white onions, halved, and thinly sliced

One 7- to 8-ounce can sauerkraut, with its juice

1 small head white cabbage, quartered, cored, and cut into chunks

1 Golden Delicious apple peeled, cored, and cut into chunks

1 small potato, peeled and finely grated

Sugar

1. Wash and dry the spareribs. Sprinkle them all over with the Five Pepper Blend.

2. In a 10-inch wide heavy-bottomed braising pan at least 3 inches deep, heat the oil and gently brown the ribs, covered, until they are golden on all sides. Shake the pan from time to time to prevent the ribs from scorching.

3. Add the ham cubes and toss them together with the ribs. When they are warmed through, stir in the bay leaves, juniper berries, thyme, caraway seeds, and paprika. Place the onions in a layer on top, cover, and sweat the ingredients over very low heat for 20 minutes, or until the onions are almost melted.

4. Add the sauerkraut and its juice and toss it thoroughly with the other ingredients. Pack in the cabbage and apple chunks rather tightly and add 2 cups of warm water.

5. Cover the pan tightly and simmer very gently for $1^1/_2$ hours.

6. Stir in the grated potato. Add a little water if the braise seems too dry. The trick is to keep the braise very moist so that it doesn't scorch. However, it should not finish brothy. Continue simmering the braise, uncovered, for 15 minutes.

7. Sugar the dish to your taste. (My godmother liked it somewhat sweet, but by all means, suit yourself.)

8. Discard the bay leaves. Serve the stew steaming hot. Boiled new potatoes are the standard accompaniment.

NOTE: Five Pepper Blend is bottled and marketed by Williams-Sonoma.

Lamb Stews

Introduction to Lamb Stews

L amb and mutton stews are the oldest meat stews in international cookery. Recent discoveries in the area once known as the Fertile Crescent strongly suggest that lamb and mutton stews were already well known in the Middle East 10,000 years before the present era. Sheep were the first animals to be domesticated by mankind for their wool, flesh, and milk; from the earliest times, sheep, and especially lambs, were also the sacrificial animals of choice, a fact well established and still attested to in the choice of lamb for celebrating the Jewish Passover, Christian Easter, and many major Muslim feasts.

Over the centuries, thousands of recipes for mutton and lamb stews evolved as sheepherding spread to Greece, Anatolia, and Asia, to Africa, to Italy, Spain, France, England, Scotland, and Ireland, then to the New World, and finally to Australia and New Zealand. In fact, sheep raising spread so rapidly that mutton and lamb quickly became accessible to the poor as food. Mutton and lamb broths and stews were stigmatized as poverty food centuries before the cattle barons imposed the priority of beef. To this day, many scorn the aroma of boiling lamb as "the smell of poverty" and are disdainful of all lamb except leg of lamb, carefully prepared to disguise its gamy taste, and rib chops grilled, preferably outside.

The longstanding bias against mutton and lamb has kept many people from trying them. Most diners love only what they are acquainted with, and, surprisingly, an incredible number of diners in the States neither know lamb nor feel inclined to try it.

Having grown up in Texas, I might have been prejudiced against lamb had my mother not been born and reared in a lamb-loving family in the northeastern United States. She taught us all, including my father, a Texan of the most macho stripe, to relish lamb. She knew the trick of removing every vestige of the fell, that thin, nacreous membrane between the skin and the flesh, which, she taught us, was the source of the gaminess. She rubbed the flesh with plenty of fresh lemon juice and olive oil. When I lived in Greece, I discovered that the Greeks, expert preparers of lamb, used the same technique.

Actually, the gamy taste of mutton—lamb that is more than twenty months old—can be appreciated and has its faithful following. Mutton makes richer-tasting stews than the younger, fresher-tasting lamb, but mutton is very difficult to obtain in the States at present. Sheep raisers have assumed that the American public dislikes the richer taste of mutton and send only lamb to market. Mutton can, with a little trouble, be ordered from your butcher. A few very special chop houses in the States still serve mutton to die-hard mutton fanciers. But one looks in vain for mutton in supermarkets. They feature only American lamb, except for a short period in late spring when frozen, thawed New Zealand lamb is occasionally available. It is a dark plum color and, although it is lamb, tastes much more like mutton than the lamb we are used to. One of the aims of this book is to present recipes with ingredients that are readily obtainable; consequently, all the stews in this chapter call for lamb. If you are a mutton lover and have a supplier, you may substitute mutton for lamb in any of the recipes that follow.

Fine lamb, once cheaper than beef, is now just as expensive; sometimes it costs even more. Make sure you get what you pay for. First-rate fresh lamb is a deep rose color, firm and ungreasy to the touch, and has a faint, sharp bouquet not unlike that of freshly chopped parsley. It should be cooked the day you buy it, but it will keep for as long as two days if well refrigerated. Ground lamb should be used at once, since its freshness deteriorates rapidly. As a rule of thumb, all stewing lamb purchased packaged from a supermarket should be washed briefly under warm running water and blotted dry. Because of its firm texture, the distribution of its fat, and its distinctive taste, lamb is ideal for stewing and braising.

It is important to trim off and discard all excess fat from lamb, limiting it to less than one quarter of the volume of the flesh. A certain amount of fat ensures the juiciness and tenderness of the meat. If, after the stew is finished, you find it a bit fatty for your taste, you can always skim off the excess. Lamb fat is viscous, hard to digest, and, in excess, to be avoided. Oil and/or pork fat may be substituted to good advantage, if necessary.

More herbs agree with the rich taste of lamb than with any other meat, providing the cook with countless opportunities to experiment; the most readily available are parsley, thyme, rosemary, oregano, chervil, savory, marjoram, mint, dill, fennel seed, and bay leaf. Lamb also goes well with generous amounts of garlic, fresh lemon juice, and fruity olive oil, all of which have a taming or balancing effect on the gaminess, whether or not the fell has been excised. Carrots, onions, potatoes, parsnips, turnips, artichokes, okra, and white beans are all complementary to lamb, as are tomatoes. Cardamom, cumin, ginger, cinammon, and orange peel are called for in various recipes to enhance the flavor of lamb but should be used with discretion.

Lamb stews are the stews I most enjoy preparing. I hope some of the joy I had in preparing these lamb stews for you will find its way into your kitchen.

A Model Lamb and Vegetable Stew

SERVES 4 OR 5

This stew employs most of the basic stew-making techniques. Once you have mastered it, you can substitute other vegetables, herbs, and flavorings, making it your own.

2 pounds lean stewing lamb, cut into bite-size pieces

1 teaspoon coarse salt

1/2 teaspoon coarsely ground black pepper

1/2 teaspoon ground cumin

3 tablespoons freshly squeezed lemon juice

3 tablespoons vegetable oil

2 large yellow onions, coarsely chopped

4 plump cloves garlic, peeled

2 large leeks, white parts only, well washed, sliced into 1/2-inch rounds

3 tablespoons finely chopped flat-leaf parsley

1 cup dry white wine

2 medium-size ripe red tomatoes, skinnned, seeded, and coarsely chopped (an equal amount of drained tinned tomatoes may be substituted)

1 bouquet garni made up of 1 rib celery, 2 bay leaves, 1 sprig fresh rosemary, and 2 sprigs fresh thyme, bound together with cotton string

3 large carrots, peeled, halved, and cut into 1/2-inch pieces

2 chicken bouillon cubes, crumbled

3 medium-size yellow potatoes, peeled and quartered

1/4 teaspoon red pepper flakes (optional)

Salt

1. Cut away and discard the excess fat and removable fell from the lamb. Wash the pieces well in a colander under warm running water and blot them dry. Sprinkle the lamb with the coarse salt, pepper, cumin, and lemon juice, working these well into the pieces.

2. Heat the oil in a large heavy-bottomed kettle over moderate heat and brown the lamb well in batches, removing the batches as they brown. Add the onions, garlic, leeks, and parsley and sauté until the onions have wilted. Return the browned lamb pieces to the kettle and toss them well with the sautéed vegetables.

3. Add the tomatoes and wine and stir well until the kettle is completely deglazed.
4. Add the bouquet garni, carrots, 4 cups of cold water, and the crumbled bouillon cubes. Stir well, reduce the heat to very low, and simmer, covered, for 1 hour, or until the lamb is fork-tender.
5. Add the potatoes and red pepper flakes and simmer, covered, for 30 minutes.
6. Skim off and discard any oil and fat that have risen to the surface around the sides of the kettle. Discard the bouquet garni. Salt to taste. Turn off the heat, allow the stew to sit, covered, for 5 minutes, then serve.

NOTE: Finely chopped fresh parsley, mint, or dill sprinkled over the stew is a welcome addition to the taste and color of the dish.

The Original Irish Stew

SERVES 6

Today, if you order Irish stew in a restaurant in the United States, you may be served a beef stew containing carrots, parsnips, green peas, cabbage, and tomatoes, as well as potatoes and onions. The original Irish stew was made with lamb or mutton and contained only potatoes and onions, salt and pepper. At serving time it was sprinkled with a little chopped parsley, if there was any at hand. Here is the recipe for the original. It is very simple and very good.

2½ pounds stewing lamb, cut into bite size pieces

2 yellow onions, cut into ½-inch slices

4 to 6 medium size potatoes, peeled and cut into ½-inch pieces

1 teaspoon coarse salt

1 teaspoon freshly ground black pepper

2 tablespoons finely chopped flat-leaf parsley

1. In a large heavy-bottomed kettle, layer the lamb in alternately with the onions and potatoes, ending with a layer of potatoes. Sprinkle each layer with salt and pepper.
2. Down one side of the pot, pour in enough cold water to come up to half the depth of the ingredients.
3. Cover the pot securely and simmer the stew over the lowest possible heat for 2½ hours.
4. Turn off the heat and allow the stew to sit, covered, for 15 minutes.
5. Sprinkle the stew with the chopped parsley and serve hot.

NOTE: If you want to be consistent in serving an entirely old-fashioned Irish meal, I suggest you accompany this with a thickly sliced cottage loaf or thin slices of Irish soda bread, and plenty of lightly salted butter. Coleslaw and pickled onions are other customary accompaniments. Provide a pitcher of cold sweet milk or buttermilk for the children and beer or freshly brewed black tea for the grown-ups. For dessert serve apple pie or a wedge of sharp Cheddar with McIntosh or Golden Delicious apples.

Lancashire Hot Pot

SERVES 6

H ot pot in one form or another is perhaps the oldest stew in the culinary repertoire of Western Europe. It is an irresistible dish that can cheer the soul and fortify the body against the coldest winter weather. I am grateful to my dear friend, Jean Fletcher, a native of Barrow-in-Furness, for sharing her collection of hot-pot recipes with me. I have experimented with several of them and come up with this version.

8 thick shoulder lamb chops, fat trimmed away and discarded

1 teaspoon coarse salt

1 teaspoon freshly ground black pepper

$^{1}/_{2}$ cup flour

$^{1}/_{3}$ cup vegetable oil

1 $^{1}/_{2}$ cups coarsely chopped yellow onions

1 $^{1}/_{2}$ cups coarsely chopped white part of leeks

2 medium-size carrots, peeled and cut into thin rounds

2 bay leaves

$^{1}/_{4}$ teaspoon dried thyme

12 freshly shucked bluepoint oysters

2 cups unsalted chicken stock

1 tablespoon brown sugar

6 medium-size potatoes, peeled and cut into $^{1}/_{2}$-inch slices

1. Sprinkle the chops with the coarse salt and pepper and dredge them well in the flour, brushing off the excess.
2. Select a large, deep, fireproof ceramic casserole with a tight-fitting lid. Set aside 2 tablespoons of the oil. Heat the rest of the oil in the casserole and brown the chops well on both sides. Allow the chops plenty of room when they are browning, or they will smother in their juice and won't brown. When they finish browning, remove the chops and set them aside.
3. Toss the onions, leeks, carrots, and bay leaves in the hot oil with a wooden spatula. Reduce the heat to very low, and keep tossing the vegetables until the onions and leeks are soft and wilted. Sprinkle in the remainder of the flour and the thyme and toss again. Place the chops on top of the sautéed vegetables in an overlapping layer. Place the oysters in a layer over the chops.
4. Heat the stock and dissolve the brown sugar in it. Pour the mixture

down the side of the casserole, so that it drowns the sautéed vegetables and chops.

5. Preheat the oven to 350°F.

6. Using a pastry brush, coat the potato slices with the remaining 2
   tablespoons of oil and layer them in, overlapping the slices on top.

7. Pour in enough hot water to reach just below the top layer of potatoes.

8. Cover the casserole with two thicknesses of foil and press the lid
   down firmly over them, sealing the stew.

9. Bake the casserole for $1^1/2$ hours. Remove the lid and the foil from
   the casserole and bake for $^1/2$ hour, or until the top layer of potatoes
   is golden brown. Serve very hot.

NOTE: It is customary to wrap a clean white napkin around the casserole and serve the dish in the receptable in which it was baked. Pickled
onions, cucumber pickles, hot mustard, and coleslaw are the usual accompaniments for this famous dish, with beer, ale, or tea to wash it down.

French Lamb Stew

*L*amb chops braised with layers of sautéed onion and thick, browned slices of potato are an old standby in French households. Having lived a long time in the Midi in my youth and acquired a definite penchant for Provençal food, when I make this Champvallon-style lamb, I give it a decidedly Provençal accent by adding tomatoes, garlic, capers, and herbes de Provence. Here's my recipe.

$^1/_4$ cup vegetable oil

2 medium-size yellow onions, halved and thickly sliced

3 large leeks, white parts only, well washed and thinly sliced

2 plump cloves garlic, thinly sliced

1 envelope ham concentrate (see Note)

4 medium-size ripe red tomatoes, skinned, halved, and seeded (drained canned tomatoes may be used)

2 bay leaves

$^1/_2$ teaspoon *herbes de Provence*

2 tablespoons bottled capers, drained

1 cup dry white wine

3 medium-size baking potatoes, peeled and cut into $^1/_2$-inch slices

1 teaspoon cracked black pepper

4 lean shoulder lamb chops

Salt

1. In a heavy-bottomed braising pan, gently heat 2 tablespoons of the oil and sauté the onions, leeks, and garlic, tossing them in the oil until they are wilted and translucent but not browned.

2. Add the ham concentrate, tomatoes, bay leaves, *herbes de Provence*, capers, and white wine and toss well. Cover and simmer gently for 15 minutes.

3. Meanwhile, heat the remaining 4 tablespoons of oil in a frying pan and fry the potato slices on both sides until golden brown. As they brown, remove the slices and set them aside on paper towels to drain.

4. Press the cracked pepper into the surface of the chops and gently brown them in the oil in which the potatoes were fried. As the chops finish browning, set them aside. Discard the oil or set it aside for another purpose.

5. Place the chops on the bed of sautéed vegetables in one layer. Cover

the braising pan tightly, reduce the heat to the lowest level, and simmer gently for 1 hour, or until the chops are very tender. If this "dry stew" seems on the point of losing it juiciness during the simmering, add a little water.

6. Salt to taste. Remove the braise to a warmed serving dish, or, if the braising pan is presentable, take it to the table and serve directly from it. The aroma is a breath of Provence!

NOTE: Ham concentrate is sold in eight-envelope packages by Goya Food, Inc. If you can't obtain it, make the substitute on page 35.

Baked Lamb, Potato, and Artichoke Stew

SERVES 4 OR 5

This is the Provençal version of the Belgian carbonade (see page 111). This version was traditionally assembled in its pot at home, then taken to the local bakery to be put in the oven after the bread had been removed. There it braised for two or three hours while the oven cooled. That slow braising takes time, it is true, but once the stew is assembled, you can simply put it in the oven and go about your business, knowing that it will be ready to serve in two and a half hours. In Nîmes it is considered one of the best defenses against the icy Mistral.

One $^1/_4$-inch-thick slice streaky salt pork, cut into $^1/_4$-inch pieces

3 tablespoons olive oil

$^1/_4$ teaspoon dried thyme

$^1/_4$ teaspoon dried marjoram

6 fresh or dried rosemary leaves

1 bouquet garni made up of 2 bay leaves, 1 large carrot, halved, and 1 branch fresh parsley, bound together with cotton string

$^1/_2$ teaspoon coarse salt

Four or five $^1/_2$-inch slices leg of lamb, bone left in

1 teaspoon freshly ground black pepper

2 globe artichokes, with their stems

1 lemon

3 medium-size potatoes, peeled and cut into $^1/_2$-inch dice

2 medium-size yellow onions, coarsely chopped

2 teaspoons vegetable oil

1 cup dry red wine

1 cup unsalted chicken stock

Salt

1. Blanch the salt pork by placing it in 2 cups of rapidly boiling water for 5 minutes. Drain it and rinse it well under cold running water, then pat it dry with paper towels. Choose a heavy, wide, ovenproof casserole or Dutch oven at least 4 inches deep. Coat the interior of the pot with the olive oil and scatter the salt pork over the bottom. Sprinkle in half the dried herbs. Place the bouquet garni in the middle.

2. Salt the lamb slices on both sides. Cover the salt pork with them. Sprinkle in the rest of the herbs and the black pepper.

3. Cut off and discard the toughest part of the artichoke stems, leaving about 1½ inches. Cut across the tops of the artichokes about ½ inch above the hearts and discard all the incised tops of the leaves. Quarter the artichokes lengthwise, through the stems. Carefully peel away and discard the tough outer cover of the stems and all the tough green parts of the leaves still adhering to the hearts. Cut out and discard the chokes. Rinse the quarters in cold water. Halve the lemon and rub the prepped artichoke quarters all over to prevent their darkening. Use the rest of the lemon to clean your fingers. Wash both your fingers and the artichokes in cold water.

4. Toss the potatoes and onions well in the vegetable oil.

5. Place the drained, quartered artichokes on top of the lamb and cover them evenly with the potatoes and onions. And the wine and stock.

6. Preheat the oven to 450°F.

7. Fit a piece of aluminum foil loosely as a cover over the ingredients, leaving about ¼ inch all around between the foil and the sides of the casserole. Pierce the foil in several places.

8. Bake for 20 minutes, then reduce the heat to 300°F, and continue baking for 2 hours.

9. Remove the foil. Add 1 cup of water. Turn off the heat, but let the stew remain in the oven for 10 more minutes.

10. Discard the bouquet garni. Salt to taste. Serve very warm but not bubbling hot.

Lamb Fricassee

SERVES 4 OR 5

Mme. Paulet was an old neighbor of mine when I lived in Aix. Her father, she told me, had been one of Cézanne's card-playing cronies. She pointed him out to me in reproductions she had of some of the famous pictures the Aixois painter did of card players. Mme. Paulet was a mine of information about Aix. We spoke of many things, among them, of course, the food of the region. Here is my version of her fricot (Aixois slang for fricassee), a soothing, delicious stew, much like a blanquette.

3 pounds breast of lamb, trimmed of all fat and cut into bite-size pieces

1 bay leaf

1/8 teaspoon *each* ground mace, ground cardamom, and dried marjoram

1/2 teaspoon freshly ground black pepper

3 tablespoons flour

1 cup milk

1 cup coarsely chopped white onion

1 cup peeled and thinly sliced carrots

3 ribs celery, coarsely chopped

1 cup peeled potatoes, in 1/2-inch dice

1 tablespoon chicken-concentrate granules

20 small white button mushrooms, wiped clean and trimmed

2 eggs

3 tablespoons freshly squeezed lemon juice

Salt

1. Cook the lamb in a pressure cooker with 4 cups of water and the bay leaf for 15 minutes.
2. Depressurize the cooker. Drain the lamb in a colander, discarding the fatty stock and the bay leaf. Rinse the lamb well with warm water.
3. Clean the pressure cooker well. Dredge the lamb with the mace, cardamom, marjoram, black pepper, and flour. Pressure cook the lamb with 3 cups of water, the milk, onion, carrots, celery, potatoes, and chicken concentrate for 15 minutes, or until the lamb is fork-tender.
4. Depressurize the cooker and simmer the *fricot*, uncovered, with the mushrooms for 10 minutes.
5. Turn off the heat and allow the stew to sit for 2 minutes.

6. Beat the eggs well with the lemon juice. Stir this mixture well into the stew, adding it little by little. The *fricot* should thicken like heavy cream.
7. Salt to taste. Do not allow the *fricot* to simmer again.
8. Serve hot on a bed of freshly cooked noodles or steamed rice.

NOTE: *Fricot* is a very nutritious, light stew; the trick to making it light lies in removing as much fat as possible from the lamb before cooking and in discarding the first fatty broth.

Piedmontese Lamb and Bean Stew with *Pistou*

SERVES 6 OR 7

O f all the landladies I had during my years in Aix-en-Provence, the most colorful was a bawdy, rude-spoken Piedmontese widow named Mme. Sciaca. She knew more secret household knacks than anyone I ever met. It was she who taught me the sole virtue of the water in which dried beans have been soaked: It will remove certain rust stains from fine linen. "Always wash the soaked beans free of it," she admonished me. "Otherwise, if you cook the beans in it, it will grind your guts and put freckles in your underwear!" She always punctuated such crudely uttered bons mots with a Rabelaisian belly laugh, and she relished my dismay. Here is a phenomenally tasty Piedmontese mountain lamb and bean stew she taught me to make. It is truly soul food on a cold night.

FOR THE STEW

- 1 pound dried Great Northern beans
- 1 teaspoon freshly ground black pepper
- 2 pounds lean stewing lamb, cut into bite-size chunks
- 1/4 cup vegetable oil
- One 1/4-inch slice smoked bacon, cut into 1/4-inch dice
- 2 cups coarsely chopped yellow onions
- 1 1/2 cups peeled and finely sliced carrots
- 1 large leek, white part only, trimmed, washed, and thinly sliced
- 2 ribs celery or fennel, finely sliced
- One 8-ounce can tomato sauce

- 2 cups peeled potatoes in 1/4-inch dice
- 1 cup coarsely chopped white cabbage
- 1/2 ounce dried porcini well washed, soaked for 15 minutes in 1 cup boiling water

FOR THE *PISTOU*

- 3 plump cloves garlic, crushed to a paste in 1 teaspoon coarse salt, using the underside of a soup spoon
- 3/4 cup finely grated Fontina cheese
- 1/4 cup finely grated Parmesan cheese
- 1/2 teaspoon dried marjoram
- 3 tablespoons best-quality virgin olive oil

Making the Stew:

1. Wash the beans well in a colander. Put them in a large heavy-bottomed kettle with 2 quarts of cold water and bring them to a rolling boil. Remove the kettle immediately from the heat and let the beans soak for at least 2 hours. You may do this the day before and soak the beans overnight, if you wish.
2. Discard the soaking water and rinse the beans well under cold running water. Clean the kettle and return the beans to it with 3 quarts of cold water. Simmer the beans, uncovered, for 1 hour. Replenish the water if necessary.
3. Meanwhile, work the pepper well into the pieces of lamb.
4. In another large heavy-bottomed kettle, heat the oil and gently sauté the bacon cubes until they color at the edges. Remove them with a slotted spoon and set them aside. Then brown the lamb in batches. Avoid crowding the lamb, and allow the pieces to brown well all over. Remove them and place them with the bacon.
5. Add the onion, carrot, leek, and celery. Toss the vegetables in the hot fat and sauté until wilted.
6. Add the beans, their liquid, and the tomato sauce. Deglaze the bottom of the kettle with a wooden spatula.
7. Add the bacon, lamb, potatoes, cabbage, the coarsely chopped porcini, and their soaking water. Stir the ingredients together, cover, and simmer gently for an hour, or until the beans and lamb are tender. While it is simmering, make the pistou.

Making the Pistou:

8. In a mortar or food processor, combine the garlic paste, the cheeses, the marjoram, and the oil. The *pistou* should be as thick as modeling clay.
9. Dilute the *pistou* with ¹/₂ cup of hot broth from the stew, then stir the mixture into the stew. Remove the kettle from the heat at once to keep the cheese creamy.
10. Salt to taste. Bring the kettle to the table and serve the steaming stew directly from it.

NOTE: This stew is a one-dish meal. Whole-grain rustic breads and a light white wine are the appropriate accompaniments. When in a great hurry, I have made this stew successfully with a large can of cannellini (if you use canned beans, add them when the lamb is almost tender so they remain whole.)

Grecian Lamb Stew

A rákhova is a tiny village that clings to Mount Parnassus, a few kilometers down the road from Delphi. It is famous for its creamy feta, a light, garnet-colored wine called kokkinélli, *and the longevity and prowess of its villagers. When I lived in Athens and went to Delphi, I always made a point of stopping in Arákhova to snack on its excellent bread, olives from nearby Amfissa, and, of course, its feta and* kokkinélli. *One day the tavernkeeper at the taberna where I usually stopped asked me to stay for lunch. It was a sunny day in early spring, full of that silvery light I have rarely seen anywhere except in Greece. The* kéfi *seemed right, and the aroma of the lamb stew persuaded me. This is my version of the Parnassian lamb stew I was served that day.*

2½ pounds lean stewing lamb, cut into bite-size chunks

2 plump cloves garlic, peeled and cut in half

5 black peppercorns, crushed

2 bay leaves

3 tablespoons freshly squeezed lemon juice

4 tablespoons flour

½ cup light vegetable oil

1 large yellow onion, thickly sliced

1 teaspoon crumbled dried oregano

6 rosemary leaves

½ teaspoon freshly ground black pepper

1 teaspoon fennel seeds

¼ teaspoon ground cinnamon

One 16-ounce can stewed tomatoes

1 cup dry white wine

2 cups coarsely chopped fresh spearmint leaves

4 cups fresh spinach, well washed and coarsely chopped

3 large russet potatoes, peeled and cut into ½-inch dice

3 cups unsalted chicken or vegetable stock

1 teaspoon sugar

Freshly squeezed lemon juice and salt

1 cup plain yogurt (optional)

2 tablespoons finely chopped fresh dill (optional)

1. Place the lamb, garlic, peppercorns, bay leaves, lemon juice, and 6 cups of water in a large heavy-bottomed kettle. Bring to a rolling boil and immediately remove from the heat.

2. Place a colander in the sink and pour the contents of the kettle into it. Discard the garlic, peppercorns, and bay leaves. Run plenty of cold water over the meat, rinsing it well. Drain well and pat the meat dry with paper towels.

3. Dredge the pieces well with the flour, patting it well into the meat. Use all the flour.

4. Wipe the kettle clean and dry it. Heat the kettle, add the oil, and when the oil hazes, brown the meat well on all sides, a few pieces at a time. Remove the meat and set it aside.

5. Reduce the heat. Sauté the onion, oregano, rosemary, pepper, fennel seeds, cinnamon, and tomatoes for 12 minutes, stirring well to deglaze the bottom of the kettle.

6. Add the wine and browned meat and stir well.

7. Scatter the mint over the stew. Add the spinach, covering up the meat and vegetables. Place the potato cubes in a layer on top, pressing them down into the greens.

8. Mix the stock and sugar and add to the kettle. Cover tightly and simmer gently for 1 hour, or until the potatoes and lamb are just tender but not overcooked.

9. Stir in lemon juice and salt to taste. If you want a typically Balkan touch, stir in the yogurt and the finely chopped dill.

10. Serve warm—*khliaros*, as the Greeks say—not hot.

Balkan Lamb with Semolina Dumplings

SERVES 6

There are countless stews in the Balkans that are called tocana, or a slight variant of that name. Without involving myself in the vehement arguments about which is the best or the most authentic, let me say simply that of all the tocana I have tasted, this one, made of lamb, is my favorite. As a stew lover, I consider it outstanding. What's more, it is easy to make; all the ingredients are available in an ordinary supermarket.

FOR THE STEW

3 tablespoons freshly squeezed lemon juice

1 teaspoon freshly ground black pepper

2¹/₂ pounds lean stewing lamb, cut into 1-inch cubes

¹/₂ cup plus 1 tablespoon flour

¹/₂ cup vegetable oil

4 cups thinly sliced yellow onions

1 cup dry white wine

1 cup unsalted chicken stock

3 plump cloves garlic, crushed to a paste with 1 tablespoon coarse salt, using the underside of a soup spoon

¹/₄ teaspoon red pepper flakes

3 ribs celery, with leaves, coarsely chopped

1 tablespoon finely chopped flat-leaf parsley

1 tablespoon finely snipped fresh chives

¹/₄ teaspoon dried thyme

1 cup tomato juice

¹/₂ cup sauerkraut juice or water

One 10-ounce package frozen whole baby okra pods, thawed (if fresh okra is available, by all means use it)

¹/₂ cup sour cream

FOR THE DUMPLINGS

¹/₂ cup milk

¹/₂ cup semolina or farina

¹/₂ teaspoon coarse salt

2 tablespoons unsalted butter

1 well-beaten egg

¹/₄ teaspoon freshly grated nutmeg

Making the Stew:

1. Work the lemon juice and pepper into the lamb. Dredge the lamb cubes well on all sides with ¹/₂ cup of the flour, brushing off the excess. Place the floured cubes on a piece of waxed paper to dry for a few minutes.

2. In a heavy-bottomed kettle or braising pan, heat the oil and gently sauté the onions until almost crisp, tossing them often to prevent burning. With a slotted spoon, remove all the onions from the oil, allowing most of the oil to drain back into the pan. Set the onions aside.
3. Sauté the lamb cubes in batches, browning them well all over. Remove the cubes as they finish browning and set them aside with the onions.
4. Discard the remaining fat from the pan. Deglaze the bottom with the wine and stock.
5. Add the onions, lamb cubes, garlic paste, pepper flakes, celery, parsley, chives, thyme, and tomato and sauerkraut juices. Stir briefly but well, cover, and simmer gently for 50 minutes.
6. Make the dumplings (see below).
7. Stir in the okra pods.
8. Mix the sour cream and the remaining tablespoon of flour until smooth and stir the mixture into the stew. Simmer for 10 minutes.
9. Add the dumplings, cover the pan again, simmer for 5 minutes, and serve the *tocana* and dumplings very hot, as a single dish.

Making the Dumplings:

1. Mix the milk, semolina or farina, and salt in a saucepan until smooth. Place the pan over medium high heat and cook, stirring the mixture constantly with a wooden spatula as it thickens.
2. When the mixture is very thick, remove the pan from the heat (but don't turn the heat off) and stir in the butter, beaten egg, and nutmeg thoroughly.
3. Return the pan to the heat, stirring the batter until it is quite thick and dry. Remove from the heat.
4. With two tablespoons dipped each time in cold water, drop the dumpling dough by neat spoonfuls into the stew. (Proceed as indicated in Step 9 in the instructions for making the stew.)

NOTE: Although the *tocana* and dumplings make a complete and sufficient dish, plain cubed boiled potatoes are often stirred into the stew just before serving. They add a completely different texture to the stew, and they stretch the *tocana*, making it possible to feed another guest, if you need to.

Sicilian *Ragù* with Rigatoni

SERVES 5 OR 6

Sicilian food is often quite distinct in taste and texture from the food of mainland Italy. The taste is sometimes complex and often extremely subtle. Many Sicilian recipes call for sweet laurel (bay) leaves, wild or domestic fennel and its seeds, orange, lemon, or citron peel, raisins, dried capsicums, and bitter chocolate as flavorings and aromatics. Sicilian sauces are often thickened with ground almonds, pine nuts, or cracker crumbs instead of flour and cornstarch. These distinctive tastes in cooking were acquired during long periods when Normans, Turks, North Africans, and Spaniards occupied the island. This lamb ragù is a case in point; it contains many of the above. It is deliciously different from other ragù pasta sauces.

3 pounds lean lamb neck bones, well stripped of their fat

1 tablespoon freshly ground black pepper

3 tablespoons unsalted butter

1½ cups coarsely chopped yellow onions

1 tablespoon fennel seeds

2 ribs coarsely chopped celery

1½ cups scraped, quartered, and thinly sliced carrots

2 bay leaves

One 2-inch piece dried orange peel, crumbled

½ teaspoon ground cinnamon

1 large fennel bulb, quartered

1 cup dry red wine

One 14-ounce can stewed tomatoes

3 cups concentrated, defatted stock

¼ cup golden raisins

½ teaspoon red pepper flakes

1 pound rigatoni, cooked al dente and drained

1 teaspoon olive oil

20 finely ground toasted almonds

3 tablespoons cracker meal

½ ounce bitter chocolate

Salt

1. Wash and dry the lamb. Sprinkle it well with the black pepper.
2. Gently heat the butter in a large heavy-bottomed stewing pot. When the butter begins to bubble, add lamb, being careful not to crowd the pieces, and brown slowly and well on all sides. The rich flavor and deep red-brown color of the stew depend on it. Remove the browned lamb and set it aside.

3. Add the onion, fennel seeds, celery, carrots, bay leaves, orange peel, and cinnamon to the pot. Toss them well in the fat with a wooden spoon so that all the vegetables are coated.

4. Bury the quartered fennel in the vegetables and layer the browned lamb over the vegetables.

5. Add the wine, 6 cups of water, tomatoes, the stock, raisins, and pepper flakes and increase the heat. When the stew begins to boil, reduce the heat to a low simmer. Skim off and discard the foam that rises for the first 15 minutes.

6. Cover the pot and simmer the stew for 2 hours, making certain the liquid always covers the meat. Add water if necessary.

7. Cook the rigatoni until *al dente*, drain well, and return to the kettle with 1 teaspoon olive oil. Shake thoroughly and set aside, covered. Do this during the last 15 minutes the stew is simmering so they finish together.

8. Meanwhile, stir the ground almonds, cracker meal, and chocolate into the stew. Simmer, uncovered, for 10 minutes, tossing the stew from time to time as it thickens.

9. Remove the pot from the heat. Discard the bay leaves. Carefully skim off and discard all the fat that has surfaced.

10. Empty the steaming rigatoni into the pot of *ragù* and toss them to-gether well. Salt to taste.

11. Arrange the dish on a large deep pasta platter and serve very hot.

NOTE: Pass freshly ground Pecorino or Romano cheese (or a mixture of both) for those who wish it. If you like, you may remove all the meat from the bones before serving it, but that somehow betrays the typical Italian country nature of the dish.

Lamb Stewed with Honey

SERVES 6

This is one of the famous stews that the North Africans prepare in the earthenware pots with curious conical tops called *tajines. Lamb and kid have been stewed with honey for thousands of years by the Arabs and Berbers of North Africa and, oddly enough, by the Mayans of Central America. The Moors introduced "honey lamb" to Spain, where it still exists in certain regions. However, this Algerian version is the finest I have tasted.*

1 medium-size eggplant, cut into $^1/_2$-inch cubes

1 heaping teaspoon coarse salt

One 2-inch cinnamon stick

$^1/_2$ teaspoon *each* ground ginger, ground coriander, ground cumin seeds, saffron threads, and red pepper flakes

3 pounds lean stewing lamb, cut into bite-size pieces

$^1/_2$ cup vegetable oil

One 14-ounce can stewed tomatoes, drained and coarsely chopped

1 cup coarsely chopped yellow onions

1 plump clove garlic, thinly sliced

2 large red bell peppers, flame roasted (see page 163), skinned, seeded, and coarsely chopped

$2^1/_2$ cups defatted lamb stock or water

5 tablespoons honey

8 to 10 small white onions, peeled, with a tiny cross cut in each end

Salt

1. Put the diced eggplant in a colander and toss well with the salt. Leave in the sink for 20 minutes to leech.
2. Toast the cinnamon stick on a dry griddle briefly. Wrap in a napkin and crush with a rolling pin. Put the cinnamon and the other spices in a mortar and pound them until uniformly fine, or process them in a miniprocessor.
3. Toss the lamb with the spices and set it aside for at least 20 minutes.
4. Rinse the eggplant well under cold running water and squeeze it out. Pat dry with paper towels.
5. In a fireproof ceramic casserole at least 2 inches deep or a heavy-bottomed braising pan, heat the oil and brown the lamb evenly in batches. Remove the batches and set them aside as they finish browning.

6. Sauté the eggplant very gently in the same casserole until it softens slightly, tossing it from time to time to make sure it doesn't stick but is not crushed to a purée. Add the tomato, onion, garlic, and bell pepper.
7. When the onion has wilted and is almost transparent, add the browned lamb. Toss all the ingredients together lightly and sauté gently for 15 minutes.
8. Skim off and discard the excess fat. Add the stock and honey, stirring everything together lightly. Cover the pot tightly and let it steam over low heat for 1 hour.
9. Add the white onions, spooning the stew over them. Add water if necessary. Simmer, uncovered, for 15 minutes, or until the onions are tender.
10. Salt to taste. Remove the stew from the heat, cover it, and allow it to sit for 5 minutes. Serve with plain boiled rice or steamed couscous.

Persian Lamb Stew

T*his is a thick, luscious, Middle Eastern ragout of lamb, yellow split peas, vegetables, and seedless grapes. It is hearty, savory, and spicy, yet wonderfully light, thanks to the consistency and slight sweetness of the grapes.*

2 pounds shoulder of lamb, with bones
1 teaspoon coarse salt
1 teaspoon cracked black pepper
1 envelope saffron seasoning (see Notes)
4 tablespoons vegetable oil
3 plump cloves garlic, thinly sliced
3 large leeks, white parts only, well washed and cut into ¹/₂-inch rounds
10 large scallions, white parts only, coarsely chopped

2 bay leaves
1 teaspoon finely crumbled dried oregano leaves
1 teaspoon cumin seeds
1 cup yellow split peas
1 tablespoon chicken-concentrate granules
1 cup Thompson seedless grapes, stemmed and washed
2 tablespoons freshly squeezed lemon juice
Salt

1. Wash and dry the lamb. Cut it into bite-size pieces. Trim away and discard all the fat and integuments, saving the bones. Work the coarse salt, pepper, and saffron seasoning into the meat and bones.
2. Heat the vegetable oil in a heavy-bottomed kettle and brown the meat and bones very well.
3. Add the garlic, leeks, scallions, bay leaves, oregano, and cumin seeds. Toss well with the lamb and bones and sauté until the vegetables wilt.
4. Add the split peas, mixing them in well, 4 cups of water, and the chicken-concentrate granules. Cover well and simmer for 50 minutes, stirring occasionally. Add water if necessary. (The peas are a classic thickening for stews in Persian cooking. They should disintegrate in cooking and make the stew thick and creamy.)
5. Prick each grape in several places with a darning needle or toothpick. Add the grapes to the stew and continue simmering for 10 minutes.

6. Add the lemon juice. Salt to taste, and fish out and discard the bay leaves and bones. Serve the stew hot on a bed of plain boiled rice or steamed bulgur.

NOTES: The saffron seasoning is produced by Goya Foods, Inc., and can be found in Latino groceries and most supermarkets.

As an appropriate and sufficient complement to this hearty ragout, serve a salad of lightly steamed tiny yellow squash or zucchini sauced with lemon juice, yogurt, and finely chopped fresh mint leaves.

Lamb with Vegetables and Bulgur Wheat

SERVES 4

This is one of the hundreds of distinctive lamb stews that form a major part of the culinary treasury of the Middle East. Instead of the habitual rice accompaniment, the stew is braised with bulgur or cracked wheat, which you may already know as the main ingredient in tabbouleh. I recommend this dish highly for its delightful taste and lightness.

1 tablespoon cracked black pepper

4 generous lean shoulder lamb chops

2 large fresh artichokes, quartered

$^1\!/_4$ cup vegetable oil

1 medium-size head garlic, unpeeled, cut in two across the cloves

1 cup dry white wine

2 cups unsalted chicken, beef, or vegetable stock

2 cups bulgur wheat

2 large peeled carrots, halved, cut into $^1\!/_4$-inch slices

8 plump shallots, thinly sliced

$^1\!/_2$ teaspoon crumbled dried sage

$^1\!/_2$ teaspoon crumbled dried oregano

3 tablespoons freshly squeezed lemon juice

Salt

1 pint plain yogurt (optional)

1. Sprinkle the cracked pepper over both sides of the chops, working it into the surface of the meat with your fingers.
2. Quarter the artichokes lengthwise. Cut off and discard the leaves, and peel and trim the stem. Remove the choke with a spoon. Rub all surfaces with half a lemon to prevent darkening.
3. In a large heavy-bottomed kettle or braising pan, gently heat the oil and brown the chops well on both sides. Remove them, once browned, and set them aside.
4. Place the two little "nosegays" of garlic, cut sides down, in the oil and brown them just until golden. Remove them and set them aside with the chops.
5. Deglaze the pan with the wine, then add the stock.
6. Stir in the bulgar.
7. Put the chops and garlic back into the pan in one layer. Add the car-

rots, shallots, artichokes, herbs, and lemon juice. Cover tightly and simmer gently for $1^{1}/_{4}$ hours, or until the chops are quite tender.

8. Ten minutes before finishing, uncover the pan and let the steam escape for 5 minutes, then cover the pan again and turn off the heat, allowing the bulgur to puff.

9. Salt to taste and serve hot. If you are serving the stew with yogurt, as many Middle Easterners do, pass a bowl of it at the table and allow each diner to add it as he or she likes.

NOTE: The secret, if secret there be, in preparing this stew perfectly is gentle heat. From the moment you apply the heat, it should be carefully maintained at the lowest possible level.

Green-Chili Lamb Stew

Green-chili stew is a favorite dish in the Santa Fe/Taos area. Each time I visit that enchanting part of northern New Mexico, I return smitten again with the unique flavor of New Mexican green chili peppers. If you, too, have a terrible yearning for northern New Mexican chili stew, you'll find that my version with lamb is easy to make and will soothe your pangs of nostalgia like the visit of an old friend.

1 scant tablespoon cracked black pepper

1 tablespoon ground chorizo mix (see Notes)

1 teaspoon ground cumin

2 pounds lean stewing lamb, cut into bite-size pieces

One $1/4$-inch-thick slice streaky salt pork, rind removed, cut into $1/4$-inch dice

2 tablespoons vegetable oil

$1/2$ cup coarsely chopped yellow onions

1 plump clove garlic, finely chopped

$1/2$ teaspoon red pepper flakes

12 ounces light beer

1 cup unsalted stock or water

One 4-ounce can whole, peeled green chilies, rinsed, drained, and cut into 1 × 2-inch pieces

2 cups peeled potatoes in $1/2$-inch dice

Salt or freshly squeezed lemon juice

1. With your fingers, work the cracked pepper, chorizo mix, and cumin well into the lamb and set it aside.
2. Pour boiling water over the salt pork cubes. Rinse them well under cold running water and blot them dry.
3. In a heavy-bottomed kettle or braising pan, heat the oil and gently sauté the pork cubes until golden. Remove and set them aside.
4. Brown the lamb in batches, raking the pieces back and forth so that they brown well all over. Remove them as they finish browning and set them aside. Discard all but 3 tablespoons of the hot fat.
5. Reduce the heat and sauté the onions, garlic, and red pepper flakes until the onion is translucent and almost melted.
6. Add the beer and stock and deglaze the bottom of the kettle with a wooden spatula.

7. Add the browned meats and the chili. Cover and simmer gently for 1 hour.
8. Add the potatoes and continue simmering the stew for $^1/_2$ hour.
9. Salt to taste. If you are following a low-sodium diet, adjust the seasoning with lemon juice.
10. Serve the stew in deep, good-size bowls.

NOTES: The chorizo mix is available in Latino groceries and in the spice section of many supermarkets.

Garnish the stew, if you like, with ripe avocado slices and a few sprigs of fresh cilantro. I ate a fiery version of this stew for the first time at the Information Center of the Acoma Indian Reservation just below Sky City Mesa, New Mexico. Clarice Valdo, the charming cook in the restaurant there, serves this stew with Indian fry bread. I suggest you do the same. If you have never tried this fluffy treat, you owe it to yourself to try it. I find fry bread, halfway between pita and a flour tortilla, superior to both. Here's the simple recipe.

New Mexican Indiana Fry Bread

MAKES 10 OR 12 BREADS

4 cups unbleached flour	1$^1/_2$ cups warm water
1 teaspoon coarse salt	(or a little more)
1 tablespoon baking powder	1 cup vegetable shortening

1. Combine the dry ingredients well in a mixing bowl.
2. Stir in the water and knead together to make a smooth, elastic, non-sticky dough.
3. Shape into a long roll. Pince or cut off pieces the size of a small lemon. Roll each lightly into a ball and pat it between your palm into a tortillalike shape about $^1/_4$ inch thick. Make a hole in the center of each with your index finger.

4. In a deep frying pan, heat the shortening. Test the heat with a small piece of dough. It should bubble and brown slowly without burning.
5. Fry the breads, one at a time, turning them so that they fry to a golden brown on both sides and fluff up considerably.
6. Blot each bread with paper towels.
7. Serve hot. The breads can be reheated in a 300°F oven, but they are best eaten straightaway.

NOTE: Like tortillas, but lighter, fry bread is perfect for tacolike eating. The freshly fried breads may also be slathered with honey or sprinkled generously with cinnamon and sugar and eaten as sweet rolls or for dessert.

Lamb with *Frikadelen* and Vegetables

SERVES 6

This is a lusty, mouthwatering Dutch stew from South Africa. Frikadelen are a type of meatball brought to the Transvaal from the Netherlands. This stew is a favorite with children; they are delighted with the little meatballs they find hiding among the lamb and vegetables.

$^{1}/_{2}$ pound ground lamb

1 slice white bread, crust removed, soaked in $^{1}/_{4}$ cup milk

1 large egg

1 tablespoon finely grated onion

1 teaspoon coarse salt

1 teaspoon freshly ground black pepper

$^{1}/_{4}$ teaspoon ground coriander

$^{1}/_{8}$ teaspoon ground nutmeg

1 teaspoon caraway seeds

1 tablespoon finely chopped fresh dill

$^{1}/_{2}$ cup flour

$1^{1}/_{2}$ pounds lean stewing lamb, cut into bite-size pieces

3 tablespoons vegetable oil

3 cups unsalted chicken stock

6 small onions, peeled and halved lengthwise

2 medium-size carrots, peeled and cut into 1-inch pieces

2 ribs celery, cut into 1-inch pieces

1 large green bell pepper, cut into $^{1}/_{2}$-inch strips

Salt

1. Mix the ground lamb well with the squeezed-out bread, egg, grated onion, $^{1}/_{2}$ teaspoon of the salt, $^{1}/_{2}$ teaspoon of the black pepper, the coriander, nutmeg, caraway seeds, and chopped dill. Beat until fluffy.

2. Wetting your fingers often, shape the mixture into balls $^{3}/_{4}$ inch in diameter. Dredge them well in the flour, brushing off and saving the excess. Place them in one layer on waxed paper. Refrigerate them while doing steps 3 and 4.

3. Sprinkle the remaining $^{1}/_{2}$ teaspoon of salt and pepper and the remaining flour over the lamb pieces, patting them well into the pieces.

4. Heat the oil over medium heat in a heavy-bottomed kettle and brown the lamb pieces in batches until they are quite brown. Remove them and set them aside.

5. Brown the meatballs evenly, remove them, and discard the fat.
6. Add the stock and deglaze the kettle. Add the meatballs, browned lamb pieces, onions, carrots, celery, and green pepper.
7. Cover the kettle and simmer gently for 1 hour, or until the lamb is fork-tender.
8. Salt to taste and serve with plain boiled rice tossed with $^1/_4$ cup golden raisins.

NOTE: This stew matures wonderfully overnight in the refrigerator; the little meatballs become particularly luscious.

West African Lamb Stew

P*eppery peanut stews are one of the hallmarks of West African cooking. The Portuguese introduced the peanut to Africa from South America. It quickly caught on as a major source of nutrition, spreading along the African seaboard. This rich, terra cotta–colored stew, thickened with ground roasted peanuts, is a favorite in West Africa. This festive version is made with lamb. I have omitted the customary dried shrimp and salt fish because I feel they overpower the subtler flavorings in the stew.*

1 cup buttermilk

3 tablespoons honey

2 tablespoons finely grated fresh ginger

2 plump cloves garlic, finely crushed

$^1/_2$ teaspoon *each* ground cayenne, mace, allspice, and cloves

3 pounds lean stewing lamb, cut into 1-inch cubes

1 tablespoon freshly ground black pepper

$^1/_2$ cup flour

$^1/_2$ cup vegetable oil

2 cups coarsely chopped yellow onions

$^1/_2$ teaspoon red pepper flakes

2 large red or green bell peppers, cut into $^1/_2$-inch strips

2 cups unsalted chicken stock

$^3/_4$ cup smooth peanut butter

One 8-ounce can tomato sauce

1 cup fresh whole baby okra pods (8 ounces frozen thawed baby okra pods may be substituted)

1 cup fresh French-cut green beans (8 ounces frozen thawed French-cut green beans may be substituted)

Salt or freshly squeezed lime juice

3 tablespoons toasted sesame seeds

1. Make a marinade by mixing the buttermilk, honey, ginger, garlic, cayenne, mace, allspice, and cloves together. Set it aside.
2. Place the lamb in a glass or enameled bowl and pour the marinade over it. With tongs, move the meat about until all the pieces are evenly coated. Cover and marinate at room temperature for 2 hours. Steps 1 and 2 may be done a day in advance, provided the marinated lamb is refrigerated.
3. Drain well and blot (do not rub) the pieces until almost dry. Work the black pepper through the meat, making sure it adheres to all the

cubes. Dredge the cubes well with the flour. Separate the cubes and place them on waxed paper to dry for 10 minutes.

4. Heat the oil in a heavy-bottomed kettle and brown the floured pieces in batches. Avoid crowding them. As the pieces finish browning, remove them with tongs and set them aside.

5. Reduce the heat and gently sauté the onions, pepper flakes, and bell pepper strips until the onions are wilted and almost transparent, but not browned. Push the vegetables aside. Tip the kettle and spoon out and discard all the fat that runs off.

6. Add the stock and deglaze the bottom of the kettle. Add the browned cubes and briefly stir all the ingredients together. Cover the pot and simmer over the lowest possible heat for 1 hour.

7. Mix the peanut butter and tomato sauce thoroughly, and stir the mixture into the stew. Add the okra pods and green beans, and simmer for 15 minutes.

8. Season to your liking with salt or lime juice. Turn off the heat, cover the stew, and let it sit for 5 minutes.

9. Transfer the hot stew to an attractive serving bowl, sprinkle the surface with the sesame seeds, and serve at once.

NOTE: This lively stew is usually served with steamed millet, couscous, or rice and various side dishes such as chopped hard-boiled egg mixed with red pepper flakes and chopped parsley; seeded, cubed papaya sauced with lime juice and finely minced chili peppers; peeled, sliced, mangoes sauced with lime juice and coarsely grated cinnamon stick; skinned, seeded, coarsely chopped ripe red tomatoes mixed with finely chopped scallions and cilantro; unsalted dry-roasted peanuts; and an assortment of chutneys.

CHAPTER FIVE

Seafood Stews

Introduction to Stewing Seafood

The internationally recognized maven of fish cookery during the thirties, Mme. S. B. Prunier, loved to repeat to her English-speaking clientele the smug old French adage: *"C'est la sauce qui fait manger le poisson."* She was well aware of the impossibility of rendering that seemingly simple saying into simple English, and she must have savored the irony, for the saying infers that the specialist must know just the right sauce for a certain fish to make the diners relish it. Fish cookery, especially French fish cookery, is one of the most demanding disciplines in professional cooking; it take years of training and experience to become a chef *poissonier* and very special talents to become a great one. In comparison, our objectives here are very modest; we are dealing only with stewing, braising, and gently simmering seafood. Yet even with our modest objectives, there are a few important fundamentals to be applied and some simple suggestions to be followed if our seafood stews, soups, and braises are to turn out well.

If you are already a true seafood lover and find the vast world of seafood passionately interesting but confusing, I recommend Alan Davidson's beautiful and informative book, *Seafood: A Connoisseur's Guide and Cookbook*. Davidson is to seafood lovers what Audubon is to bird lovers.

When undertaking these or any other seafood dishes, it is practical to remember that seafood is highly perishable; it should be from the catch of the day, if possible, and always of the highest quality. Find yourself a reliable fishmonger to whom you can confide your needs, and become his or her regular and demanding client.

When shopping on your own, however, it is very important to recognize the signs by which knowledgeable shoppers judge the freshness of seafood. At its freshest, seafood has no smell, or it simply smells of the sea or of the fresh water where it was caught. The slightest sulfuric scent indicates that the catch has been out of its native waters for some time. Icing slows the process of decomposition in seafood but cannot stop it. Always examine the eyes; in freshly caught fish, they are bright and bulging. They recede and grow dull in a matter of hours after the fish has been landed. Don't be afraid to pry open the gills with your fingers and inspect them. They should be bright pink or red, not dull or faded. Finally, the texture of freshly caught fish is firm and somewhat resistant. The flesh begins to soften immediately once the fish is filleted.

In judging the freshness of crustaceans, we must depend pretty much on smell and appearance. Generally speaking, crustaceans, even those that have been thawed (most of the shrimp and prawns offered to us for sale are delivered frozen to the fishmonger), should have lustrous shells and be far from limp.

In buying shellfish, be sure they are alive. Never buy any shellfish whose shells are permanently ajar. Those that do not close their shells quickly of their own accord when tapped are no longer alive.

A couple of rules of thumb should be followed when cooking seafood: Most fish disintegrates quickly when simmered; most mollusks and crustaceans toughen. Fortunately, there are standard solutions to these problems. If you are making a thick soup or stew of many small fish, their disintegration may be intentional. Many seafood stews, however, should not be simmered or boiled. There are some noteworthy exceptions, and one of them is bouillabaisse, which must boil furiously for a scant 10 minutes to trick the abundant olive oil into combining with the broth. Even in preparing bouillabaisse, however, it is wise to delay putting the more delicate fish into the kettle until 5 minutes before finishing the stew; otherwise they will be reduced to an unappetizing heap of bits and bones while yielding their delicious broth.

There is, of course, a drawback in not simmering fish for a stew or soup. The fish will remain recognizable and attractive, but their contribution to the savor of the stew will remain faint—too subtle, in fact, for most tastes. How, then, is the stew maker to proceed? One of the classic solutions is to enhance the flavor of the fish by poaching it first for a very short time in a *court bouillon*, removing it, setting it aside, reducing the *court bouillon*, then finishing the stew, adding the poached fish at the end. The other classic solution is to compensate for the subtle flavor of the lightly cooked fish by adding several tablespoons of fish concentrate made by simmering fish heads, spines, and trimmings with aromatics, wine, and sometimes a little Cognac or brandy, and refining or clarifying the reduction. In classic kitchenese, this concentrate is referred to as a *fumet*. (The term designates the quintessential aroma and savor of game, certain rare mushrooms such as truffles, and in this instance, seafood.)

Recipes for *court bouillon* and *fumet de poisson* can be found at the end of this chapter.

When in a hurry, you may, of course, enhance the taste of a fish stew with fish bouillon cubes (Knorr, the Swiss company makes them) or an instant fish stock marketed under the name of Seabags, distributed by Summers Trading Co. of Passaic, New Jersey. Both are reliable friends to have on hand in your pantry. Dried bonito flakes, known as *katsuobushi*, are another handy surrogate. They are a staple in Japanese cooking, and I have had no trouble finding them in Japanese groceries. You simply steep a heaping tablespoon of the flakes in a cup of boiling water. The result is a clear, full-bodied fish stock, made with as little trouble as making a cup of tea with a teabag.

Stock for Poaching Fish

MAKES 1¾ CUPS

1 plump shallot, thinly sliced

1 small leek, white part only, well trimmed, split lengthwise, and well washed

1 small rib celery, thinly sliced

1 small carrot, peeled and cut into thin rounds

One ½-inch piece fresh ginger, peeled

1 sprig flat-leaf parsley

½ teaspoon dried thyme

1 bay leaf

½ pound fish trimmings and heads, gills removed from heads

¼ cup red wine vinegar

6 black peppercorns, bruised

Salt

1. Put all the ingredients and 2 cups of cold water in a medium-size heavy-bottomed pan and bring to a rolling boil. Reduce the heat to low and simmer for 15 minutes, skimming off and discarding the froth that rises.
2. Simmer for 15 more minutes and salt to taste.
3. Place three thicknesses of dampened cheesecloth in a large strainer and filter the stock. Discard all the solids.

NOTE: The stock (or *court bouillon*) is now ready for poaching fish. If you are planning to use it at once, cool it first. Standard practice is to start poaching fish in cold stock. Hot stock seals the surface albumen and causes the fish to poach unevenly. One cup of milk is often added to the *court bouillon* along with some thin slices of lemon when poaching nonoily fish. For oily fish, 2 tablespoons of dry red or white wine may be added, as well as a few drops of brandy or dry sherry.

You may have neither the time nor the inclination to make a genuine *fumet de poisson*, or concentrated fish stock, but I encourage you to prepare it at least once in order to taste the difference between a seafood stew or soup enhanced with a little *fume de poisson* and one in which the taste has been reinforced with commercial concentrates, or not reinforced at all. Making your own *fumet* is a snap once the ingredients are simmering, and you will have the satisfaction of producing something special from those parts of the fish you always paid for but were in the habit of discarding or simply leaving with your fishmonger.

Concentrated Fish Stock

*I*f you and your family are fond of fish, I suggest you make a large batch of this concentrate and freeze it in individual zippered plastic bags. Frozen, it will keep for 3 months. Unfrozen, a batch will keep for about 3 days, covered and refrigerated. To keep it longer, you must either freeze it or keep reheating it to the boiling point every other day. Ask your fishmonger to provide you with extra fish heads and bones from nonoily saltwater fish. Some fishmongers now charge for these trimmings, but most, I find, are happy to give them to you.

2 pounds fresh fish heads, spines, and trimmings from nonoily saltwater fish such as whiting, sole, flounder, monkfish, or the like, gills removed and discarded, spines broken up into manageable lengths

1 small white onion, thinly sliced

1 medium-size carrot, thinly sliced

1 rib celery, cut into 2 or 3 pieces

1 small leek, white part only, split and well washed

2 branches flat-leaf parsley

½ teaspoon dried thyme

1 bay leaf

½ teaspoon fennel seeds

2 cloves

6 peppercorns, bruised

½ cup dry white wine

3 tablespoons red wine vinegar

½ teaspoon sugar

½ teaspoon coarse salt

1 jigger (1½ ounces) Cognac or brandy (optional)

1. Put all of the ingredients in a wide, heavy-bottomed braising pan with 6 cups of cold water.
2. Heat the ingredients slowly and cook this *court bouillon* just below the simmering point for 2 hours, or until the liquid has reduced to one quarter of its volume. Some cooks hasten this process by boiling the *court bouillon* rapidly, but it spoils the freshness of the taste.
3. Discard the solids and strain the stock through three thicknesses of dampened cheesecloth. The concentrated stock or *fumet* is ready to be used.

NOTE: In addition to enhancing the taste of fish stews and soups, a few drops of this concentrated stock in sauces meant to be served with fish will give those sauces a real flavor boost.

Old-Fashioned Oyster Stew

SERVES 4

Fifty years ago, when there were far more oyster bars in every large American city than there are now, oyster stew was the great favorite of late-night revelers. Having drunk a bit too much, they stopped by an oyster bar to steady themselves with a steaming bowl of this bracing stew before weaving their way home. The stew was also generally believed to be a panacea for ailing children. At our house it was the only good thing about being confined to bed. My mother would serve it to us on a large tray, lending a little importance to our indisposition. There would be her oyster stew, hot and fragrant, in our favorite bowl, with those curious little round, puffed crackers (that never made their appearance under any other circumstances) bobbing about on the surface. It was my mother's ritual for making us feel better, and it certainly worked.

3 tablespoons unsalted butter	3¹/₂ cups milk, scalded
2 tablespoons flour	¹/₂ cup half-and-half
¹/₈ teaspoon hot paprika or ground cayenne	1 teaspoon Worcestershire sauce
	1 tablespoon dry sherry (optional)
2 or 3 dozen freshly shucked oysters, with their juice	Salt

1. Melt the butter in a wide, heavy-bottomed braising pan and stir in the flour and paprika.
2. When this roux is sizzling, add the oysters and their juice, and combine them with the roux, stirring them for about 3 minutes, or until the oysters curl.
3. Add the scalded milk, cream, Worcestershire sauce, and sherry, stirring them in well with a wooden spatula or whisk. Cook the stew just below the simmering point for 5 minutes.
4. Remove the stew from the heat. Let it sit for 10 minutes, covered. Salt to taste. Heat again gently until steaming and serve in deep bowls. Place plenty of oyster crackers within easy reach.

NOTE: Our grandfather Wilhelmi, an old Philadelphian passionately fond of oyster stew, thought it barbaric to spice the stew with paprika.

He added a dash or two of vinegar from a bottle of Tabasco peppers, claiming it was the proper way to "hot up" the stew. I've eaten it both ways and have "hotted it up" with black pepper, as well. Frankly, I can't say which version is best. I like them all.

Creamy Clam Chowder

SERVES 4 OR 5

*I*n the foreword to the genial little book Alpha Beta Chowder, *Jeanne Steig opines, ". . . chowder is a robust goop . . . more akin to stew than soup." I concur heartily and feel that any clam chowder worth its name should be robustly thick and goopy. Those are adjectives that can usually be applied to a good New England clam chowder. The tradition goes back a long way. Think of the clam chowder Mrs. Hussey served up to Ishmael and Queequeg on their first evening in Nantucket, with its hazelnut-size clams and flakes of salt pork—obviously a great one. I have eaten truly great chowders in Boston's North End. But, ironically, I had the greatest one ever last year in the Shockoe Slip District of Richmond, Virginia. I have tried to reproduce it here. In the interest of those who live far from the sea, I have called for tinned clams. Should you have a pint of freshly shucked clams on hand, however, use them instead, putting in the clams themselves only 5 minutes before the finish. Remember that fresh clams toughen quickly if simmered a few minutes too long. They need only to be heated through.*

Two 10½-ounce cans minced clams, with their juice (that's lots of clams, but I doubt your diners will complain!)

One ¼-inch-thick slice very lean salt pork, cut into ¼-inch cubes

1 small white onion, coarsely chopped

2 tablespoons finely chopped green bell pepper

3 tablespoons flour

2 cups milk, scalded

1 cup half-and-half

⅛ teaspoon *each* ground sage, thyme, and cayenne

3 medium-size potatoes, boiled, peeled, and cut into ½-inch cubes

Salt and freshly ground black pepper (see Note)

1. Strain the juice from the clams into a bowl, and reserve the clams and juice.
2. In a large heavy-bottomed kettle, gently render the salt pork until the cubes are golden but not dry and hard. Remove the cubes with a slotted spoon and set them aside. Pour off and discard all but 3 tablespoons of the dripping.
3. Add the onion and bell pepper and sauté for 5 minutes, scraping the

vegetables back and forth with a wooden spatula. Sprinkle in the flour and toss until it is no longer white.

4. Add the reserved clam juice, scalded milk, half-and-half, sage, thyme, cayenne, and 1 cup of hot water. Stir well, scraping the bottom to prevent the chowder's scorching, and cook just below the simmering point for 10 minutes.

5. Add the potatoes, chopped clams, and pork bits. Reduce the heat to very low and continue to cook for 10 minutes. Remove from the heat, and salt and pepper to taste.

6. Let the chowder mature for 5 minutes and serve in deep bowls. Place plenty of oyster crackers and saltines within easy reach.

NOTE: Richmond clam-chowder fanciers seem to prefer cracked pepper to the finely ground. I admit that when you bite into tiny fragments of cracked black pepper, they bite back, giving an added nip to the experience.

Mussels in Cream

SERVES 4

Brussels is famous for its fish and shellfish stews, especially its stewed mussels. I shall never forget the first time I visited that great city. At one of the many good restaurants on the Grande Place, I ate a mountain of mussels stewed in cream and aromatics. That, I am told, is the most popular way of preparing mussels in the Low Countries, and it certainly is a fine, tasty way to do them. The recipe varies slightly from town to town, but in the main, this is the standard Flemish recipe. Use only small or medium-size, very fresh, catch-of-the-day mussels.

4 or 5 dozen very fresh small mussels, scrubbed and debearded

2 tablespoons coarse salt

1 teaspoon cornmeal or oatmeal

3 plump shallots, sliced paper-thin

1 small white onion, coarsely chopped

1 branch fresh thyme

1 bay leaf

2 branches flat-leaf parsley

$^1/_2$ cup dry white wine

$^1/_4$ teaspoon freshly ground white pepper

1 teaspoon flour

1 tablespoon unsalted butter

1 cup half-and-half

$^1/_8$ teaspoon ground cayenne

Salt

1. Put the mussels in a large pan with the salt and enough cold water to cover well. Sprinkle in the cornmeal to encourage them to void their sand. Allow the mussels to sit for 30 minutes, then rinse them in a colander under cold running water. Discard any mussels that are permanently open.

2. Place the shallots, onion, thyme, bay leaf, parsley, white wine, and white pepper in the bottom of a large, heavy-bottomed kettle. Place the mussels over these ingredients, cover tightly, and set over low heat.

3. When the wine boils, turn off the heat and let the kettle sit, covered, for 5 minutes.

4. Carefully decant the liquid from the kettle into a small saucepan without disturbing the mussels or the sand that will have accumulated on the bottom during the stewing. Leave the mussels covered so that they will stay hot.

5. With your fingertips, mix the flour and butter into little pellets.

6. Heat the stewing liquid with the half-and-half to a gentle simmer. Throw tiny balls of the flour-and-butter mixture into the simmering sauce, whisking to dissolve them.

7. When the liquid has thickened slightly, add the cayenne and salt to taste. Simmer very gently for 5 minutes, then turn off the heat.

8. Heap the hot mussels into four deep bowls. Discard any that have remained closed, and the herbs and debris that remain at the bottom of the kettle. Pour an equal amount of sauce over each heap of mussels and serve at once. Provide bowls for the shells and plenty of thick slices of crusty bread to mop up the sauce, which is a marvel.

Caleb's Catfish Stew

SERVES 6

When I was a small child in north central Texas, all the rivers, lakes, and creeks teemed with catfish of every size and description. Legendary ones of monstrous size succeeded for years in evading the best anglers. One known locally as Ol' Rip was finally landed and proved to weigh an incredible sixty-three pounds. The giant was auctioned off and purchased at great expense by a local politician, whose intention it was to throw a great public fish fry and use the occasion to electioneer. Ol' Rip proved too large to fillet and fry in corn-meal, so a venerable soul-food cook named Uncle Caleb converted the enormous fish into three washtubs of catfish stew. I doubt that Uncle Caleb's recipe was ever set down on paper; in those days, old recipes were circulated by word of mouth, liberally sprinkled with "Seems like we done it thisaway. . . ." Like so many of the remembered recipes in this collection, I had to reconstitute this one by asking many old cooks, then adapting their collective wisdom. Nevertheless, I want to give credit to that wonderful old cook whose catfish stew delighted so many of us, so I am calling the recipe Caleb's.

Nowadays filleted catfish is available in many supermarkets. This stew is an ideal way to serve it. The trick is making the dark roux—a simple job easily and perfectly done with very low heat and lots of patience.

6 slices lean smoked breakfast bacon, cut into 1/2-inch pieces
3 tablespoons vegetable oil
6 tablespoons flour
2 small white onions, coarsely chopped
1 small green bell pepper, cut into 1-inch squares
1 large ripe red tomato, skinned, seeded, and coarsely chopped
6 cups hot fish stock (see page 215), or 2 cubes fish bouillon dissolved in 6 cups boiling water

1/4 teaspoon ground cayenne
1/4 teaspoon ground cloves
1/4 teaspoon ground allspice
3 tablespoons Worcestershire sauce
1 1/2 pounds thick catfish fillets, cut into bite-size pieces
1/4 teaspoon cracked black pepper
Salt

1. In a large heavy-bottomed kettle, gently render the bacon just until it begins to brown, not crisp. With a slotted spoon, remove the bacon to a plate and set it aside. Carefully remove all bits from the drippings, even if you have to strain the fat, or the bits will burn and spoil the roux.

2. Add the vegetable oil to the dripping in the kettle, then add and slowly brown the flour, scraping it continuously back and forth with a wooden spatula. Producing the nut-brown roux will require 12 to 15 minutes. As it finally changes color from old ivory to a darker hue, it will begin to smoke. Reduce the heat and continue to scrape the bottom of the kettle continuously. If you brown the roux slowly and keep scraping the bottom, it won't burn.

3. When the roux is the color of a hazelnut, add the onions, bell pepper, and tomato and combine them well with the roux. Continue to rake this heavy mass for 5 minutes, breaking it up constantly so that all the vegetables get a chance to wilt.

4. Add the hot stock, stirring to deglaze the kettle and combine the roux smoothly with the stock. Then stir in the cayenne, cloves, allspice, and Worcestershire sauce and simmer, covered, for $^{1}/_{2}$ hour, scraping the bottom of the kettle well from time to time to make sure the stew does not "catch" and scorch.

5. Add the catfish, the reserved bacon, and the black pepper. Stir to distribute, and simmer, covered, for 5 minutes. Turn off the heat and let the stew sit for 5 minutes.

6. Salt to taste and serve at once in deep bowls.

NOTES: The traditional accompaniment to this stew is cornbread, hot and fragrant from the oven.

The stew may be made as much as a day in advance, provided it is well refrigerated. (The catfish does not usually disintegrate with reheating, provided you reheat the stew gently.) If there is any stew left over, it can be extended later by adding water or fish stock and *fideos* (see page 244) or canned white hominy (see Note, page 148). Dilute the stew first, then bring it slowly to a simmer. Add the pasta or hominy and continue simmering gently until it is cooked to your taste.

Bouillabaisse

Without a doubt, bouillabaisse (BOO yuh bess) is the most famous fish stew in the world. Bouillabaisse lore is vast and well worth a few minutes of our time. This delicious dish belongs by right to Marseille but is claimed by the entire Côte d'Azur. Like most regional favorites, bouillabaisse is simple and basic; finessing it does not make it better, only more impressive. It is quickly prepared, and it requires no special equipment. Despite vociferous claims to the contrary, there is no unique, secret, best recipe for bouillabaisse though everyone thinks he has it!

Purists insist that without such uniquely Mediterranean fish as rascasse and small local rockfish, your bouillabaisse will lack authenticity. I concede the point, though I consider it moot. I am no purist. I am, however, deeply devoted to good food, and I agree with that most French of French adages: "When thrushes are lacking, one eats blackbirds." I say it would be a pity to deprive yourself of a good bouillabaisse because you have neither rascasse nor rockfish, so use the best alternatives and carry on.

2 to 3 pounds firm-fleshed, nonoily saltwater fish, scaled or skinned, gutted, gills removed, well washed, and blotted with paper towels (I suggest such familiar fish as cod, ocean perch, monkfish, conger eel, red snapper, whitefish, whiting, 1 or 2 blue crabs, and a handful of whitebait, if you can find them easily)

¹/₂ cup light olive oil

1 large yellow onion, thinly sliced

2 plump cloves garlic, crushed

3 large ripe red tomatoes, skinned, seeded, and coarsely chopped

20 saffron threads, toasted (see page 161)

4 medium-size potatoes, boiled until al dente, peeled, and sliced into ¹/₄-inch rounds

1 tablespoon coarse salt

1 teaspoon freshly ground white pepper

¹/₄ teaspoon ground cayenne

1 bouquet garni made up of 3 branches dried fennel or ¹/₂ teaspoon fennel seeds, 3 branches flat-leaf parsley, 1 branch fresh thyme, 1 tiny twig fresh rosemary, and one 1 × 3-inch piece dried orange peel, all tied together with cotton string or wrapped in cheesecloth and secured

12 to 18 slices day-old French bread, cut ¹/₂ inch thick

1. Leave the small fish whole, once cleaned, but cut the larger ones across the spine into 2-inch pieces. Use the heads. (You can remove them when you serve the stew, if you choose.) If you are using crab, remove and discard the apron and the upper shell. Hack the bodies into two or three pieces, and detach the claws. Pull out and discard the gills. Rinse all the fish, including the crab, in a colander and drain them well.

2. In a large heavy-bottomed kettle, heat the oil and gently sauté the onion and garlic until the onion is transparent. Add the tomatoes and increase the heat. Stir this *soffritto* with a wooden spatula until it becomes a paste.

3. Steep the saffron for 30 seconds in $^1/_2$ cup of boiling water and add it to the kettle, using the mixture to deglaze the bottom. Remove the kettle from the heat.

4. Arrange the potatoes in layers over the *soffritto*. Carefully layer in the smaller fish and crab, then the larger fish, and sprinkle in the salt, white pepper, and cayenne.

5. Add the bouquet garni and 7 cups of rapidly boiling water. Cover the kettle and boil the stew rapidly for 10 minutes, no longer.

6. Discard the bouquet garni. Carefully remove the fish and potatoes and arrange them on a platter. Place several slices of bread in each shallow soup plate and ladle the hot broth over them.

7. Serve at once. Your guests should help themselves to the fish and potatoes. The broth and bread are eaten first, then, in the same plate, the fish and potatoes.

NOTE: It is customary to provide a sauceboat of *rouille*, a peppery, mayonnaiselike sauce greatly prized by bouillabaisse fanciers. A dollop of *rouille* is usually stirred into the bouillabaisse broth to liven it up. A recipe for the sauce follows.

Rouille

his sauce exists all around the northern shores of the Mediterranean. It is called by various names, and the recipe varies slightly from place to place, but it is basically the same, and it is the only really piquant condiment generally accepted by the Provençals and Catalans, who, unlike their North African neighbors, are not great lovers of peppery food. As a matter of fact, they are so abstemious in the use of this sauce that it is a source of great merriment to them when a foreigner can be induced to close his mouth on an undiluted spoonful. In Provence the sauce goes by the name rouille—*literally rust—because of its color. In Catalonia it is called* romesco, *suggesting some connection with Roman times—a doubtful claim that I shall not belabor. The Provençals add their version of this sauce to their fish soups; the Catalans mix it with mayonnaise as a dressing for poached seafood. There is one notable difference between the two versions. Where the Provençals use soaked bread, the Catalans use ground, toasted almonds and hazelnuts.*

2 plump cloves garlic, crushed
1 teaspoon coarse salt
½ teaspoon ground cayenne
1 slice white bread, crust removed and discarded, soaked in water and squeezed out
1 egg yolk, at room temperature

¼ cup fruity olive oil, at room temperature
3 tablespoons hot broth from the bouillabaisse (alternatively, 3 tablespoons of hot water will do)

1. Put all of the ingredients except the broth in a miniprocessor or blender and pulse until smooth. (The sauce was originally made in a mortar and pounded with a pestle, but it takes much longer and sometimes doesn't emulsify at all.)
2. With the machine running, add the broth to the mixture, drop by drop. When the sauce is as smooth as mayonnaise, spoon it into a sauceboat and serve.

NOTE: If the *rouille* is not served at once, cover it and keep it in a cool place (but not in the refrigerator). If it should separate, simply pulse it again before serving.

Red Mediterranean Chowder

*T*his robust red chowder is a hybrid. It combines the best qualities of Cata-lan sarsuela, Portuguese açorda, Livornese zuppa di pesce, and Aegean kakaviá, yet it is none of them. Its fresh taste and light, peppery bite will delight you as it has already delighted my family and friends. I call for canned tomatoes here because their ripeness and taste can be depended upon. Of course, if you have that many fine, ripe red tomatoes available, by all means use them instead.

One 20-ounce can Hunt's sliced or wedge-cut stewed tomatoes, with their juice

One 14-ounce can whole peeled stewed tomatoes, coarsely chopped, with their juice

1 cup dry red wine

3 cups fish stock (see page 215) or unsalted, defatted chicken stock

3 cups soft bread crumbs from day-old Italian or French bread

1 medium-size yellow onion, finely grated

1 large leek, white part only, split, well washed, and coarsely chopped

4 plump cloves garlic, finely crushed to a paste with 1½ teaspoons coarse salt, using the underside of a soup spoon

½ cup finely chopped flat-leaf parsley

½ teaspoon *each* red pepper flakes (more if you like), ground cinnamon, ground cumin, and whole fennel seeds

2 bay leaves

36 littleneck clams, well scrubbed

24 medium-size raw shrimp, scissored down the back, deveined, well washed, shells left on

One 6-ounce can crabmeat, picked over, rinsed, and drained

½ pound ocean perch fillets, skin left on, cut into bite-size pieces

Salt and pepper

½ teaspoon Angostura bitters (optional)

1. Put the tomatoes and their juice, the wine, stock, bread crumbs, onion, leek, garlic paste, parsley, pepper flakes, cinnamon, cumin, fennel seeds, and bay leaves in a large, deep, heavy-bottomed kettle and stir them together well. Simmer, covered, for 1 hour, scraping the bottom with a wooden spatula from time to time to prevent scorching. After

1 hour, turn off the heat and let the stew sit for 15 minutes. You may prepare the stew up to this point hours in advance or the day before, if you like, allowing the stew more time to sit and mature. (Refrigerate the stew if you make it a day in advance.)

2. Meanwhile, put the clams in a deep skillet with a cover. Heat them slowly for 15 minutes, then remove them from the heat. When they cool enough to handle, shuck them, discarding the shells and any clams that have not opened. Put the clams in a bowl and carefully decant their juice over them, taking care not to pick up any sand they may have released. Set the bowl of clams and their juice aside.

3. When the stew is ready, add the clams and their juice, the shrimp, crabmeat, and the perch. Stir the fish in gently with a wooden spoon. Heat the stew again gently to just below the simmering point and let it cook for 5 minutes. Salt and pepper to taste, and stir in the bitters. Serve the stew very hot in deep bowls, dividing the seafood among them.

NOTE: If sweet basil or cilantro are in season, garnish each bowl with a sprig of either. I also suggest you pass a cruet of your finest olive oil for those who might fancy a little of it floated on the surface of this wonderfully oil-less, fatless stew. Plenty of good Italian bread is in order, as well. Don't blanch at the amount of bread already in the stew—the cups of crumbs are completely transformed in simmering. In any case, the complex carbohydrates are very good for you.

Aegean-Style Squid

SERVES 4 OR 5

This is my favorite way of stewing medium-size squid. The accompanying sauce and vegetables peg the recipe immediately as Aegean, and so it is. The islanders stew the squid with whatever vegetables they have. For the okra, you may substitute $^1/_2$ pound fresh, well-washed, stemmed spinach or very tender young green beans, topped and tailed.

3 medium-size squid, cleaned, drawn, and dressed (see Note)

3 tablespoons light olive oil

5 small white onions, quartered

8 plump cloves garlic, halved lengthwise

$^1/_4$ teaspoon *each* cracked black pepper, ground cumin, dried oregano, dried thyme, and fresh or dried rosemary

1 bay leaf

6 branches flat-leaf parsley, tied in a bundle with cotton string

2 ribs celery, cut into $^1/_4$-inch diagonal slices

2 medium-size carrots, peeled and cut into $^1/_4$-inch rounds

1 Anaheim, New Mexican, or sweet frying pepper, halved and cut into 6 or 8 pieces

One 7-ounce can tomato sauce

$^2/_3$ cup dry white wine

1 cup fish stock (see page 215), 1 Seabag (see page 214), or 1 cube fish bouillon dissolved in 1 cup hot water

16 or 20 tender okra pods, trimmed (thawed, frozen okra may be substituted)

$^1/_4$ teaspoon ground cinnamon

1 tablespoon freshly squeezed lemon juice

1 teaspoon finely crumbled dried dill (if fresh dill is available, use an equal amount, finely chopped)

1. Cut the squid tentacles and swimming flaps into $^1/_2$-inch pieces. Cut the pouches into fourths, lengthwise. Lay them flat, insides up, and crosshatch them at $^1/_4$-inch intervals with a very sharp knife, taking care not to cut completely through. Cut the crosshatched pieces into 1-inch squares. Set the cut-up squid aside.

2. Heat the oil in a heavy-bottomed kettle and sauté the onions until wilted, tossing them often with a wooden spatula. Add the garlic and

squid and toss them together with the onions, sautéing for just 3 minutes.

3. Add the cracked pepper, cumin, oregano, thyme, rosemary, bay leaf, and parsley and toss again thoroughly.
4. Add the celery, carrots, Anaheim pepper, tomato sauce, wine, and fish stock, deglazing the bottom well.
5. Simmer gently, covered, for ½ hour, or until the squid is fork-tender but not soft.
6. Stir in the okra pods, cinnamon, lemon juice, and dill and continue simmering, uncovered, for 15 minutes. Turn off the heat and salt the stew to taste.
7. After 5 minutes, discard the parsley bundle and the bay leaf, and serve the stew with plain boiled rice, pilaf, or instant couscous.

NOTE: Squid can often be purchased pan-ready at good supermarkets. Be sure you check the date on the package, and refuse any packaged squid that is surrounded by a milky fluid, an indication that the squid has been improperly thawed from frozen stock. If you purchase fresh squid that has not been cleaned, drawn, or dressed, here are the simple steps for preparing it:

Work over a large bowl of water or over a colander under cold running water. Gently pull the tentacles loose from the pouch. Drop the tentacles and viscera into the colander. Find the pen, a long, semitransparent piece of cartilage. Draw it out and discard it. Rinse out the pouch. Starting near the opening, peel off the thin purplish skin. With a sharp knife, cut off and save the two swimming flaps on each side of the pouch. Turn the pouch inside out and rinse it again. Set it aside. Lay the tentacles and viscera on a cutting board and cut the tentacles loose just above the eyes. Unless the recipe requires the ink from the ink sac, discard it. Press out and discard the beak, a circular piece of cartilage fixed where the tentacles meet. Rinse the tentacles. The squid is ready to be used in the recipe you have chosen. If you are not using the squid at once, put the pouch, swimming flaps, and tentacles in a bowl of cold, slightly salted water or in a plastic bag, and refrigerate.

Stuffed Squid Niçoise

SERVES 6

S tuffed squid is a dish prized all around the Mediterranean. I have at least a dozen recipes for it, each from a different area. They differ mainly in the ingredients used in the stuffing. In Catalonia, ground pork is often added to the stuffing. In Greece and the Aegean, rice, spinach, dill, and oregano are favored. Along Italy's endless coastlines, squid is usually stuffed with grated Parmesan, bread crumbs, and garlic. This recipe from Nice is distinguished by a little tuna in the stuffing. I heartily recommend this method of preparing squid to those who may be trying this fish for the first time. I encourage you not to be daunted by the length of the recipe; it really isn't so complicated.

6 medium-size squid, cleaned,
   drawn, and ready for use
   (see Note, page 231)

FOR THE SAUCE

3 tablespoons light olive oil

2 large yellow onions, coarsely
   chopped

2 plump cloves garlic, crushed

3 medium-size ripe red tomatoes,
   skinned, seeded, and coarsely
   chopped (off-season, substitute
   one 14¹/₂-ounce can stewed
   tomatoes, with their juice)

1 cup dry white wine

1 cup fish stock (see page 215), or
   1 Seabag (see page 214),
   dissolved in 1 cup boiling
   water

1 bouquet garni made up of
   2 branches flat-leaf parsley,
   1 branch dried thyme, 1 bay
   leaf, and one 1 × 2-inch piece
   dried orange peel, all bound
   together with cotton string

10 saffron threads, toasted and
   finely crumbled (see page 161)

Salt and black pepper

1 tablespoon vegetable oil

2 small scallions, white parts only, finely chopped

1 tablespoon finely chopped green bell pepper

1 tablespoon finely chopped flat-leaf parsley

2 slices white bread, crusts removed, soaked in $^1/_4$ cup dry white wine

$^1/_4$ teaspoon finely crumbled dried chervil

$^1/_4$ cup freshly grated Parmesan cheese

1 large egg yolk

$^1/_4$ teaspoon freshly ground black pepper

$1^1/_2$ ounces (about half a small can) light water-pack tuna

Salt

Lemon wedges

Chopped flat-leaf parsley

1. With a sharp knife, excise the swimming flaps from the squid without perforating the pouches, and chop them up finely with the tentacles. Set aside.

2. Prepare the sauce: Heat the olive oil in a heavy-bottomed kettle and gently sauté the squid, raking the pouches and chopped bits back and forth through the oil for 3 minutes. Be careful! Frying squid is notorious for spattering hot oil about. With a slotted spoon, remove the pouches, wipe them with paper towels, and set them aside.

3. Add the onions and garlic to the rest of the squid and continue to sauté until the onion is wilted. Add the tomatoes and make a standard *soffritto* by raking the ingredients back and forth until they form a thick paste.

4. Add the wine, stock, bouquet garni, and saffron. Deglaze the pan thoroughly, and simmer the sauce gently for 20 minutes.

5. Meanwhile, make the stuffing: Heat the vegetable oil in a small skillet; gently sauté the scallions, bell pepper, and chopped parsley for 3 minutes, and remove them immediately from the heat.

6. Put the soaked bread, chervil, Parmesan, egg yolk, black pepper, and tuna in a bowl and mix them together well. Incorporate the sautéed vegetables and beat until light. Add a few drops of water if the stuffing seems too dry. Cover the stuffing and chill it for 10 minutes in the freezer.

7. Stuff the squid pouches, leaving a little room for expansion in cooking, and fasten each opening loosely with a toothpick. Wipe the pouches clean. If there is a little stuffing left over, mix it into the sauce.

8. Place the stuffed pouches in one layer in the sauce. (It should almost cover them.) Add a little water if necessary. Braise the stuffed squid gently, covered, for $1/2$ hour, turning the squid from time to time. If the level of the sauce sinks, add more water.

9. Discard the bouquet garni, and salt and pepper the sauce to taste, shaking the kettle to distribute the seasoning throughout.

10. Remove the toothpicks from the squid, taking care not to burn your fingers. Place the squid in a deep dish and spoon the sauce over them. Garnish with lemon wedges and chopped parsley.

NOTE: The usual accompaniments for this dish are plain boiled rice or gnocchi, but I find fluffy mashed potatoes super with it—not a Mediterranean combination, but one of those great alliances one sometimes discovers by chance. *De gustibus* . . .

Spanish Shrimp Stew

*I*n 1845 the French novelist Alexandre Dumas journeyed to Spain. Being the gourmet that he was, he literally ate his way across the Iberian Peninsula. In the kitchen of a fellow Frenchman living in Madrid, he tested many of the dishes he preferred and published some of the recipes. Here's one of his favorites; I have updated it and made it more specific. With its classic soffritto and its picada *thickening of ground toasted almonds and cracker crumbs, it remains an exquisite, entirely Spanish way of stewing shrimp. The stew makes a good first course, served hot in deep soup bowls, or a light main course, served traditionally on slabs of toasted country bread. It is also fine on nests of boiled rice or tossed with linguine.*

1 tablespoon coarse salt

$^1/_4$ cup dry sherry

1 bouquet garni made up of 3 sprigs flat-leaf parsley, 1 bay leaf, and 2 sprigs fresh thyme, bound together with cotton string

3 slices fresh lemon

1 Seabag or 1 cube fish bouillon (see page 216)

1 pound medium-size raw shrimp, scissored down the back and deveined, shells left on

6 tablespoons ($^3/_4$ stick) unsalted butter

2 tablespoons olive oil

3 medium-size white onions, finely grated

8 medium-size ripe red tomatoes, finely grated, skins discarded (off-season, canned, whole, skinned tomatoes may be substituted)

2 plump cloves garlic, finely grated

20 blanched, toasted almonds, finely ground

4 soda crackers, finely crushed

$^1/_4$ teaspoon ground cayenne

Salt

Finely chopped flat-leaf parsley

1. In a narrow heavy-bottomed kettle, heat 4 cups of water with the salt, sherry, bouquet garni, lemon slices, and the fish concentrate. Bring to a boil and toss in the shrimp. As soon as the mixture comes to a boil again, remove the kettle from the heat. With a slotted spoon, remove and discard the lemon slices. Remove the shrimp to

a colander and run cold water over them. Peel them, set the shrimp aside, covered, in a cool place, and save the shells.

2. Heat 3 tablespoons of the butter and 1 tablespoon of the olive oil in a frying pan and fry the shrimp shells gently for 15 minutes, tossing them with a wooden spatula from time to time. Make sure that the butter doesn't brown. Add the shrimp-poaching water and simmer for 10 minutes. Strain, pressing all the liquid out of the shells. Discard the shells and return the bouquet garni to the liquid. Continue boiling the liquid with the bouquet garni until it has reduced to half its volume.

3. Meanwhile, in a wide braising pan, heat the other 3 tablespoons of butter and the remaining tablespoon of olive oil. When the butter is bubbling, add the grated onion, tomatoes, and garlic. Simmer for 15 minutes. Add the reduced fish stock to this *soffritto*, discarding the bouquet garni. Stir in the crushed almonds, cracker crumbs, and cayenne and simmer for 15 minutes.

4. Add the shrimp and simmer just long enough for them to heat through. Remove the kettle from the heat, salt to taste, and serve at once as indicated in the headnote, sprinkled with a little finely chopped parsley.

Shrimp and Black Bean Bisque

This rich, mocha-hued bisque, with its subtle bite and elusive flavor, is very special. My old traveling companion Zen Alvarez and I discovered it many years ago on our first visit to Cascais. We had been exploring the cliffs all morning and were, as usual, famished. We found a good restaurant at the very top of the cliffs and were soon oohing and aahing over this unusual bisque. We had never eaten anything quite like it.

Years later, finding myself in Lisbon, I set out with another friend to find the restaurant again. It was one of those Portuguese winter days when the Atlantic punishes the whole area with whips of icy rain. In spite of the weather, we found the restaurant and were served the bisque again. All the manager would tell me about the dish was that it was made of black beans and a black shrimp found only along that coast. The dish seems to be far more Caribbean or Brazilian than Portuguese. Whatever its origin, it is outstanding and deserves to be better known. I am happy to pass my recipe along to you.

3 tablespoons light olive oil

2 tablespoons unsalted butter

$^1/_2$ pound raw, medium-size shrimp, shelled (save the shells), deveined, cut in half lengthwise, then 3 times across, kept moist in a little lightly salted water

2 allspice berries, coarsely cracked

1 plump clove garlic, finely crushed

1 large, yellow onion, finely grated

2 medium-size ripe red tomatoes, skinned, seeded, and coarsely chopped (off-season, substitute one 7-ounce can tomato sauce)

2 tablespoons finely chopped cilantro

1 large green bell pepper, flame-roasted (see page 163), peeled, cored, and coarsely chopped

One 16-ounce can black beans, well rinsed and drained

1 cup cooked rice

2 cups Fish Stock (see page 215), or 1 Seabag (see page 214), dissolved in cups hot water

$^1/_2$ teaspoon baking soda

5 *pequin* chilies (see Note page 137), finely crumbled (wash your fingers well after crushing them), or $^1/_4$ teaspoon ground cayenne

1 cup half-and-half

2 tablespoons dark rum

Salt

1 teaspoon finely grated orange peel

1. In a wide, heavy-bottomed braising pan, heat the oil and butter and gently sauté the shrimp shells with the allspice and garlic for 7 minutes. Toss the ingredients frequently so that they sauté evenly. Remove the pan from the heat and strain out the fat, pressing the shells against the sieve to extract every drop of the highly flavored fat. Discard the shells and return the fat to the pan.

2. Add the onion and sauté until it becomes a light-golden mass. Add the tomatoes, cilantro, and bell pepper, and stir together well with a wooden spatula. Sauté for about 5 minutes.

3. Add the black beans, rice, and stock. Stir together well until heated through and remove from the heat.

4. Using a food processor or blender, process the ingredients into a smooth purée.

5. Return the purée to the pan and stir in the baking soda and crumbled chilies. When the mixture is just below the simmering point, stir in the half-and-half and rum. Continue to cook below the simmering point for 5 minutes, then stir in the drained shrimp pieces and orange peel. Cook for 2 more minutes. Turn off the heat and allow the bisque to sit for 3 minutes.

6. Ladle the bisque into deep warmed bowls and garnish each with a single leaf of fresh cilantro. Pass a bowl of warm, crisp *migas* to sprinkle into the bisque. The recipe follows.

Portuguese-Style Fried Bread Crumbs (Migas)

MAKES ABOUT 1 CUP

Those are many kinds of migas in Iberian cooking; some are savory and are added to soups or served with fried eggs; some are sweet and are eaten for breakfast with hot chocolate or coffee. The following recipe is for lightly flavored savory ones to be eaten with the preceding bisque in lieu of croutons.

1 loaf day-old French or Italian
  bread
$^1/_2$ teaspoon ground cinnamon
$^1/_2$ teaspoon onion powder

$^1/_4$ teaspoon coarse salt
3 tablespoons vegetable oil or
  fruity olive oil

1. Halve the loaf lengthwise and dig out the soft part of the bread in large flakes with a fork. Pull them apart into pieces that are still fragments and not small crumbs. You should have about 1$^1/_4$ cups.
2. Put these *migas* in a paper bag with the cinnamon and onion powder and shake them until the flavorings have been lightly distributed throughout.
3. Spread the *migas* out on a tea towel or paper towel. Dissolve the salt in 1 cup of warm water and sprinkle the *migas* until they are quite damp, but not soaked. It isn't necessary to use the whole cup of water.
4. In a large heavy-bottomed kettle, heat the oil and toss the *migas* in it with a wooden spatula, gently browning them until they are golden. This will take about 10 minutes.
5. Empty the *migas* into a bowl and serve them at once, while they are still hot and crisp. Provide a large serving spoon so that your guests may serve themselves as they see fit.

NOTES: Should you have to make the *migas* well in advance, spread them on a metal baking tray and crisp them again in the oven at 350°F just before serving time. Provided they are completely cooled and dry, *migas* can be stored for a few days in a tightly closed jar or cookie tin and reheated, but it is better to make them fresh.

The Portuguese sometimes add minute bites of fried chorizo and hot pepper to *migas* and serve them with a glass of wine. The sweet breakfast type are made according to the recipe above, omitting the onion powder but adding more cinnamon and plenty of sugar to the bag before shaking them. These sweet *migas* are delicious with stewed fruit or yogurt.

Ton's Paella

SERVES 5 OR 6

In many ways, paella is to the Costa Brava and the Zona Oriental of Spain what bouillabaisse is to the Côte d'Azur and Provençal shoreline of France. Both are Mediterranean seafood stews with world reputations. Both are considered typical. The two dishes differ greatly, however. Bouillabaisse is brothy—indeed, the broth is the important thing—whereas paella is the most famous of the sopas secas, and it is the flavor and texture of the rice that count. Marseille is the putative birthplace of bouillabaisse, as Valencia is the putative birthplace of paella, but that does not prevent any hamlet, restaurant, family, or cook laying claim to the best recipe for either of these great dishes.

A good paella is savory and full-bodied. The rice should turn out moist and slightly creamy, and, as in a good risotto, the center of each grain should be slightly resistant. The taste of the rice depends up the sofrito, or sofregit, as it is called along the Catalan coast, and the light bouquet of the stock, and its texture depends up proper simmering. If you don't have a paella, the correct name for the shallow, wide, two-handled metal pan in which the paella is prepared, use a similar earthenware cazuela or a large frying pan. It must be wide, shallow, and flameproof.

Paella is the perfect beach or picnic meal for a family. The pans are designed to be propped up on stones a few inches from the ground, so that sticks can be poked under them and kindled. (Unlike a barbecue, a paella requires a brief, hot flame, not coals.) I ate my first authentic paella one summer in the early fifties while camping out with fellow students on a beach outside Alicante. There, on the ground alongside her shack, a Mother Courage-like canteen operator prepared a huge paella for us in twenty minutes. We knelt on the ground around it and ate it directly from the pan, Gypsy-style.

Here is my Catalan cousin Ton's recipe for a simple but very good paella to be made in the kitchen at home. Remember, it is the care with which the rice is prepared, not the number of fish, crustaceans, and shellfish, that determines the success of the dish.

2 plump shallots, sliced paper-thin

1 bay leaf

1/2 cup dry white wine

12 or 16 medium-size very fresh mussels, scrubbed and bearded

3 tablespoons light olive oil

1 small rib pork chop, meat and bone cut into 6 or 8 pieces

1 small squid, cleaned, drawn, and cut into small pieces (see page 231)

12 medium-size raw shrimp, scissored down the back, deveined, and well washed

1 small white onion, finely chopped

1 plump clove garlic, finely crushed

1/4 small green bell pepper, finely chopped

1 tablespoon finely chopped flat-leaf parsley

3 medium-size ripe red tomatoes, skinned, seeded, and finely chopped (off-season, substitute one 14 1/2-ounce can stewed tomatoes, well drained and finely chopped)

2 1/2 cups short-grain rice

12 saffron threads, toasted and finely crumbled (see page 161)

5 cups Fish Stock (see page 215) or 2 Seabags (see page 214) dissolved in 5 cups hot water

1/2 cup freshly shelled green peas or thawed, frozen green peas

1/4 teaspoon freshly ground black pepper

1 bottled pimiento, rinsed and cut into lengthwise strips

2 lemons, quartered

1. Put the shallots, bay leaf, and white wine in a heavy-bottomed saucepan, and pile the mussels on top. Cook over moderate heat for 7 minutes, covered, shaking the pan from time to time. If the mussels haven't opened, continue simmering for 3 more minutes. If they have, turn off the heat and let the mussels sit for 3 minutes with the cover still on. With a slotted spoon, remove the mussels to a bowl and set them aside, discarding any that have not opened. Carefully decant the juice, leaving any sand in the bottom of the saucepan. Set the juice aside. Discard the sand, shallots, and bay leaf.

2. Heat the oil in a 12-inch paella or frying pan and gently brown the pork and pork bones until golden. Remove from the pan and set aside.

3. Sauté the squid and shrimp in the pan for 3 minutes, raking them about with a wooden spatula. Take care! Frying squid often spatters and pops. Remove the squid and shrimp and reserve them with the pork.

4. Add the onion, garlic, and bell pepper and sauté until the onion is transparent, raking the vegetables back and forth frequently. Add the parsley and tomatoes and reduce to a paste, continuing to rake the mixture about so that it cooks through.

5. Add the rice, stirring until all the grains are coated. Stir the saffron and the juice from the mussels into the fish stock and pour the mixture into the rice. Stir gently, deglazing the pan thoroughly. Stir in the peas (if you are using fresh ones), pork, squid, and black pepper. Simmer over high heat for 7 minutes, stirring only once.

6. Place the shrimp evenly over the surface and bury them a little in the simmering rice. Do not stir. Distribute the mussels evenly over the surface as well. Continue to simmer for at least 5 minutes. Test the rice. If it is dry and not yet ready, add a little water. The trick is to bring the rice almost to the finished point, then remove the pan from the fire and cover it with a cloth or folded newspaper (the usual cover in Catalonia). If you are using thawed frozen peas, add them at this point, and let the paella sit, covered, for 5 minutes. (Some cooks swear that the paella, once removed from the fire, should be placed on a coil of damp towels.) Decorate the surface of the paella with the pimento slices and lemon wedges and serve at once.

NOTE: Paellas can be made with *fideos* (see page 244) instead of rice. They can be made without seafood, or with a great assortment of meats, such as chicken, rabbit, and sausages, in addition to seafood. However, such impressive paellas can be inappropriately greasy. The simplest are best.

Seafood and Vermicelli Paella

SERVES 4 OR 5

This dish, called fideuà, is a regional favorite along the Catalan coast. According to Manuel Martinez Llopis, the great authority on Iberian cooking, this pasta-based paella dates back at least to the thirteenth century. Until this century, the fideos, a kind of elbow spaghetti from which the dish derives its name, were almost the size of macaroni, but today they are generally tiny, like vermicelli. They are packaged in twists and sold in Latino groceries almost everywhere in 6-ounce and 12-ounce cellophane bags.

Like all paellas, fideuà is a sopa seca, one of those typically Hispanic dishes that start very soupy and finish creamy and risottolike, with most of the sauce absorbed. Also like paella, fideuà can be made with anything from chicken to assorted sausages. This particularly fine one is made with monkfish, shrimp, and a rich fumet, which you must have on hand before starting.

6 cups rich fish stock,
   3 tablespoons Concentrated
   Fish Stock (see page 216), or
   1 Seabag (see page 214)
3 tablespoons vegetable oil
8 or 10 medium-size shrimp,
   scissored down the back,
   deveined, well washed, and left
   in the shell
4 pieces ¹/₂-inch-thick boned
   monkfish tails (about ¹/₂
   pound), cut into bite-size pieces

1 large yellow onion, finely grated
12 ounces *fideos*, broken into
   2-inch pieces (about 1 handful
   per person, as the old
   cookbooks say)
1 large, very ripe red tomato, soft
   interior finely grated, skin
   discarded
10 saffron threads, toasted and
   crumbled (see page 161)
Salt

1. Heat the stock, or its substitute mixed in 6 cups of water, to the simmering point.
2. In a 12-inch paella pan or flameproof *cazuela*, heat the oil and sauté the shrimp and monkfish briefly on all sides. Remove them and set them aside.
3. Add the grated onion and sauté until most of the juice has evaporated and it is almost golden, then add the *fideos* and stir them as they

absorb most of the oil. Sauté for about 3 minutes, but don't allow the pasta to brown. Add the grated tomato and stir in thoroughly.

4. Mix the saffron with a little of the hot fish stock and let it steep for 30 seconds, then add it and the rest of the stock to the paella pan, stirring everything together briefly. Salt to taste. Smooth the surface, and do not stir again. Simmer for 10 minutes, then add the shrimp and monkfish, distributing them evenly over the surface. Continue to simmer for 5 minutes, or until the pasta has absorbed most of the sauce.

5. Turn off the heat, cover the pan with a cloth or newspaper, and allow the pasta to puff for 5 minutes. Place the paella pan in the middle of the dining table and serve at once.

NOTE: As a typical first course, serve an *ensalada catalana* composed of the light inner leaves of romaine, olives, quartered tomatoes, and hard-boiled eggs, and slices of several luncheon meats, such as boiled ham, salami, and cooked sausages. Catalans eat their salads before, never after, the main course. They also prefer saucing them simply with coarse salt, fine vinegar, and choice olive oil, to which they help themselves from the *vinagreta* that is customarily placed on the table before the first course.

Salt Cod in Lemon-and-Dill Sauce

SERVES 4

In the late fifties, I was privileged to spend several days on two occasions with the monks at the sixteenth-century monastery of Varlaam at Meteora in Macedonia. Staying in that surrealistic aerie, perched almost 1000 feet in the air, was truly a heavenly experience. I ate at a common table with the monks and the abbot. The food was plain but very good. While I was there, this succulent stew of salt cod, potatoes, and onions, flavored with lemon and dill, was served several times as the principal dish. I found it a most delectable way to prepare salt cod.

Here is my modernized version of the monks' ancient recipe. For this or any other salt-cod recipe, you need prime-quality, moist, thick, center-cut salt cod. Salt cod is making a reappearance on restaurant menus and in many supermarkets. If you have trouble finding it, ask your fishmonger to order it for you. (Salt cusk, often sold in the States, is not a satisfactory substitute.) The dish works very well, too, substituting fresh cod steaks for the salt cod; that variation follows this recipe.

Four 3-4 inch pieces first-rate
    white salt cod, $1/2$ to 1 inch
    thick
$1 1/2$ cups low-fat or skim milk
$1/2$ teaspoon fennel seeds
1 bay leaf
$1/4$ cup light olive oil
2 medium-size yellow onions,
    peeled and quartered lengthwise
2 plump cloves garlic, thinly sliced
2 medium-size potatoes, boiled,
    peeled, and cut into $1/8$-inch
    rounds
1 cup soft bread crumbs from day-
    old Italian or French bread
3 tablespoons flour

$1/2$ teaspoon freshly ground white
    pepper
$1/2$ cup dry white wine
$1/2$ cup Concentrated Fish Stock
    (see page 216), or 1 Seabag
    (see page 214), or 1 cube fish
    bouillon dissolved in $1/2$ cup hot
    water
3 tablespoons freshly squeezed
    lemon juice
12 bottled capers, rinsed and
    crushed (optional)
1 teaspoon finely crumbled dried
    dill or finely chopped fresh dill
Salt

1. Soak the cod for 24 hours in cold water, changing the water several times.
2. Rinse the cod and put it, skin side up, in a pan large enough to accommodate four pieces without crowding them. Add the milk, fennel seeds, and the bay leaf, and cook just below the simmering point for 30 minutes.
3. Remove the pan from the heat and allow the cod to cool in the milk. Discard the milk, seeds, and bay leaf. Blot the cod and set the fillets aside.
4. Heat the oil in a heavy-bottomed braising pan and gently sauté the onions and garlic until they are transparent and wilted but not browned. Add the potatoes in one layer over them. Mix the bread crumbs and flour and sprinkle them over the potatoes.
5. Bury the cod fillets, skin sides down, in the crumbs in one layer and sprinkle in the white pepper. Add the wine, the stock (or its dissolved substitute) mixed with $1^1/2$ cups of warm water, the lemon juice, and the crushed capers. Give the pan a few gentle shakes to combine these additions. Simmer, covered, over very low heat, shaking the pan from time to time, for 30 minutes, or until the sauce is as thick as cream and the cod flakes easily with the tines of a fork.
6. Sprinkle in the dill, salt to taste, if necessary, and serve lukewarm. The cod in its sauce is superb if refrigerated overnight and served cold for lunch.

NOTE: At Varlaam this dish is considered Lenten fare. It can be made festive, however, by sprinkling it liberally with toasted slivered almonds, delicately browned sliced garlic, and some thinly sliced bits of bottled pimiento. With these garnishes, the dish bears a striking resemblance to several Basque versions of stewed salt cod.

Fresh Cod Steaks in Lemon-and-Dill Sauce

SERVES 4

Four 3-4 inch fresh cod or scrod
    steaks, 1 inch thick, cut across
    the spine in rounds, bones and
    skin not removed
$^1/_2$ teaspoon coarse salt

2 tablespoons flour
$^1/_4$ cup light olive oil
All the other ingredients follow
    the olive oil listed in the
    preceding recipe

1. Salt the steaks and dredge them lightly with the flour, brushing off and saving the excess.

2. Heat the oil in a heavy-bottomed braising pan that will accommodate the steaks in one layer without crowding them, and quickly brown them, 2 minutes on each side. Remove them to a plate and set them aside.

3. Proceed with Step 4 of the preceding recipe, using the oil remaining in the pan after the fish steaks are browned to sauté the onions and garlic. Add the potatoes and floured bread crumbs as specified.

4. Follow Step 5, but do not add the fresh cod steaks until the last 5 minutes of braising, after the sauce has thickened. Then proceed with Step 6. Remove the fresh cod steaks from the pan very carefully with a metal spatula; they are far more delicate than the salt cod. Spoon the rich sauce over the fish.

Swordfish Steaks Provençale

SERVES 4

This dish is a repository of nineteenth-century Provençal cooking techniques and flavorings. Raïto, as it is known, was originally a highly seasoned ragout of salt cod prepared in Provençal households the afternoon of Christmas Eve, a day of fast and abstinence, to be eaten as a collation before setting off for midnight mass. I remember eating raïto in Les Baux de Provence where I went one mistral-tormented Christmas Eve in the early fifties to record the carols of Saboly during the Mass. The raïto of salt cod was the only thing on the menu in the small restaurant, but it was tasty, I was hungry, and I was grateful for it.

The dish takes far less time to prepare and becomes quite festive when swordfish replaces the desalinated cod. The traditional dish was prepared with dried tomatoes or tomato paste, since there were no fresh tomatoes in Provence at Christmastime. I suggest you make the dish in high summer, when sun-ripened tomatoes and fresh basil are plentiful. It will be an excellent departure from the usual grilled swordfish.

$^1/_2$ teaspoon coarse salt

$^1/_2$ teaspoon freshly ground black pepper

3 tablespoons flour

Four 3-4 inch swordfish steaks, 1 inch thick

$^1/_4$ cup light olive oil

10 walnut halves

3 medium-size yellow onions, thinly sliced

5 plump cloves garlic, thinly sliced

4 or 5 flat anchovy fillets, coarsely chopped

$^1/_8$ teaspoon crumbled dried thyme

8 crumbled dried rosemary needles

$^1/_4$ teaspoon fennel seeds

2 bay leaves

2 tablespoons coarsely chopped flat-leaf parsley

20 golden raisins, rinsed

3 medium-size, very ripe red tomatoes, soft inner parts finely grated, skins discarded

$^1/_2$ cup dry red wine

$^1/_2$ teaspoon finely grated orange peel

2 tablespoons bottled capers, rinsed

12 oil-cured black olives, pitted

12 leaves fresh basil, coarsely torn (optional)

1. Salt, pepper, and lightly flour the swordfish steaks. Brush off and reserve the excess flour.

2. Choose a heavy-bottomed braising pan large enough to accommodate the steaks without crowding them. Heat the oil and quickly brown the steaks on both sides. Remove them at once and set them aside.
3. Brown the walnuts in the same oil, tossing them well. Remove them and set them aside.
4. Reduce the heat. Add the onions, garlic, anchovies, thyme, rosemary, fennel seeds, bay leaves, parsley, and raisins. Sauté, tossing vigorously with a wooden spatula, until the onions wilt.
5. Grind the walnuts to a fine meal in a miniprocessor and mix them with the reserved flour. Sprinkle this mixture into the sauté, stirring it in well. Add the tomatoes and continue sautéing until the mixture is a thick paste.
6. Add the wine and 1 cup of boiling water. Stir well and simmer for 20 minutes.
7. Place the swordfish steaks in the pan and spoon the sauce over them. Add the orange peel, capers, and olives and simmer, covered, for 10 minutes.
8. Remove the pan from the heat. Allow the *raïto* to cool and mature for 5 minutes.
9. Serve hot on plain boiled rice. Scatter a few torn basil leaves over each steak.

Tuna and Shrimp with Peppers and Garlic

SERVES 4

*A*fter trying many versions of this clear, peppery fisherman's stew from the northern coast of Spain, I have developed my own, combining what I feel are the best qualities of several. Marmitako, as it is called, is the Basque adaptation of marmite, the French name for the venerable cast-iron kettle in which most stews used to be made, as well as the stews those kettles produced. The dish is reminiscent of the vegetable soup many of our grandmothers used to make routinely for supper, except that it contains peppers and lots of chopped garlic, and fish is simmered in the soup for the last 7 minutes. A good marmitako can be made with red tuna, bonito, or salmon, and I have even heard of one made with mackerel. This one, untraditionally, contains shrimp as well as tuna; that is my addition, and I think you will like it. I prefer preparing the stew in a wide braising pan for better control of the timing. The fish must, on no account, be overcooked.

3 tablespoons light olive oil

1 strip lean breakfast bacon, finely chopped

1 large leek, white part only, well washed and coarsely chopped

1 small white onion, coarsely chopped

2 medium-size carrots, peeled, quartered lengthwise, and coarsely chopped

2 ribs celery, coarsely chopped

3 tablespoons Concentrated Fish Stock (see page 216), or 1 Seabag (see page 214)

1/2 cup dry white wine

4 medium-size potatoes, peeled and halved, each half cut into 3 pieces

2 large green or red bell peppers, flame-roasted (see page 163), and cut into 2-inch squares

1/4 teaspoon red pepper flakes or ground cayenne

Salt

One 1-pound piece red tuna 1/2 inch thick, divided into 4 pieces

1 tablespoon finely chopped flat-leaf parsley

5 plump cloves garlic, very finely chopped

20 medium-size raw shrimp (about 1/2 pound), scissored down the back, deveined, and well washed, the shells left on

1. Heat the oil gently in a wide, heavy-bottomed braising pan. Add the bacon, leek, onion, carrots, and celery and toss thoroughly until the oil disappears. Gently sweat these ingredients over low heat, covered, for 20 minutes, tossing them from time to time to prevent scorching.
2. Add the fish stock or Seabag, 2½ cups of cold water, the wine, potatoes, bell peppers, and red pepper flakes. Simmer, covered, for 40 minutes.
3. Salt to taste. Make a nest in the stew for each of the tuna pieces and place them deep in the vegetables. Sprinkle evenly with the chopped parsley and garlic. Arrange the shrimp over the parsley and garlic in one layer. The shrimp should be almost covered with the broth. (If necessary, add a little hot water.) Simmer, tightly covered, for 7 minutes, or until the tuna is poached uniformly white and the shrimp have just turned pink. Do not overcook.
4. Divide the tuna, shrimp, vegetables, and broth among four large soup plates, and serve very hot. Provide thick slices of soft-crumbed, crusty bread for dunking and extra bowls for the shrimp shells.

NOTE: Should you have to prepare this dish several hours in advance, proceed through Step 2, then reheat and add the tuna and shrimp 7 minutes before serving time. One of the great joys of this stew is finding the tuna and shrimp done *à point*.

CHAPTER SIX

Vegetable and Fruit Stews

Introduction to Vegetable
and Fruit Stews

Vegetable and fruit stews have always been a major part of world cuisine. Both here and abroad they frequently seem to be down-home favorites that don't often find their way into our everyday meals, probably because meat, fowl, fish, and dairy products outrank them in our too-often food-foolish, affluent society. Also, it is generally thought that down-home favorites require far more time to prepare than most people think they can spare. Both of those attitudes need to be reconsidered and changed.

The U.S. Department of Agriculture reminded us recently with its Food Guide Pyramid that we should eat three times as many dishes made of vegetables, fruits, and grains as we do, leaving the meat, fowl, fish, and dairy products for once or twice a week and for special occasions. Ironically, that is how most of our grandparents ate, as did their parents and grandparents before them. They left us a rich legacy of recipes for vegetable and fruit dishes, many of them for delicious, now unusual, stews. I found hundreds of them when looking for stews for this collection.

If the boiled-to-death peas and carrots, cabbage, potatoes, and stewed prunes of delis, diners, and school cafeterias have turned you against stewed vegetables and fruits, I challenge you to rediscover them in these wonderful old recipes. Here are a few things to remember when shopping for and preparing vegetables and fruits:

Insist on freshness. There is no more appetizing aroma than that of fresh-picked fruits and vegetables. That aroma is the first thing to dissipate once they have been picked. It is a sure sign of freshness, so learn to smell produce, and don't feel inhibited about it. The nutritional value of vegetables and fruits lessens the longer they are kept, so try to find a reliable farmers' market and patronize it. Get to know the vendors. Ask them questions, especially about produce you don't recognize or know about. If you depend on a supermarket for your vegetables and fruits (and most of them nowadays are quite reliable), know what day of the week the produce arrives and shop accordingly.

Examine closely what you are buying. The skin should be firm, smooth, bright in color, unbruised, unspotted, and clean. Organic produce, because it is raised without insecticides, can be less visually attractive when you buy it, but find a reliable dealer.

If you plan to keep leafy produce several days, remove and discard any bruised or damaged leaves. Wash and blot the leafy vegetables dry and store them in the vegetable compartment of the refrigerator without crowding them. Do not store tomatoes in the refrigerator; it causes their interior cells to rupture and soften. Place them loosely in a brown paper bag in a cool, not cold, place.

Vegetables and fruits should be used as soon as you have prepared them. Wash everything well and scrub with a vegetable brush if necessary. Beware of leaving peeled, cut-up vegetables in water. It leaches away the water-soluble nutrients.

Unless otherwise indicated, cook vegetables and fruits as little as possible, so that they remain somewhat resistant. Each vegetable and fruit has its own cooking time. Hard root vegetables such as potatoes and carrots require longer cooking than others. When stewing, add the harder vegetables first, the softer ones later, so that they maintain their identity and aren't reduced to a hodgepodge.

It is impossible here to give you a course in vegetable and fruit cookery. Both are extensive, delightful worlds for you to discover on your own. There are dozens of fine books on both, some dedicated to only one vegetable or fruit. Interest yourself in becoming a modest specialist; you, your family, and your guests will be the better for it. If you are a conscientious food budgeter, you won't be able to resist taking advantage of the savings in making vegetables and fruits a larger part of your menus. Of course, if you really want to learn about vegetables and fruits, follow Voltaire's advice and, like Candide, find a plot, even a small one, and "make your garden grow." Nothing will teach you as much about vegetables, fruits, and *yourself.*

Vegetarian Chili

R ecipes for vegetarian chili abound. Too many are, frankly, bad. Here is a recipe for chili sin carne I put together at the request of some of my vegetarian friends. I am no vegetarian, and this recipe makes use of beans and tomatoes, ingredients this old-fashioned Texas chili maker would never think of putting in chili con carne, as you can see from my recipe on page 86. If you are a vegetarian, however, and have a terrible yen for chili con carne, this thick, dark, rich substitute is not only very satisfying, it is low in fat, high in protein, very high in complex carbohydrates, and entirely vegetarian. Of all the brands of canned beans I tried for this recipe, Goya pintos and black beans kept their textures the best when simmered.

1 cup dried green lentils, well washed and picked over

1 bay leaf

2 dried *ristra* peppers (see page 142), stemmed, seeded, and torn in half, lengthwise

1 medium-size eggplant, peeled and cut into $1/2$-inch cubes

$1^1/2$ tablespoons coarse salt

6 tablespoons vegetable oil

2 medium-size white onions, coarsely chopped

$1/2$ medium-size green bell pepper, coarsely chopped

1 garlic head, cut crosswise just above the root to expose the ends of the cloves, root section discarded, sheath housing the cloves left intact

2 tablespoons chili powder

$1/2$ teaspoon hot paprika (more, if you like your chili very spicy)

1 teaspoon ground cumin

1 teaspoon finely crumbled dried oregano leaves

$1/4$ teaspoon ground nutmeg

One $14^1/2$-ounce can chunky tomatoes, with their juice

One 16-ounce can pinto beans, with their juice

One 16-ounce can black beans, with their juice

Salt

1. Place the lentils, bay leaf, and peppers in a large heavy-bottomed kettle with 6 cups of cold water. Bring to a rolling boil; boil for 5 minutes, then reduce the heat to very low and simmer gently for 1 hour,

taking care to keep the lentils covered by adding a little hot water from time to time.

2. Meanwhile, toss the eggplant cubes with the salt. Place them in a colander in the sink with a small weighted plate on top, and allow them to leach for 20 minutes. Rinse them well in cold water, squeeze out the water by hand, and pat them dry with paper towels.

3. Heat the oil in a large heavy-bottomed frying pan and brown the eggplant cubes. Remove them with a slotted spoon and set them aside on absorbent paper. Discard or reserve for another use all but 2 tablespoons of the oil.

4. Gently sauté the onions, bell pepper, and garlic head until the onion and pepper have wilted.

5. Remove the pieces of *ristra* pepper from the lentils. Scrape the softened red pulp from the skins and add it to the *soffritto*, discarding the skins. Stir the *ristra* pulp into the *soffritto* with the chili powder, paprika, cumin, oregano, nutmeg, and the tomatoes and their juice, and bring to a boil.

6. Empty the contents of the frying pan into the lentils and stir together. Add the pinto beans and their juice, the black beans and theirs, and the browned eggplant cubes. Add warm water to cover and simmer gently for $1/2$ hour. From time to time, scrape the bottom of the kettle with a wooden spatula to prevent the chili from scorching, but do not stir more than necessary.

7. Salt to taste, and serve in deep bowls. Don't discard the braised garlic head. At my house we vie for it; we love picking it apart and savoring the tightly bound cloves.

NOTE: Veteran Texas chili con carne aficionados traditionally "hot up" their chili with Tabasco sauce, and they prefer eating it with saltines, not bread or corn tortillas. I usually make the following salsa cruda for those who prefer it to the bottled hot sauce.

Salsa Cruda

MAKES ABOUT 1 CUP

*T*his is a simple, fresh, crunchy hot sauce that is excellent for giving almost any stew an added zest. It is an easy but distinctive dip for corn chips and a wonderfully fresh-tasting kicker for a Bloody Mary.

2 medium-size firm ripe red
  tomatoes, seeded and finely
  chopped
1 medium-size white onion,
  peeled and finely minced
3 fresh serranos or 1 fresh
  jalapeño pepper, stemmed,
  seeded, and finely minced

12 cilantro leaves, finely chopped
$^{1}/_{8}$ teaspoon sugar
1 teaspoon freshly squeezed lime
  juice (optional)
Salt

1. Combine all of the ingredients in a ceramic or glass bowl and mix well.
2. Cover the bowl and refrigerate for 3 to 6 hours.
3. Stir well and serve.

NOTE: This sauce is at its best after 6 hours of refrigeration, but it starts to fade quickly thereafter. Leftover sauce should be discarded.

Texas Pinto Beans

SERVES 6

Despite the popular commercial success of pinto beans stewed with tomato, onion, garlic, salt pork, chili peppers, and various spices and herbs, sold under such names as ranch-style, cowboy, ranch-house, chili beans, and the like, anyone who knows beans about beans, as the old saying goes, recognizes that pintos are at their best—and at their least windy—when cooked the ancient Mexican way, with nothing but water and, if available, a pinch of epazote, a dried herb (Chenopodium ambrosioides) available in Mexican groceries. Whatever sauces and flavorings the diner may prefer should be added after the beans are thoroughly cooked. If you taste pintos simmered slowly this simple way, you will have to agree that their natural meaty savor is far superior without the heavy flavorings.

2 cups dried pinto beans, washed and carefully picked over
1/2 teaspoon dried epazote (optional)
1 teaspoon sugar (optional)

1 small clove garlic, peeled
1/4 cup melted lard, dripping, or vegetable oil
Salt

1. Place the beans in a large flameproof *cazuela* or heavy-bottomed kettle with 8 cups of cold water and very gently bring them to a rolling boil. Let the beans boil for 2 minutes, then turn off the heat and let them sit for 1 hour.
2. Drain and rinse the beans, then return them to the kettle. Add the epazote, sugar, garlic, and 8 cups of warm water. Simmer the beans very gently for 3 hours, or until the beans are creamy and soft but the majority of the skins still unbroken. Add hot water as necessary; the beans should always be slightly covered with liquid while cooking. Dried beans catch and burn very easily, so check them from time to time.
3. Stir in the fat gently with a wooden spoon, salt to taste, and serve warm.

NOTES: Pintos cooked this way were the daily staple of early settlers in the West. They loved eating the beans with chopped raw onion, pepper sauce, and freshly baked corn bread. It was customary to add a hunk of salt pork during the last hour of simmering, to be divided up at serving time.

It is standard practice to make refried beans from these pintos. Here's how: In a large heavy-bottomed skillet, fry 1 tablespoon of finely chopped onion in 3 tablespoons of lard or dripping for a few seconds, then add the cooked beans and their juice. When the juice is bubbling, crush the beans against the bottom and sides of the skillet with a pestle or potato masher until they are smoothly puréed. Stop cooking the purée when it has reached the desired texture, some like it loose, some very dense. Remove the skillet from the heat, salt to taste, and serve warm. This dish requires a certain amount of fat, otherwise the consistency will be chalky and the beans will quickly lose their fresh taste.

Hopping John

SERVES 6

In South Carolina it is believed that if you eat hopping John on New Year's Day—some say before noon—you will have good luck in the coming year. No one really knows why this old Southern favorite of black-eyed peas and rice, flavored with a ham bone and spiced with hot red pepper, is called hopping John, though amusing explanations abound. What we know for sure is that the black-eyed pea, which is not a pea at all but a cousin of the Asiatic mung bean, came to the Gullah low country of South Carolina with Nigerian slaves. Rice, another Asian import, arrived a little later, but it was quickly discovered that rice and beans were a perfect combination, and rice-and-bean stews became a standard item of regional cooking throughout the South, the Caribbean, and both Central and South America. Those stews have endured. An unorthodox vegetarian hopping John can be made by substituting vegetable bouillon cubes for the ham bone and adding a little olive oil. I find it a little short of soul food, but it's very good.

1 pound black-eyed peas
1 medium-size yellow onion, coarsely chopped
$^1/_2$ medium-size green bell pepper, coarsely chopped
1 ham bone, or $^1/_2$ pound piece smoked bacon, rind left intact, the bacon sliced through at $^1/_4$-inch intervals to the rind, widthwise

$^1/_4$ teaspoon red pepper flakes (more, if you prefer your hopping John very spicy)
1 cup long-grain rice
Salt

1. Pick over the black-eyed peas well and rinse them in a colander using cold running water.
2. Put the rinsed peas with three times their volume of cold water in a large heavy-bottomed kettle. Heat slowly and maintain at a rolling boil for 2 minutes. Turn off the heat and let the peas plump for 1 hour.
3. Add the onion, green pepper, ham bone, pepper flakes, and more cold water to cover. Simmer gently for 40 minutes, or until the peas are tender but still firm. Keep replenishing the kettle with hot water, since the peas will absorb a lot. Stir as little as possible.

4. Add the rice, mixing it in well. Continue simmering for 15 minutes, then remove from the heat, cover, and let the rice puff for 3 minutes.
5. Remove and cut up whatever ham is attached to the ham bone, or, if you used bacon, slice through the rind, and return the meat to the kettle. Serve the hopping John right from the kettle in which it was cooked.

NOTE: Stewed collard greens (recipe follows) and an iron skillet of golden-crusted, hot-from-the-oven corn bread are the perfect accompaniments to this grandfather of all soul-food stews. A bowl of coarsely chopped, salted, rinsed, and drained raw onion and a bottle of pickled peppers or Tabasco sauce should be provided for those who favor them. Plenty of sweet butter should be on hand for the hot cornbread. Buttermilk, sweet milk, or iced tea are commonly drunk with this meal, but cold beer is also a good soul-food mate.

Stewed Collard Greens

S tewed field greens are one of the joys of country cooking, whether they are prepared in the soul-food manner of this recipe, in an Italian-style minestra, or a Greek-style *horta*, and the iron-loaded, fibrous greens are so good for us. This recipe specifies collards, but turnip, mustard, kale, beet, or a mixture of greens may be substituted.

3 large bunches young collard greens (about 3 pounds)
1 tablespoon coarse salt
1 pound streaky salt pork, rind removed, cut into 1/2-inch cubes (an equal amount of cubed leftover ham may be substituted)

1 tablespoon cider vinegar
1 teaspoon sugar
1 medium-size yellow onion, coarsely chopped
2 medium-size potatoes, peeled and cut into 1-inch cubes
Salt

1. Put the collards in the sink, sprinkle them with the coarse salt, cover with cold water, and let them soak for 10 minutes. Give the leaves a good washing in the salted water. Drain away the salted water and rinse the greens well, leaf by leaf, under cold running water, discarding any that are blighted. With a sharp paring knife, cut away and discard any tough stems. Shake the leaves and let them drain.
2. In a large heavy-bottomed kettle or Dutch oven, brown the pork cubes. Remove the cubes with a slotted spoon and set them aside. Discard the fat. Deglaze the kettle with 2 cups of water. Add the vinegar, sugar, onion, potatoes, and the pork cubes. Layer the greens on top. Cover the kettle tightly and simmer gently for 1 hour.
3. Salt to taste and either serve in the kettle itself or in a large bowl that will accommodate the greens, potatoes, pork cubes, and the pot liquor.

NOTE: Provide a bottle of pickled hot peppers, a bottle of Tabasco sauce, or both. Crusty, freshly baked corn bread to crumble into the pot liquor is de rigueur.

Stewed Yellow Squash

SERVES 6

Thisʰⁱˢ simple stew is a summer treasure, so tasty that in high summer, when yellow squash is abundant, I make it several times a week. Because it is so savory and luscious, children love it for supper; because it is so light and digestible, their grandparents do, too!

2 slices lean breakfast bacon,
  finely chopped
3 medium-size white onions,
  thinly sliced
6 medium-size yellow squash,
  sliced into ¹/₄-inch rounds

Pinch ground sage (optional)
¹/₈ teaspoon dried thyme leaves
  (optional)
Salt and black pepper

1. In a medium-size heavy-bottomed braising pan, gently heat the chopped bacon until it begins to render its fat. Add the onions, tossing them well with the fat and the bacon bits. Add the squash and toss well again. Nothing should be allowed to brown.
2. Add the sage, thyme, and ¹/₂ cup of cold water. Cover the pan tightly and simmer for 20 minutes, or until the squash is tender.
3. Salt and pepper to taste and serve hot.

NOTE: As children, we were quite happy to make our supper of large bowls of this stew, huge slices of bread and butter, and glasses of cold milk.

Sweet-and-Sour Tomato Stew

SERVES 4

This dish was brought to Texas from the East Coast by the earliest Anglo settlers, who called it " 'mater puddin'." During the Depression years it acquired the title "poor folks' stew." My mother used to prepare it on Wednesdays or Fridays during Lenten season. Back in those pre–Vatican II days, it was a "make-do dish" for a day of fast and abstinence, but as children we loved its sweet-and-sour taste and looked forward to it. My mother's version, nearer the original, was made with white bread only. My version uses both white and pumpernickel for better flavor, color, and texture. Traditionally, this dish was made with canned tomatoes, but you may substitute fresh ripe tomatoes. I was delighted to discover recently that this dish is known from Maine to the West Coast.

2 tablespoons vegetable oil

1 medium-size yellow onion, finely chopped

1 rib celery, finely chopped

1 plump clove garlic, finely chopped

$^1/_8$ teaspoon freshly ground black pepper

$^1/_8$ teaspoon ground sage

1 tablespoon brown sugar

One $14^1/_2$ ounce can whole peeled tomatoes, chopped, with their juice

2 slices white sandwich bread, crusts removed, cut into $^1/_2$-inch cubes (about $^1/_2$ cup)

2 slices dark pumpernickel bread, crusts removed, cut into $^1/_2$-inch cubes (about $^1/_2$ cup)

Salt

2 tablespoons finely chopped flat-leaf parsley

1. Heat the oil in a large, deep, heavy-bottomed skillet. Add the onions, celery, garlic, pepper, sage, and sugar, and sauté until the onions have almost melted (about 7 minutes), stirring continuously with a wooden spatula.

2. Add 1 cup of warm water and deglaze the pan. Add the tomatoes and simmer gently for 20 minutes.

3. Fold in the bread cubes and simmer gently for 10 minutes, stirring occasionally. The bread thickens the stew and must be scraped from the bottom occasionally or it will catch and scorch.

4. Salt to taste, sprinkle with parsley, and serve hot.

NOTE: Although this dish, accompanied by bread and butter and a glass of milk, was our Lenten collation years ago, today I find it too meager as a main course. It is a very good side dish, however, with grilled pork chops, roast pork, or baked ham.

Creole Peanut Soup

SERVES 6

There are many creole recipes for peanut or groundnut soup. They abound throughout the South and the Caribbean Islands. Many have been so "bridge-clubbed" that they are bland travesties of their former selves, but this one seems nearer its African origin than most; it has a distinctive, earthy flavor, and it is delightfully spicy.

3 tablespoons unsalted butter

2 tablespoons vegetable oil

2 medium-size scallions, white parts only, finely chopped

1 small clove garlic, finely minced

1 medium-size carrot, peeled, quartered, and thinly sliced

1 medium-size yellow squash, quartered and thinly sliced

1 small green or red bell pepper, finely chopped

1/2 cup finely grated white cabbage

1 medium-size white turnip, finely grated

5 cups unsalted or low-sodium chicken stock

3 tablespoons flour

1/4 teaspoon ground hot paprika or ground cayenne

1/2 teaspoon ground *quatre épices* (see Notes)

1 cup creamy peanut butter

1 large bay leaf

1 tablespoon cane syrup or honey

6 dried shrimp tails (optional), all bits of shells removed, finely ground or pounded (see Notes)

1/4 cup half-and-half

1 tablespoon Angostura bitters

Salt

1/2 cup oven-toasted croutons

1. In a large heavy-bottomed kettle, heat the butter and oil until sizzling and gently sauté the scallions, garlic, carrots, squash, bell pepper, cabbage, and turnips, raking them back and forth with a wooden spatula, until they are transparent. (This should take about 10 minutes.)
2. Meanwhile, heat the stock to the boiling point.
3. Add to the vegetables the flour, paprika, and *quatre épices* and sauté for 4 minutes.
4. Stir in the hot stock, a little at a time, until uniformly mixed. Simmer very gently for 10 minutes.

5. Stir in the peanut butter, using a whisk, if necessary. Add the bay leaf, syrup, and ground shrimp tails. Simmer gently for 20 minutes, scraping the bottom of the kettle frequently to prevent scorching.
6. Remove from the heat. Fold in the half-and-half and Angostura bitters, and salt to taste.
7. Serve hot in shallow soup plates, garnished with a few croutons.

NOTES: The exquisite combination of spices known as *quatre épices* can be found in food specialty shops under the brand name Select Origins. A good substitute is McCormick Chinese Five Spice.

The tiny salt-dried shrimp are sold in small cellophane packages in most Latino groceries.

This is excellent chilled and served cold. Garnish it with dollops of unsweetened whipped cream, sprinkled with finely snipped fresh chives.

Hearty Lentil Stew

SERVES 6

*L*entils have been a staple for ten thousand years—at least a thousand years longer than any other legume. They are cheap, available, rich in protein and carbohydrates, and low in fat, which makes them even more nutritious than soybeans. In France this old country recipe is called bonne femme, which in French approximates down-home or homemade in our kitchenese.

1¹/₂ cups brown lentils, carefully picked over

2 medium-size carrots, peeled, quartered, and thinly sliced

3 tablespoons unsalted butter

¹/₂ cup streaky salt pork, coarsely chopped

1 small white onion, coarsely chopped

3 plump cloves garlic, finely chopped

1 medium-size sweet Italian frying pepper, finely chopped

3 tablespoons flour

1 cup unsalted chicken stock

1 medium-size ripe red tomato, skinned, seeded, and coarsely chopped

¹/₄ teaspoon each finely crumbled dried thyme and sage

¹/₄ teaspoon ground cumin

¹/₄ teaspoon freshly ground black pepper

Salt

1. Wash the lentils well and put them in a large heavy-bottomed kettle with the carrots and 8 cups of cold water. Bring the water to a rolling boil. Boil for 2 minutes, then reduce the heat to very low and gently simmer the lentils until tender, about 45 minutes.

2. Meanwhile, in a heavy-bottomed skillet, heat the butter and slowly sauté the pork, onion, garlic, and frying pepper until they are transparent. Stir in the flour until it is absorbed, then add the stock and stir with a wooden spatula until the mixture is smooth and thick, like heavy cream.

3. Stir this thickened *mirepoix* into the lentils, then mix in the tomato, thyme, sage, cumin, and black pepper. Simmer gently for 20 minutes, scraping up the bottom occasionally to make sure it doesn't scorch, and adding warm water when necessary.

4. Salt the stew to taste. If there is time, let the stew sit for as long as an hour, then gently heat it again. Serve in deep soup bowls. Provide cruets of your best red wine vinegar and best olive oil for those diners who, according to custom, like to add them to their stew.

NOTE: In the area around Foix in the Pyrenees, this stew is often garnished with a mixture of fried croutons and browned julienned onions. However, I find the stew already very substantial, and quite satisfying without those embellishments.

Green Lima and Noodle Stew

I was introduced to this bean stew as a child when I was taken one summer by friends to visit their childhood home in the piney woods near Evans, Georgia, where we spent the entire summer. The food was entirely different from any I had known at home. The grandmother in the family produced this dish often for us, using fresh green limas from her garden. Now, almost half a century later, I have no way of finding out how she came by that recipe, the only one like it I have encountered in Southern cooking. Years later, when my Italian friends made pasta e fagioli for me, I found myself thinking of Granny Martin's stew.

3 cups freshly shelled baby lima beans, or two 10-ounce packages thawed frozen green baby lima beans

$^1/_2$ cup coarsely chopped streaky salt pork

3 medium-size scallions, white parts only, coarsely chopped

2 cups flour, plus extra flour for kneading

2 large eggs

$^1/_2$ teaspoon coarse salt

$^1/_4$ teaspoon freshly ground white pepper

$^1/_4$ teaspoon freshly grated nutmeg

1 teaspoon vegetable oil

3 tablespoons unsalted butter or olive oil

$^1/_4$ cup half-and-half (optional)

Salt

1. In a large heavy-bottomed kettle, bring 4 cups of water to a rolling boil. Add the beans, salt pork, and scallions. Reduce the heat and simmer, covered, for 20 minutes.

2. Meanwhile, place 2 cups of the flour in a mound on a clean, hard work surface. Make a crater in the center and place the eggs, salt, pepper, nutmeg, and oil in it. Combine the ingredients little by little, using your fingertips. Add flour if needed to make a very dense, kneadable dough. Knead vigorously for 5 minutes, then roll the dough into a ball, wrap it in plastic wrap, and place the bundle in the freezer for 15 minutes.

3. Remove the dough, unwrap it, and grate it into rivels (tiny dumplings), using the coarsest side of a box grater. If you don't have a box grater, make the rivels by pinching off tiny bits of the dough. Keep them small. Spread the rivels on a clean tea towel and allow them to dry a little.

4. When the lima beans are tender, sprinkle in the rivels, a handful at a time, stirring them in with a wooden spatula. Simmer, covered, for about 10 minutes, or until the rivels are cooked through.
5. Remove the kettle from the heat. Fold in the butter and the cream, and salt to taste. Let the stew sit, covered, for 5 minutes.
6. Serve hot in soup plates.

NOTE: Granny Martin served oversized, fresh-from-the-oven buttermilk biscuits with this stew. If you want another dish to accompany this one, Stewed Collard Greens (see page 263) are just the ticket, and you can never go wrong with a platter of sliced, sun-ripened tomatoes alongside.

Greek Lima Bean Stew

*I*f you like beans, this old Ionian recipe will surely please you. This dish is sometimes made in Greece with fava beans, which, I suspect, were the basis of the original version of this recipe, since broad beans were eaten around the Mediterranean centuries before the lima arrived. I must admit, however, that I prefer this dish made with giant limas. When shopping for giant limas for this recipe, buy only those beans that have shiny, unbroken skins. If the majority of the skins are split, it means the limas are more than a year old and will shed their skins and cook to pieces. If you were making a puréed soup that would be fine, but not for this dish.

2 1/2 cups (1 1/8 pounds) dried shelled giant lima beans, carefully picked over and well washed

3 tablespoons olive oil

1 large yellow onion, peeled, halved, and thinly sliced

1 medium-size carrot, peeled, quartered, and thinly sliced

1 small bulb sweet fennel, cut into six pieces lengthwise

1 rib celery, finely chopped

2 plump cloves garlic, finely minced

1/2 teaspoon red pepper flakes

1 bay leaf

2 tablespoons tomato paste

1/2 teaspoon sugar

Salt

1. Place the beans in a large heavy-bottomed kettle with 6 cups of cold water. Heat the beans to the boiling point, boil them for 2 minutes, then turn off the heat and let them soak for 1 hour.

2. Meanwhile, heat the olive oil in a large heavy-bottomed skillet and sauté the onion, carrot, fennel, celery, and garlic for 7 minutes, tossing them continuously with a wooden spatula. Remove the pan from the heat and set aside.

3. Rinse the beans well and return them to the kettle with 6 cups of cold water, the sautéed vegetables, the pepper flakes, and the bay leaf. Simmer very gently for 1 1/4 hours. Maintain the liquid at about 2 cups, replenishing it with hot water. The stew should be juicy but not soupy.

4. Dilute the tomato paste in 1 cup of hot water. Add the sugar, stir the mixture into the stew, and simmer again for 15 minutes.
5. Test the beans. They should be done but not mushy. If necessary, simmer them longer.
6. Salt the stew to taste, and serve at once.

NOTE: It is customary to provide very good olive oil and red wine vinegar as condiments for these beans. Most of the Greeks I know like these beans well anointed. A *choriatikí* salad of tender inner leaves of romaine, quartered tomatoes, sliced raw sweet onion, rings of bell pepper, feta sprinkled with dried oregano leaves, and oil-cured black Greek olives is the typical accompanying dish. The salad is usually placed in the center of the table so that the diners may spear what they want from it with their own forks. Of course, a few loaves of fine-textured, white Greek bread would be in keeping, too, if you can find them locally; otherwise, Italian loaves are a good substitute.

Middle Eastern Okra Stew

SERVES 6

I t is believed that okra originated in India and was taken to the Middle East and Africa by traders. Much later, it was brought to the New World by African slaves. Until recently, except for pockets of immigrants from India and the Near East, the consumption of okra in the States was confined to the South. When I was growing up in Texas, okra—called "okree" by old-timers—was a much-appreciated summer vegetable in the cooking of the region. It was usually fried in cornmeal or stewed with tomatoes, onions, and yellow squash. Here is an okra stew, much like the ones I knew at home, which I discovered and enjoyed in Greece. It makes a very interesting addition to a vegetarian diet, but it is useful, too, as a delicious and unusual accompaniment for meat and fish dishes.

2 pounds fresh young okra pods, the tinier the better (see Note)

3 tablespoons freshly squeezed lemon juice

3 tablespoons unsalted butter

2 tablespoons finely chopped fresh mint leaves

2 medium-size yellow onions, coarsely chopped

3 medium-size ripe red tomatoes, skinned, seeded, and coarsely chopped

1 tablespoon finely chopped flat-leaf parsley

1 tablespoon finely chopped fresh dill

$1/4$ teaspoon freshly ground black pepper

1 cup unsalted vegetable stock, or 1 vegetable bouillon cube dissolved in 1 cup boiling water

$1/2$ cup short-grain rice, washed and drained

Salt

1. Wash the okra pods. With a sharp paring knife, cut off the stem of each pod without perforating the pods themselves. Soak them for 30 minutes in 4 cups of water acidulated with the lemon juice.
2. In a large heavy-bottomed kettle, heat the butter gently and sauté the mint and onions until the onions are transparent. Add the tomatoes, parsley, dill, and pepper, stirring them about for about 10 minutes, until the *soffritto* is reduced to a paste.
3. Drain the okra pods, saving 1 cup of the acidulated water. Add the pods, 1 cup of acidulated water, and the 1 cup of stock to the mix-

ture in the kettle. Stir well and simmer, covered, over low heat for 45 minutes.

4. Stir in the rice. There should still be enough liquid in the kettle to cover the solids. If not, add a little hot water. Simmer, covered, for 12 minutes, or until the rice is tender.

5. Salt to taste and serve warm.

NOTE: If fresh okra is not available, substitute two packages of thawed frozen whole okra pods, but reduce the simmering time to 30 minutes. There is a new (to me) burgundy okra on the market. It is deep purple and a little crispier than the bright green types. I have tried it and recommend it. If you use it, add 15 minutes to the simmering time.

Turkish Stuffed Eggplant

SERVES 6

K*nown as* imam bayildi, *this is one of the best-loved dishes in the Middle Eastern repertoire. It requires considerable attention, but it sounds more difficult than it is. I can assure you that if you care enough to make it, lovers of Middle Eastern food will appear out of the woodwork to beg you to make it for them. In the best* imam bayildi, *the eggplant becomes almost transparent, honeylike, and ready to melt in your mouth. We are told that the title means "the Muslim priest fainted," though no one seems to know whether he swooned from sheer delight on tasting the dish or from learning how much oil his wife had used in preparing it.*

6 plump Japanese eggplants, as uniform in size as possible

2 tablespoons coarse salt

2 medium-size yellow onions, coarsely chopped

$^1/_2$ cup light olive oil

6 medium-size ripe red tomatoes, 3 skinned, seeded, and finely chopped, 3 sliced $^1/_2$ inch thick

9 plump cloves garlic, peeled, 3 finely crushed, 6 left whole

2 teaspoons sugar

2 tablespoons finely chopped flat-leaf parsley

$^1/_2$ cup soft white bread crumbs

3 tablespoons freshly squeezed lemon juice

$^1/_4$ teaspoon freshly ground black pepper

$^1/_2$ teaspoon fennel seeds

3 tablespoons dry red wine

1. Stem the eggplants without puncturing the skin around the stems. With a potato peeler, remove four $^1/_2$-inch-wide strips of skin down the length of each eggplant. Leave $^1/_2$ inch of the skin on each end intact so that the eggplants do not disintegrate or collapse during braising. With a sharp paring knife, make a deep incision down the center of each of these peeled areas. The objective is to be able to force a little stuffing into the incisions without tearing the eggplants. At this point, force salt into each of the slits; salt the peeled areas as well. (Use the entire 2 tablespoons of salt.) Put the eggplants aside and let them leach for at least $^1/_2$ hour.

2. Put the chopped onion in a small saucepan with 1 cup of water and boil rapidly for 3 minutes. Drain the onion and set aside.

3. Rinse the salt out of the eggplants with warm running water, squeeze them out gently, and blot them dry with paper towels. Force some of the onion into the incisions.

4. In a large heavy-bottomed kettle or braising pan, heat the oil and sauté the eggplants for 5 minutes, turning each one several times. Remove them and let them cool enough to handle.

5. Mix the chopped tomatoes, the remaining onion, the crushed garlic, the sugar, and the parsley together and force some of the mixture into each of the incisions. Arrange the eggplants neatly and snugly in a single layer in the oil left in the braising pan. Drape a slice of tomato over the middle of each eggplant. Place a little of the remaining stuffing on each slice of tomato. If any stuffing is left over, scatter it over the eggplants. Sprinkle the tomato slices with the bread crumbs, lemon juice, pepper, and fennel seeds, and place 1 of the whole cloves of garlic on each. Mix the wine with 1 cup of warm water and pour the mixture into the oil. Simmer, covered, over the lowest possible heat for 1 hour, or until the eggplants are very tender. If the pan juices have not reduced to a few spoonfuls, remove the cover, increase the heat, and reduce them.

6. Allow the eggplants to cool in the kettle. Using a spoon and a spatula, carefully remove the eggplants to a nonreactive dish that will hold them all. Taste the pan juices that have accumulated in cooling and adjust the taste with salt, sugar, and lemon juice, if necessary. Pour the juices over the eggplants. Cover and refrigerate.

NOTE: *Imam bayildi* keeps very well for a week if refrigerated. A very small amount of finely grated fresh orange peel and a few leaves of fresh mint are complementary garnishes for this marvelous dish. Remember that the dish is considered a splendid *mese*, or hors d'oeuvre, but is never eaten as a main course.

Tunisian Stew with Scrambled Eggs

SERVES 6

V ersions of this dish, known as chekchouka (chek CHOO kah), abound in North Africa, but this Tunisian one, to my mind, is the best of the lot—the most complex and exciting. Those who already love Mexican ranch-style eggs won't find it hard to love this dish. Neither will vegetarians.

¹/₄ cup light olive oil

2 medium-size white onions, coarsely grated

2 plump cloves garlic, finely chopped

2 medium-size frying peppers (Anaheims or Italian frying peppers) cut into 1-inch squares

3 medium-size ripe red tomatoes, skinned, seeded, and coarsely chopped

¹/₈ teaspoon *each* ground cinnamon, cardamom, cloves, nutmeg, and cayenne

¹/₄ teaspoon finely grated orange peel

One 10-ounce package frozen green beans, thawed

One 9-ounce package frozen artichoke hearts, thawed

1 cup dry white wine

6 large eggs

2 tablespoons finely chopped cilantro leaves

1. In a deep heavy-bottomed braising pan, heat the oil and sauté the onion, garlic, and frying peppers until limp, stirring them frequently with a wooden spatula.

2. Add the tomatoes, spices, orange peel, green beans, and artichoke hearts and toss thoroughly. Add the wine and ¹/₂ cup of warm water. Stir the liquid into the stew without letting the vegetables disintegrate.

3. Place two sheets of aluminum foil over the top of the pan and force the lid down on them to seal in the stew. Lower the heat and cook the stew very gently for ¹/₂ hour.

4. Salt to taste.

5. Beat the eggs with 6 tablespoons of cold water and stir them into the stew. Turn off the heat, cover the pan tightly, and let it sit for 5 minutes.

6. Turn out onto a large, warm serving platter. Sprinkle with the chopped cilantro and serve at once.

NOTE: This is a substantial main course for a good lunch. Serve with plain or saffron rice and a green salad, all of which can be accommodated on large dinner plates and eaten at the same time. Toasted pita bread and plenty of Salsa Cruda (see page 258) complete the meal. What to drink? The North Africans would say buttermilk. I suggest iced tea or, if the weather is cold, hot herbal tea. If your guests insist on alcohol, beer goes better with North African food than wine.

Potato, Leek, and Cabbage Stew

SERVES 4

Here is a one-pot Flemish prescription for resisting the rigors of bone-cold, dank winter days in the Low Countries—or anywhere else. This is hefty country fare, but tasty and consoling, the kind of food our hardworking ancestors used to look forward to after a long day of heavy outdoor work. Serve it steaming as a main course. Follow it with a salad of mixed greens, a generous cut of aged Gouda, a choice of fresh apples, and, of course, good light rye bread, and you have a completely Flemish supper. Light beer or cider are appropriate beverages to wash down all this country food and lighten your spirits in the process. I have had this stew in Amsterdam, sprinkled liberally with crisped bacon bits. You may want to try it that way. As it stands here, however, it makes a very good vegetarian dish.

8 tablespoons (1 stick) unsalted butter, melted

5 medium-size yellow potatoes, peeled and cut into $^1/_8$-inch rounds

3 medium-size leeks, white parts only, split, well washed, and thinly sliced

1 medium-size head white cabbage, cored and finely shredded

$^1/_4$ teaspoon freshly ground black pepper

$^1/_2$ teaspoon coarse salt

$^1/_8$ teaspoon freshly grated nutmeg

$1^1/_2$ cups low-fat milk

$^1/_4$ cup fresh oven-toasted bread crumbs

1. Dip a pastry brush in the melted butter and lightly coat the bottom and sides of a medium-size heavy-bottomed kettle.
2. Layer in the potatoes, leeks, and cabbage consecutively. Brush each round of potato with melted butter, and sprinkle each of the layers with a little pepper, salt, and nutmeg.
3. When all the vegetables have been layered in, add the rest of the butter and pour in the milk down one side. Seal the kettle with two thicknesses of aluminum foil and press the lid down tightly on them to seal in the stew.
4. Cook the stew for 45 minutes over the lowest possible heat. Break the seal and test the doneness of the vegetables. If they are still too

raw and tough, reseal and cook for another 10 minutes. The Dutch often cook this stew for more than an hour, but I prefer the vegetables crisp and distinguishable. Cooking them longer reduces them to a mush; however, by all means, suit yourself.

5. With a wooden spatula, toss the layers together and transfer the stew to a large warmed bowl. Sprinkle with the bread crumbs and serve hot.

NOTE: It is customary to serve a large pitcher of fresh milk with this dish so that those who care to may souse it to their liking—a standard rural practice with certain stews and soups all over Western Europe. Children seem to love adding milk to the stew.

Polish Vegetable and Barley Stew

SERVES 6

This is a fast-day version of the famous Polish stew called Krupnik. *More elaborate versions often contain everything from beef bones to chicken giblets. I chose this version for my vegetarian friends.* Krupnik *belongs to the vast family of gruel soups that were the main source of everyday nourishment on farms all over Europe during the Middle Ages. This version is hearty enough for almost anyone, but I recommend it highly for both young and old who may be convalescing and must give their stomachs a rest. It is wonderfully easy to digest.*

1 ounce dried Polish mushrooms or porcini

1 medium-size yellow onion, finely chopped

1 medium-size carrot, peeled, quartered, and thinly sliced

1 cup topped and tailed, very finely sliced green beans

$^1/_2$ cup freshly shelled green peas or thawed frozen green peas

1 tablespoon unsalted butter

$^1/_2$ cup pearl barley

3 medium-size yellow potatoes, peeled and cut into $^1/_2$-inch dice

Salt and freshly ground black pepper

1 cup sour cream

2 tablespoons finely chopped fresh dill

1. Soak the dried mushrooms in 2 cups of boiling water for 30 minutes. Remove them with a slotted spoon and rinse them briefly in a sieve under warm running water. Pat them dry with paper towels and chop them coarsely.

2. Filter the soaking water through a sieve lined with three thickenesses of dampened cheesecloth to remove any sand. Put the filtered water, mushrooms, chopped onion, carrot, green beans, and peas in a large heavy-bottomed kettle with 8 cups of cold water. Bring to a rolling boil, then reduce the heat and simmer for 20 minutes.

3. Meanwhile, heat the butter in a skillet and sauté the barley for 2 minutes, stirring it with a wooden spatula to make certain all the grains are coated and shiny. Do not allow the barley to brown.

4. Add the barley and potatoes to the kettle and continue to simmer for 45 minutes, or until the barley is tender. The stew risks nothing by longer simmering.

5. Salt and pepper the stew to taste and serve hot in large deep bowls with a generous dollop of sour cream and a sprinkling of finely chopped dill. Polish rye bread, both light and dark, spread with sweet butter, make good accompaniments.

NOTE: If there is any leftover stew, next day add water or milk, a few chopped scallions, and some chopped fresh mushrooms, and simmer gently until the scallions and mushrooms are tender.

Venetian Rice and Green Peas

SERVES 4

*I*f you are looking for a delicious, comforting, light, quickly prepared dish for supper after a hectic day at work and don't want to exasperate yourself with culinary complications, this may be the perfect choice. It is a famous Venetian dish whose name (risi e bisi) literally means rice and green peas—but it's so much more!

4 tablespoons (¹/₂ stick) unsalted
   butter
2 tablespoons light olive oil
3 thin slices prosciutto, finely
   chopped (¹/₄ cup finely cubed
   leftover ham may be
   substituted)
3 medium-size scallions, white
   parts only, coarsely chopped
¹/₄ teaspoon dried sage leaves,
   finely crumbled
2¹/₂ cups freshly shelled tender
   young green English peas, or
   two 10-ounce packages thawed
   frozen green peas

4 cups unsalted, defatted chicken
   stock or two 13¹/₂-ounce cans
   low-sodium chicken broth,
   defatted
2 cups short-grain rice
2 tablespoons finely chopped
   flat-leaf parsley
3 tablespoons freshly grated
   Parmesan cheese
Salt and freshly ground white
   pepper

1. In a medium-size heavy-bottomed kettle or braising pan, heat 2 table-spoons of the butter and all the oil and gently sauté the prosciutto, scallions, and sage until the prosciutto begins to crisp but not brown.
2. Add the peas and toss them in well. Add 1 cup of the stock, bring it to a rolling boil, and deglaze the pan.
3. Add another cup of the stock, stir in the rice, and simmer for 10 minutes.
4. Add the remaining 2 cups of stock without stirring the stew, and continue simmering for 5 or 10 minutes, or until the rice and peas are tender and most of the liquid has been absorbed or has evaporated. The dish, as served in Venice, is never soupy.

5. Remove the pan from the heat. Add the remaining 2 tablespoons of butter, the chopped parsley, and the Parmesan, and toss well.
6. Salt and pepper to taste and serve at once.

NOTE: For an unorthodox but excellent version of this dish, substitute one 10-ounce package of thawed frozen artichoke hearts for half the amount of green peas. By all means provide extra freshly grated Parmesan at the table for the diners who desire it.

Fruit Stew with Custard Topping

*T*his rough country dish—or some version of it—probably dates back to the
Middle Ages. It can be eaten for dessert, if you like, though it is eaten
more often as the main dish for supper at many farms in the Auvergne. It is one
of those substantial dishes so beloved in the Massif Central of France, where
hardworking farm folk have stout appetites. I like to serve the dish as a dessert in
late summer or early fall, using whatever fruit is in season. It is neither a cobbler
nor a cottage pudding, but it may remind you of both. To my mind it is better
than either.

4 large tart apples, peeled, cored, and quartered

6 medium-size Bosc pears, peeled, cored, and quartered

8 pitted prunes, soaked for $^1/_2$ hour in warm water and drained

$^1/_4$ cup golden raisins, soaked for $^1/_2$ hour in warm water and drained

$1^1/_2$ cups sugar

2 cups dry red wine

Peel of 1 lemon, in a single spiral

1 tablespoon vanilla extract

8 tablespoons (1 stick) unsalted butter

$^1/_4$ cup flour

3 eggs

$^1/_4$ cup low-fat milk

1. Put all the fruit in a large, heavy-bottomed, ovenproof kettle. (I use a black cast-iron Dutch oven.) Sprinkle half the sugar ($^3/_4$ cup) over the fruit, and pour in the wine. Add the lemon peel and vanilla. Bring the wine to a rolling boil, then reduce the heat to very low.
2. Dot half the butter ($^1/_2$ stick) over the fruit, and set the rest aside. Simmer the fruit, uncovered, for 30 minutes.
3. Preheat the oven to 400°F.
4. In a large bowl, whisk the flour, eggs, remaining $^3/_4$ cup sugar, and milk together for 5 minutes.
5. Remove the kettle from the heat. Discard the lemon peel and test the juice. It should not be sour, nor too watery. If it needs more sweetening, add extra sugar. If it needs thickening, return the kettle to the heat and reduce it a bit, increasing the heat.
6. When you judge the juice to be right, give the batter another whisk-

ing and pour it over the fruit, covering it evenly. Use the remaining $^1/_2$ stick of butter to dot the surface and bake for 30 minutes, or until golden brown.

7. Take the kettle to the table and serve your guests directly from it. Provide sugar and cream for those who wish them.

NOTE: This dish may be served hot or cold. In summer I find it particularly delicious cold, with milk or cream.

Quince and Citrus Compote

SERVES 4 OR 5

This is an old recipe from the days when we spent much of every summer making jams, jellies, and marmalades. It was given to my mother by Minnie Culps, an early settler in north central Texas, who said her family had brought the recipe with them from Kentucky. When I was a child, nearly every farm in our region had a quince tree. The raw fruit, always hard as wood and tasteless, would, when simmered for half an hour, yield prodigious amounts of pectin, take on an exquisite taste, and turn a red-amber color. For all those reasons, quince was a wonderful help in making preserves from other fruit.

This old-fashioned compote is lovely on toast at breakfast, or at any time as a snack with yogurt. At my house we like to eat it along with a cut of strong cheese like Manchego, a pleasant habit we picked up from our Latino friends. The compote and cheese balance each other wonderfully.

The quince has almost disappeared from greengrocers' displays today. It is so rare that when I buy quinces in early fall at the farmers' market, other shoppers often ask me how to prepare them. Quince is worth knowing if you are fond of marmalade. If you are interested, ask your greengrocer to obtain some for you.

3 large quinces, wiped free of their velvety bloom, peeled, quartered, cored, and thinly sliced (save the peelings, cores, and seeds)

2 large lemons, peeled, depithed, and thinly sliced (save the seeds)

2 small oranges, peeled, depithed, and thinly sliced (save the seeds)

3 tablespoons finely chopped candied ginger

One 2-inch cinnamon stick

4 cloves

2 cups sugar

3 tablespoons honey

1. In a large, nonreactive, heavy-bottomed kettle, place the quince, lemon, orange, and ginger; add almost enough water to cover them (about 2 cups). Bring to a boil, and boil for 5 minutes, then reduce the heat and simmer gently for 45 minutes, stirring minimally from time to time to prevent scorching. Add a little water if the mixture seems to be losing its juiciness.

2. Meanwhile, put the quince peelings, cores, seeds, cinnamon stick,

and cloves in a small nonreactive saucepan with enough water to cover, and simmer for 40 minutes. Strain the liquid into the other kettle, pressing the pulp against the sieve to extract as much pectin as possible. Discard the solids.

3. With a wooden spoon, combine the sugar and honey with the compote, stirring until the sugar is completely dissolved. Simmer gently for 20 minutes, or until the quince is pink and almost transparent.

4. Test for sweetness and add a little more sugar, if necessary, but remember that this is compote, not jam or preserves.

5. Transfer the compote to a glass bowl, cover loosely with a cloth, and let it sit for 12 hours at room temperature before serving.

NOTE: Tightly covered and refrigerated, this compote will keep well for about 10 days.

Rhubarb Compote

Rhubarb, an old-time physic thought to be a blood purifier, has gained favor recently as an easily grown kitchen-garden plant whose tartness gives an added fillip to other fruit in pies and compotes. This is my favorite recipe for stewing it in a compote. Delightful as a kind of marmalade, it can be eaten by the bowlful as a dessert with vanilla ice cream. Served with roast fowl, it is a nice substitute for the ubiquitous cranberry sauce.

1 cup dry white wine

1 cup sugar

$^1/_4$ teaspoon coarse salt

1 teaspoon vanilla extract

$^1/_8$ teaspoon ground cayenne

One 2-inch cinnamon stick

4 cloves tied up in cheesecloth

1 pound very fresh young rhubarb, ribs only, ends and coarser strings removed, thinly sliced

2 large Granny Smith apples, peeled, quartered, cored, and thinly sliced

12 large, ripe strawberries, stemmed and halved

1 tablespoon finely chopped candied ginger

1. Heat the wine to just below the boiling point and dissolve the sugar and salt in it, stirring in the vanilla after the sugar is dissolved.
2. Place the cayenne, cinnamon stick, and cloves in the bottom of a medium-size heavy-bottomed kettle. Layer the rhubarb, apples, strawberries, and ginger over them and pour on the wine mixture. Bring to a boil, then lower the heat and simmer, covered, for 20 minutes, stirring from time to time. Skim off and discard the froth that rises.
3. Remove and discard the cinnamon stick and the little bundle of cloves.
4. Test the compote for doneness and sweetness. The fruit should remain somewhat distinct and should not be cooked to a purée, nor should it be too sweet.
5. Transfer the compote to a glass bowl and allow it to cool.

6. The compote may be eaten as is, served in small glass bowls, or embellished with vanilla ice cream or yogurt. It may also be mixed with 2 cups of heavy cream whipped and sweetened, as in the great English dessert rhubarb fool. If you opt for making the fool, serve it with slices of pound cake and sprinkle the fool with a dash of freshly grated nutmeg.

T oday the food-supply network in the United States is highly effi-
cient and very competitive. Your local grocers can obtain almost
anything, and they can help you with the more unusual items if you ask
them. I also suggest you take a good look in the Yellow Pages of your
telephone directory under "Food" or "Groceries." It is a good way to
get acquainted with those who supply your area. Get to know the sup-
pliers by name.

The following directory is meant for those of you who prefer dealing
directly with sources. The list is minimal but, with two exceptions, the
dealers listed there will send you a free catalog on request.

Southwestern, Mexican, and Amerindian
Peppers and Corn Products

Albuquerque Traders
P.O. Box 10171
Albuquerque, NM 87114
505-897-1650

Jane Butel's Pecos Valley Spice Co.
142 Lincoln Ave.
Santa Fe, NM 87501
800-468-8226

The Santa Fe School of Cooking
The Shop
Upper Level/Mercado Plaza
116 West San Francisco St.
Santa Fe, NM 97501
505-983-4511

Latino, Spanish, and
Caribbean Products

Goya Foods Inc.
100 Seaview Drive
Secaucus, NJ 07096
201-348-4900
no catalog

Herbs, Spices, and Nuts

Gel Spice Co. Inc.
48 Hook Rd.
Bayonne, NJ 07002
800-922-0230

General Spice Inc.
238th St. and St. Nicholas Ave.
South Plainfield, NJ 07080
212-227-8351

Harry and David
2518 South Pacific Highway
Medford, OR 97501
503-776-2121

Pepper House International
Outside CA: 800-858-3828
California: 818-960-4733

Pete's Spice
174 First Ave.
New York, NY 10009
212-254-8773

San Francisco Herb Co.
250 14th St.
San Francisco, CA 94103
800-227-4530

The Spice Market
664 Bergen St.
Brooklyn, NY 11238
718-636-6300

Salt Cod, Salt Scrod, and Salt Haddock

Balducci's
424 Sixth Ave.
New York, NY 10011
212-673-2600

Iron Gate Products
520 Barretto St.
Bronx, NY 10474
212-757-2670

Gazin's, Inc.
P.O. Box 19221
New Orleans, LA 70179
504-482-0302
catalog $1.00 (refundable)

Legal Sea Foods
33 Everett St.
Boston, MA 02134
Outside MA: 800-343-5804
Massachussets: 617-254-7000

Middle European Products

Paprikas Weiss Importer
1546 Second Ave.
New York, NY 10028
212-288-6117

Rice, Beans, Creole and Cajun Seasonings, Etc.

N'awlins Lous-e-ana Connections, Inc.
1031 St. Ferdinand St.
Suite B
New Orleans, LA 70117
800-237-2325
506-943-3400

Seabags and Many Other Wonderful Things

Williams-Sonoma
Mail Order Department
P.O. Box 7456
San Francisco, CA 94120-7456
800-541-2233

INDEX

About the Author

JACQUES BURDICK was born in Texas and educated in the United States, France, Spain, and Greece. The recipient of two Fulbright grants to France, he has devoted his life to twin passions: the theater and food. He recently retired from the chairmanship of the theater department at the University of Missouri–Kansas City but remains Emeritus Professor of Theater both there and at Adelphi University on Long Island, where he still teaches and directs. A long-time resident of Manhattan, Burdick has taught in several cooking schools in the tri-state area. He has been joint owner and chef of a restaurant on the Costa Brava and spends his summers cooking and writing in France and Catalonia. He is the author of *French Cooking en Famille*.